SCOTTISH LITERATURE INTERNATIONAL

Gateway to the Modern: Resituating J. M. Barrie

Edited by
VALENTINA BOLD
and ANDREW NASH

Occasional Papers: Number 18
Association for Scottish Literary Studies

Published by
Scottish Literature International
Scottish Literature
7 University Gardens
University of Glasgow
Glasgow G12 8QH

Scottish Literature International is an imprint of
the Association for Scottish Literary Studies

www.asls.org.uk

ASLS is a registered charity no. SC006535

First published 2014

A CIP catalogue for this title
is available from the British Library

ISBN 978-1-908980-02-1

ALBA | CHRUTHACHAIL

ASLS acknowledges the support of Creative Scotland
towards the publication of this book

Contents

Contents (continued)

Acknowledgments

We would like to acknowledge the formal support of the School of Interdisciplinary Studies of the University of Glasgow, and the Association of Scottish Literary Studies (ASLS), which made possible the 2010 Dumfries conference upon which this volume is based. David Borthwick, lecturer in literature with the School, was an able co-organiser alongside Valentina Bold, and the Peter Pan Moat Brae trust and the Theatre Royal, Dumfries also provided input. Margery Palmer McCulloch, of the ASLS, was a particular source of support for this volume, and deserves especial mention, alongside Duncan Jones, who oversaw the book as it went into production. Valentina would like to extend her thanks to her own darling boys, Hayden and Kieran.

Abbreviations

References to Barrie's main works, given parenthetically in the text, are to the following editions:

ALI   *Auld Licht Idylls* (1888), Uniform Edition (London: Hodder & Stoughton, 1930).

DE   *The Plays of J. M. Barrie in one volume*, ed. A. E. Wilson ['The Definitive Edition'], (London: Hodder & Stoughton, 1942).

EE   *An Edinburgh Eleven* (1889), Uniform Edition (London: Hodder & Stoughton, 1926).

FMJL   *Farewell Miss Julie Logan* (1932), in *Farewell Miss Julie Logan: A J. M. Barrie Omnibus*, ed. Andrew Nash (Edinburgh: Canongate, 2001).

GH   *The Greenwood Hat, Being a Memoir of James Anon: 1885–1887* (London: Peter Davies, 1937).

LWB   *The Little White Bird* (1902), in *Farewell Miss Julie Logan: A J. M. Barrie Omnibus*, ed. Andrew Nash (Edinburgh: Canongate, 2001).

MO   *Margaret Ogilvy* (1896), Uniform Edition (London: Hodder & Stoughton, 1931).

PP   *Peter Pan* (1904), *Peter Pan and other plays*, ed. Peter Hollindale (Oxford and New York: Oxford University Press, 1995).

PPKG   *Peter Pan in Kensington Gardens* (1906), in *Peter Pan in Kensington Gardens; Peter and Wendy*, ed. Peter Hollindale (Oxford and New York: Oxford University Press, 1991).

PW   *Peter and Wendy* (1911), in *Peter Pan in Kensington Gardens; Peter and Wendy*, ed. Peter Hollindale (Oxford and New York: Oxford University Press, 1991).

ST   *Sentimental Tommy* (1896), Uniform Edition (London: Cassell, [1930]).

TG   *Tommy and Grizel* (1900), Uniform Edition (London: Cassell, [1928]).

WT   *A Window in Thrums* (1889), Uniform Edition (London: Hodder & Stoughton, 1928).

Introduction

VALENTINA BOLD and ANDREW NASH

J. M. Barrie is a writer of elusive depth and complexity, whose life and literary creations continue to inspire writers, readers and theatre-goers worldwide. In 2010, the one hundred and fiftieth anniversary of his birth was celebrated with events around the world, from library exhibitions and theatrical performances to a Google doodle. The inspiration for this volume came from an academic conference held that year in the town of Dumfries, where Barrie attended the local academy from 1873 until 1878, later recalling these years as the happiest of his life. Augmented by additional new work, the result is the very first collection of academic essays on Barrie which attempts to do at least some justice to the extraordinary range of his literary achievement.

Barrie's fluctuating critical fortunes have been well documented. The spectacular fall from grace that set in soon after his death has prompted its own analysis of why a writer so esteemed by his own generation could be so harshly criticised by the next and, sadly, still overly neglected today.[1] As with his near contemporary Robert Louis Stevenson, biographical studies of Barrie continue to outweigh critical assessments. The revival of interest in Barrie's writing and in new performances of his plays which has taken place over the last thirty years is a sign that his work is being taken more seriously by critics, historians and practitioners of the theatre (if not necessarily the novel), as well as scholars of children's literature and Scottish literature. Nevertheless, a recently published *Companion to Modern British and Irish Drama, 1880–2005* gives his work only one passing reference (to *Peter Pan*), while a companion to *fin de siècle* literature does not mention him at all.[2] Distressingly, a modern essay collection on his most famous creation categorically asserts that 'J. M. Barrie's critical reputation rests on one work: *Peter Pan*'.[3]

This volume sets out to challenge that claim by considering the remarkable variety of Barrie's writing against its many literary and cultural contexts. The range of Barrie's achievement has perhaps counted against his critical reputation: a novelist once considered the equal of Meredith and Hardy; the most successful dramatist of the early twentieth century; the creator of a children's classic that has refused to grow old; not to mention underestimated contributions as an essayist and humorist; the multiplicity of genres within which Barrie worked has perhaps prevented him from being taken to the centre of critical discussions in any one area of literary criticism or history. His originality as a writer has also been a problem. Contemporary reviewers of both the novels and plays were often reduced to describing them as 'Barrie-ish', 'Barrie-esque' or 'all Barrieness'.[4] In her *Modern Drama in Europe* (1920), Storm Jameson concluded: 'his work eludes definition, as does the work of all men who are masters of their art. There is nothing like it in the whole of modern drama'.[5] Originality can be an obstacle, however, when it comes to placing an author in defining categories or traditions. Is Barrie predominantly a novelist or a playwright? Is he Victorian, Decadent, Edwardian or Modernist? The title of this collection – *Gateway to the Modern* – acknowledges the difficulty of answering these questions but attempts to embrace it in a more positive and productive light that has hitherto been the case. What emerges is a writer fully immersed in the literary and intellectual culture of his day. In his *Critical History of English Literature* published in 1960, David Daiches judged that Barrie 'was quite out of touch with the new literary movements of his time'.[6] The essays in this volume mount a detailed and compelling challenge to that assessment, exploring the many ways in which his way can be illuminated when read alongside various literary, cultural, theatrical, and philosophical contexts of the period.

The book is divided into three sections. The first considers Barrie's achievement as a dramatist, and explores how his mastery of the theatre made him an early enthusiast for, and proponent of, the cinema. Jan McDonald discusses Barrie's relationship with his theatrical contemporaries, notably Shaw, Galsworthy and Harry Granville Barker. She traces his involvement in theatrical controversies, such as Ibsenism and the stage portrayal of the New Woman and the suffragette, and campaigns, including the fight against censorship and the movement for the establishment of a repertory theatre. Barrie emerges from this detailed analysis as a writer whose theatrical vision contrasted with the 'essentially optimistic world view' of his contemporaries, and whose originality lies in the 'pervasive performative element' of his work, which 'links with his use of metatheatricality as a vessel for his commentary on current theatrical practice.' This point is picked up directly by Anna Farkas, who discusses Barrie's metatheatrical critique of the Victorian dramatic tradition in plays produced between 1900 and 1915. As Farkas reminds us, it was Shaw who judged that Barrie's plays had confirmed 'the final relegation of the Nineteenth Century London theatre to the dust-bin'. Her chapter shows convincingly that in plays such as *The Wedding Guest* (1900) and the much neglected *Alice Sit-by-the-Fire* (1905), Barrie's playful deconstruction of the sexual problem play swept aside established theatrical forms and 'prepared the stage for a new type of heroine and a different kind of play about gender relations.'

Farkas is ultimately concerned with establishing Barrie's 'modernity as a playwright', a task also pursued by R. D. S. Jack in his chapter on the later drama. Building on work in his most recent book on Barrie, *Myths and the Mythmaker* (2010), which considers the author's early development, Jack extends his reach to consider the mature dramas, from *Quality Street* (1902) to *Dear Brutus* (1920). Drawing on Barrie's undergraduate lecture notes, particularly those from Professor David Masson's classes on 'Rhetoric and Belles Lettres', Jack proposes an alternative model for reading Barrie's 'Shakespearean' romances, one alert to the range of modal variety that Barrie inherited and 'modernised' from Masson's classes and his published Shakespeare lectures. Such an approach, as Jack persuasively demonstrates, presents Barrie as a 'unique modernist', whose multi-layered texts and embrace of open endings serve as 'accurate mirrors of a doubtful age'.

The final chapter in this first section demonstrates how Barrie's modernity, and his interest in the potentiality of form, extended to early cinema. Jonathan Murray considers Barrie's reciprocal relationship with the new medium, discussing his own satirical – yet serious – contributions to the genre written and produced during the First World War, and also examining the many ways in which his life and work has proved irresistible to other filmmakers, including Alfred Hitchcock. Murray shows how Barrie's enthusiastic engagement with the infant medium of cinema manifested itself in 'satirical culture-clash comedies that pre-empted postmodernism's subsequent interest in the self-referential aspects of artistic and popular cultural production'. More recently, cinematic representations of Barrie's work have taken the form of transformations of *Peter Pan* and interpretations of the author's biography. Murray concludes his chapter by critically examining the distortions and simplifications of these reworkings of text and life.

The essays in the second section concentrate mainly on Barrie's prose, and are concerned with the complex matter of his place in literary tradition, particularly traditions in Scottish literature. Douglas Gifford offers a detailed analysis of Barrie's final prose work, the novella *Farewell Miss Julie Logan*, placing it in the context of his fiction as a whole and alongside other Scottish narratives of the supernatural, from Burns to Buchan. Uncovering striking continuities in form, theme, setting and language, Gifford shows how Barrie's story connects with a rich heritage of Scottish writing dealing ambivalently with the supernatural and embodying forms of narrative duality. Whereas Gifford looks back to identify the cultural roots of Barrie's fictional flowering, Andrew Nash looks forward to consider the presence of his work in modern and contemporary literature. Rehabilitating the notion of the sentimental as one of Barrie's appealing strengths rather than a weakness, Nash convincingly traces Barrie's connections with, and influence on, modernist novelists, such as D. H. Lawrence and Ford Madox Ford, and a range of modern Scottish writers including James Kelman, Alasdair Gray, Muriel Spark and John Burnside. The discussion of Spark throws opens the door for more detailed comparison of their work, with the possibility of viewing *Memento Mori*, for instance, as a creative response to *Peter Pan* read as a revenant ballad.

Much of the responsibility for the prevailing view that Barrie is tangential to major developments in Scottish literature belongs to Hugh MacDiarmid. In her chapter, Margery Palmer McCulloch reconsiders the relationship between these two writers, exploring some of the reasons behind MacDiarmid's hostility to a writer whom he considered in 1926 to have 'long severed any effective connection he ever had with Scottish life or thought'.[7] Rightly judging the two writers to belong to separate generations, McCulloch nevertheless shows that MacDiarmid's attitude to Barrie was perhaps not as negative as is commonly assumed, and that both shared something in common in their recognition of the artistic possibilities of the Scots language.

The final section, 'Peter Pan's Connections', explores neglected aspects of the background and intellectual contexts of this iconic play, and also shows its direct effects on audiences. Paul Fox explores *Peter Pan in Kensington Gardens*, identifying a liminality within the work as it brings together precise topography, imaginative reconstruction (temporal as well as physical), elements of performance and the Decadent aesthetic, exemplified by a key section in John Davidson's 'Thirty Bob a Week'. Rosemary Ashton complements this with a demonstration of the importance of a real place – Bloomsbury, the home of the Darling family – for the play version of the text. Ashton traces the significance of Bloomsbury to Barrie, both personal and literary, building up a much clearer picture of the literary London in which he moved and worked, an under-researched aspect of his biography and writing career. In a different vein, Ralph Jessop examines some of the philosophical ideas that underlie *Peter Pan*. Focusing on the notion of make-believe and transformation, Jessop presents the play as a profoundly modernist text, utilising oppositional discourses (scepticism – grounded in Barrie's Scottish philosophical education and, specifically, in the work of David Masson and Thomas Carlyle – versus wonderment; independence of thought and adventure versus utilitarian beliefs) to construct escapist possibilities. Valentina Bold returns us from make-believe to the real (at least in part), considering a set of letters written by children to the first Wendy, Hilda Trevelyan. Bold demonstrates the impact of the play on its first, and youngest, audiences, several of whom went on to have distinguished and adventurous lives, but also reveals their complex, multiple response to Wendy as a fictional character and Trevelyan as actress.

J. M. Barrie and the story of Peter Pan have most recently inspired the planning for a Children's Centre for Literature in Dumfries. The centre will be based at the conserved house and garden at Moat Brae in Dumfries, where Barrie played out as a boy the games that would later inspire the story of Peter Pan. The Peter Pan Moat Brae Trust is now at an advanced stage of planning for the centre, which will not only celebrate the Barrie and Peter Pan heritage, but more generally seek to promote a better understanding and interpretation of Scotland's literary and cultural heritage for children and young people. This will be done through a year-round programme of activities, events, workshops and exhibitions. A unique attraction at the centre will be the reinvention of the garden, inspired by Neverland, and laid out to entice children into a world of imagination, discovery and outdoor play. The final chapter of this volume, introduced by Hugh McMillan and related to Dumfries Academy's children's collection *On the Grass Cloud: Poems for the Peter Pan Garden*, which he edited, shows that the play still has relevance for children, perhaps especially those who, as Barrie did, have lived in Dumfries.

It is the editors' hope that this volume will assist in Barrie's ongoing literary re-evaluation. By presenting him as an inherently modern writer, we want to show that his work, often dismissed in the later twentieth and early twenty-first century, provides a true 'gateway to the modern', which is at once original, consciously intellectual, and emotionally engaging.

Notes

1 For an incisive investigation of this problem, see R. D. S. Jack, *Myths and the Mythmaker: A Literary Account of J. M. Barrie's Formative Years* (Amsterdam & New York: Rodopi, 2010), chapter 1.

2 Mary Luckhurst (ed.), *A Companion to Modern British and Irish Drama, 1880–2005* (Oxford: Blackwell, 2006); Gail Marshall (ed.), *The Cambridge Companion to the Fin de Siècle* (Cambridge: Cambridge University Press, 2007).

3 Donna R. White and C. Anita Tarr (eds), *J. M. Barrie's Peter Pan In and Out of Time: A Children's Classic at 100* (Lanham, Maryland: The Scarecrow Press, 2006), p. vii.

4 See Leonee Ormond, *J. M. Barrie* (Edinburgh: Scottish Academic Press, 1987), p. 149; review of *The Little White Bird*, *Times Literary Supplement* (14 November 1902), p. 339.

5 Storm Jameson, *Modern Drama in Europe* (London: Collins, 1920), p. 211.

6 David Daiches, *A Critical History of English Literature* (1960), rev. edn, 2 vols (London: Mandarin, 1960), II, p. 1108.

7 Hugh MacDiarmid, *Contemporary Scottish Studies* (1926), ed. Alan Riach (Manchester: Carcanet, 1995), p. 17.

PART I: DRAMA AND FILM

1. Barrie and the New Dramatists

JAN McDONALD

Introduction

William Archer in *The Old Drama and the New* described Barrie as 'a writer
so intensely individual as to elude classification and stand absolutely alone
in our dramatic literature'.[1] J. C. Trewin failed to find accommodation for
him in 'the great house' that was *The Edwardian Theatre*, 'uneasy in the
drawing room, hardly for the study, not entirely for the playroom, he refuses
to be categorised'.[2] There is likewise uncertainty about whether he belonged
in the commercial world of London's West End stage or in the revolutionary
New Drama movement whose principal promoters were William Archer,
G. B. Shaw, Harley Granville Barker, and John Galsworthy. Sheldon Chaney,
writing in 1914, places Barrie firmly within the latter group: 'the new English
school of dramatists, including Shaw, Galsworthy and Barrie, is by every
test the greatest in achievement and the greatest in promise in the dramatic
world today'.[3] Thomas Dickinson disagrees: 'in a time in which revolt had
become something of a convention, Barrie has been distinguished by standing
apart from the protestants [...] Barrie is no reformer, no joiner of new
groups'.[4] Jean Chothia settles for compromise: Barrie 'stands between the
Society dramatists and the writers of minority drama whose themes he
often absorbed into lighter, less testing plotting and characterisation'.[5]

Initially it might appear that Barrie and the 'protestants' had little in
common. Advocates of radical revision of both current theatrical conventions and the conservative consumerist ideology that the bourgeois drama
promoted, the reformers sought to establish an 'alternative' theatre, independent of commercial considerations. The long run system, based on a
profit-making imperative, which they believed inhibited both creative
opportunities for actors and the development of emergent playwrights,
should be replaced by a repertory system with matinees devoted to experimental new work; the engagement of fashionable 'stars' by an ensemble
company of equals with equal remuneration, and the reactionary ethos of
Society drama by a repertoire that promoted 'a critical and dissenting attitude

to conventional codes of morality.'[6] The New Drama, nurtured in the *ad hoc* productions of the private theatre societies of the 1890s, briefly found a home at the Court Theatre (1904–07) and at the Savoy (1907–08) under the management of Granville Barker and J. E. Vedrenne.

The major part of Barrie's theatrical activity was conducted on the West End commercial stage or its New York equivalent. Many of his works ran for many months and were regularly revived. He was associated from the outset of his playwriting career with successful theatre managers. The leading roles in his dramas were played by 'star' performers or 'stars' were created by appearing therein. His plays, and his principal producer, Charles Frohman, called for elaborate innovative settings, the houseboat in *Walker, London* (1892) and the island in *The Admirable Crichton* (1902), being only two examples. He did not as a rule address current social or political issues overtly, as Shaw and Galsworthy often did, and as Barker did from time to time. Yet Barrie regularly engaged with the theatrical radicals and their campaigns. This chapter will examine: first, the personal relationships between Barrie, Shaw, Galsworthy and Barker; second, the manner in which the playwrights contributed to the theatrical controversies of the period; and, finally, some critical opinions of Barrie's plays expressed by the New Dramatists.

Friends and Neighbours

Despite differences in the their political philosophy, in their dramaturgy and in the theatrical spheres in which they operated, Barrie, Shaw, Barker and Galsworthy were friends, and for many years close neighbours. It was Barker who suggested that Barrie move into Adelphi Terrace House where the Barkers and Galsworthys resided. Shaw lived opposite, 'so near that the tale went (quite untruly) that [they] could throw things into each other's windows'.[7] Letters and anecdotes reveal many social visits, communal sheltering from air raids during the First World War, shared lunches and dinners, often at their favourite restaurant, Romano's. The moral support provided by Barker on the occasion of Barrie's divorce was reciprocated during the harrowing period prior to final separation of Barker and Lillah McCarthy in 1918.

Barrie was probably closest to Galsworthy. Both began their literary careers as novelists – Galsworthy's *Fraternity* (1909) was dedicated to Barrie

– and each was skilful at adapting his private persona to meet social demands. On meeting Galsworthy, Barrie described him thus in a letter to the Duchess of Sutherland: 'a queer fish like the rest of us. So sincerely weighed down by the out-of-jointness of things socially [...] but outwardly a man-about-town, so neat, so correct – he would go to the stake for his opinions, but he would go courteously raising his hat'.⁸ Galsworthy regularly consulted Barrie on drafts of his plays, and appointed him his representative at rehearsals for the production of *The Forest* in 1924. Barrie, as Chancellor of the University of Edinburgh (from 1930), was instrumental in the awarding of Honorary Degrees to Barker and Galsworthy.

On Shaw's relationship with Barrie, Dennis Mackail wrote: 'Secretly these two might never fully appreciate each other's gifts, and neither perhaps was unduly anxious to laugh at each other's wit – Barrie most certainly not; but there was appreciation for all that'.⁹ In his obituary of Barrie in the *Sunday Graphic*, Shaw called him 'a most affectionate creature'. Although 'shy' and 'even secretive', 'when you did meet him he was charming'. 'You couldn't help liking Barrie, and you couldn't help liking his work.'¹⁰

A light hearted collaboration occurred in 1914 when Barrie, Barker, and Shaw, together with William Archer and G. K. Chesterton , participated in the creation of a bizarre escapade. Barrie wanted to include a piece of filmed material in the piece he was writing for Gaby Deslys, *Rosy Rapture* (1915), and this involved the cream of London's *literati* in an excursion to the country where they performed a spoof Western movie with a script created by Barrie under the direction of Barker.¹¹

Controversies and Campaigns

Ibsen and Ibsenism

Granville Barker asserted that Ibsen's work 'is and must be imitated by almost every dramatist coming after him. Like Ibsen or loathe him, our European drama is Ibsenised'.¹² The first translations of Ibsen's plays to be shown on the London stage belonged to that group of his work known as 'social prose dramas', namely, *A Doll's House* in 1889, followed by *Pillars of Society*, *Ghosts*, *Rosmersholm*, and *Hedda Gabler* in 1891. Each examines the ways in which events of the past 'haunt' contemporary life and how heredity and environment combine to shape a character's destiny. All have a woman in a leading role, a woman who finds herself at odds with conventional social values and common assumptions about gender identity. Conservative critics expressed outrage at what they saw as sociological tracts advocating disruption of the *status quo*, focussing on sordid tales of neurotic, unstable women and the deviant behaviour of degenerate men.

In 1891, the Ibsen controversy was at its height with six productions of his plays in London, including the notorious private production of the unlicensed *Ghosts* by the Independent Theatre Society in March, prompting William Archer's article 'Ghosts and Gibberings' in the *Pall Mall Gazette*, which ridiculed the complacent narrow-mindedness of the critics and the London establishment.[13] 1891 also saw the production of Barrie's satire, *Ibsen's Ghost*,[14] and the publication of Shaw's essay, *The Quintessence of Ibsenism* – two contrasting responses from two dramatists, each at the outset of his theatrical career.[15]

Had Barrie been seeking to win favour with the leaders of the nascent alternative theatre movement, the fact that his first successful professional production was a burlesque on the work of its prophet and progenitor would hardly have been diplomatic. Even the timing of its opening performance might be seen as a direct challenge. *Ibsen's Ghost*, starring the popular comic actor, J. L. Toole, was presented at his Theatre on 30 May, the afternoon before the last night of *Hedda Gabler*, produced by Elizabeth Robins, one of Shaw's 'high priestesses of Ibsen', and supported by William Archer, Ibsen's champion and pioneer of the New Drama. Barrie's play proved a box office 'hit' and continued in the repertoire until the end of the season.

However, the question arises as to how much of this success can be attributed to Barrie. He wrote the script, but Toole, whose name appeared in the subtitle, 'Toole Up-to-Date', was the 'author' of the production. Barrie's original was altered by cutting large sections of dialogue, by adding improvised 'gagging' or 'thickening', as Toole called it, by introducing the actor's own 'spoof' of a popular mime play, *L'Enfant Prodigue*, and, most significantly, a piece of comic business in which he 'transformed' himself into Ibsen. According to the reviewer in the *Era* this transformation was the highlight of the production. 'If anything will extinguish the Ibsen craze, it will be the apparition of Ibsen at Toole's, and the uproarious fun accompanying it.' In performance, Barrie's parody of Ibsen's plays became a vehicle for Toole's idiosyncratic brand of comedy. William Archer noted in his review in the *World*: 'as yet, indeed, we have only seen the "business" of Mr

Toole's part. I intend to return in a week or so, in hopes of hearing the dialogue.'[16]

Clement Scott, the arch-anti-Ibsenite, was delighted. 'I don't suppose that Mr. J. M. Barrie thinks seriously about the subject one way or another. I did and I do. But some of us have shouted it out in court; he has laughed it out.'[17] In fact, the production did little to offend the Ibsenites, despite Barrie's later hinting that his 'soap-bubble was meant to fall upon [Ibsen's] more weird idolators' rather than on Ibsen himself.[18] William Archer in his review had generously called it 'A piece of genuinely witty fooling which ought not to be missed'. Later in life, Barrie was to acknowledge Ibsen as 'the greatest craftsman that ever wrote'[19] and 'the dramatist I have always known to be the greatest of his age'.[20]

Shaw's *The Quintessence of Ibsenism*, originally delivered as a lecture to the Fabian Society as part of a series entitled 'Socialism and Literature', interpreted Ibsen's plays as indictments against the tyranny of social conventions that destroyed the identity of the individual. Written for a radical audience, it omitted any reference to Ibsen's poetic language, his use of symbolism, and his innovations in theatrical technique. Ibsen always denied that he was a social philosopher and resented his plays being treated as propaganda rather than as dramatic art, but Shaw's *Quintessence* had considerable influence on his reception in Britain. 'Ibsenism' came to mean three things; a belief in a socialist political philosophy; a resistance to unthinking adherence to social convention; and a belief in creating a new role for women in society. The New Dramatists, radicals both politically and theatrically, were likewise committed to writing plays with a serious social purpose, in some cases with an overt agenda of social reform. Although Shaw's assessment of Ibsen is flawed, it remains instructive in examining the works of Shaw himself and of his fellow playwrights.

Shaw's 'butchering of Ibsen to make a Fabian holiday' and the sacrifice of Barrie's satirical critique to the self-promotion of a star may contribute little to an understanding of Ibsen's work *per se*, but Barrie and the radicals continued to comment on the contemporary theatre, albeit employing differing critical methods. Archer and Shaw were adept at using their journalistic reviews to challenge theatrical conventions. They, together with Barker, wrote monographs and scholarly essays.[21] Only Barker wrote a play *about* the theatre, his elegiac *Farewell to the Theatre* (1916).

Barrie, on the other hand, frequently chose the theatrical form itself to expose the limitations of contemporary drama and theatre practice. *Alice-Sit-By-The-Fire* (1905) satirises the inherent artificiality and false presumptions of the 'well made play' and the conventions of Society drama on the well-worn theme of 'women with a past'. William Archer, writing in the *World*, commenting that the play is 'an effective piece of dramatic criticism', goes on: 'It is like a commentary-in-action upon my article of last week; but it will do more [...] to render impossible the play of artificial situation and mendacious self-sacrifice.'[22] *A Slice of Life* (1910), Barrie's burlesque of the 'problem play', was described by the *Times* reviewer (2 July 1910) as 'a masterpiece of most delicate and searching dramatic criticism'. In *Rosy Rapture*, the revue sketch Barrie wrote for the glamorous Gaby Deslys, he highlights 'the silliness of "musical comedy" with its incompetent chorus [and] the grotesqueness of melodrama.'[23] *Punch: A Toy Tragedy* (1906) brings together the 'old' drama and the 'new' as the dated and unfashionable marionettes have to give way to 'Superpunch' or the 'New Man' in the guise of none other than G. B. S. himself.[24] When Shaw's *Press Cuttings* (1909) was refused a licence because living characters were presented on stage, he protested that he himself had been thus represented 'by no less well-known an author than [his] friend Mr J. M. Barrie.'[25] Barrie claimed that 'Superpunch' was not designed to resemble Shaw but Granville Barker playing John Tanner in *Man and Superman* at the Court Theatre in 1905, whose make-up rendered him a Shavian 'look-alike'. Barrie's metatheatrical critical commentaries, although less sustained than those of Shaw, Archer or Barker, share much in substance.

The 'Woman' Question

There was a growing demand for reform of gender inequality in Britain from the 1880s until the outbreak of the First World War. The theatre was harnessed to promote the campaign for women's suffrage, from the sketches of the Actresses' Franchise League to the full length propagandist drama, *Votes for Women!*, by Elizabeth Robins, directed by Barker at the Court in 1907. More generally, a reassessment of the nature of women, sexual relationships between men and women, and the political and social rights of women were pervasive themes in the plays of the New Dramatists. Notable examples include Shaw's *Mrs Warren's Profession* (1894), *Man and Superman* (1902), *Getting Married* (1908), and *Pygmalion* (1913). Barker in *The Madras*

House (1910) observed the sorry plight of working women, 'superfluous' single women, women as objects of the male gaze, and idle middle-class 'ladies', a comprehensive catalogue of wasted opportunity and sexual discrimination. Galsworthy exposed the plight of women confronted by prejudice and economic hardship, for example, Mrs Jones in *The Silver Box* (1906), the strikers' wives in *Strife* (1909), and Ruth Honeywill in *Justice* (1910).

In Barrie's dramas there are many representations of strong women, indeed even 'heroic' women, who have a powerful influence on the action.[26] However, in the context of the 'Woman' Question his position is somewhat ambiguous. In asserting that women *already* have power over public institutions, such as politics and the law, but a power that is exerted in the domestic sphere and channelled through the covert manipulation of a male agent, Barrie shows himself to be fundamentally a reactionary.

'Plain' Maggie Wylie, the heroine of *What Every Woman Knows* (1908), is virtually 'sold' in matrimony by her brothers to the impecunious student, John Shand. Through the application of her intelligence and energy 'behind the scenes', he becomes a successful politician, only latterly coming to realise her essential contribution to his rise to power. The women's movement was not impressed by the view that a woman's effective impact on society and on public life could/should be exerted only indirectly through a male relative. A review of the play's revival at the Old Vic in 1960 makes the point: 'it was to a large extent, in its 1908 meaning, a betrayal of women. Its arguments were those of the anti-suffragette.'[27] Indeed, the play's title was copied for the title of a Scottish anti-suffrage pamphlet.[28]

In the second act, Barrie introduces (significantly, set partly offstage) a group of suffragettes. John is to make a speech in support of their cause, secretly written, of course, by Maggie. This short scene at first sight has little significance for the plot, but Barrie's reply when it was suggested that it be cut from the published text, is revealing:

> The suffrage must stand, for though there is so little of it, it is an integral part of the play. It only 'dates' the play to the extent of showing the action takes place a few years ago and I think it should give opportunities for the society-ladies to wear dresses that will be more interesting than absolute present-day – probably those long tight skirts (of which I see myself making some play).[29]

Is this scene 'an integral part of the play' because it is an ironic comment on the fact that, while the radical women believe they need the support of a man in their cause, it is a 'womanly' woman, Maggie, who has actually written the key speech? Or was it simply that Barrie just wanted to introduce stage business with the 'long tight skirts'? One must agree with Barker's comments, unsurprising from the author of *The Madras House*, 'the political part is trivially dealt with'.

A manipulative woman of a different kind appears in *The Adored One* or *The Legend of Leonora* (1913), the only play by Barrie ever to be booed by an audience. The first act, later *Seven Women* (1913), succinctly made the point that the female character is multifaceted and flexible in assuming a variety of roles, including those of the Mother, the Suffragette, the Murderess, and so on. In the subsequent act, Leonora (interestingly the full name of Ibsen's Nora in *A Doll's House*) murders a man in a railway carriage because he will not shut the window to accommodate her ailing child. At her trial, playing the 'sacred' role of mother and of the 'womanly' woman, she charms the judge and jury and is acquitted. The failure of this version led Barrie to revise the script so that the murder and the trial take place in a dream.

The diversity of the critical reception of this drama is revealing. A large proportion of the press regarded it as an anti-suffrage play. The reviewer in the *Illustrated London News* proposed that it might be 'a parable on the lawlessness of Militant Suffragism and its immunity from punishment'.[30] Channing Pollock in the *Green Room Book* called it 'the greatest, and gentlest, anti-woman suffrage play ever written'.[31] Others dismissed it as a failed attempt at a *pro-suffrage* play. Walbrook in *Barrie and the Theatre* grieved that 'the Feminist wave had caught [Barrie] in its clasp and temporarily washed away his sense of humour'.[32] The *Times* (4 September 1913) quoted the author: '[Barrie] said he was trying to show that a new spirit had grown up among women but he is mistaken if he thinks that modern women would agree that their future lies with wayward, inconsequential feeble-minded creatures of the type portrayed in Leonora'. R. D. S Jack argues that such critics failed to appreciate the irony of the outcome. '[Leonora] has shown how women may conquer male society while still entrapped in its institutions.'[33] In other words, Leonora and Maggie Wylie are manipulative sisters under the skin.

Richard Burton in his review of the 1918 edition of Barrie's plays concludes: 'In his treatment of women he is the great champion of the old-fashioned woman of charm and truly feminine influence. As Shaw gave us the New Woman, so Barrie the woman who has no date, because she stands for the Eternal Feminine.'[34] But Shaw similarly portrayed Candida Morell, Jennifer Dudebat, Lady Cicely Waynefleete, and that 'boa constrictor', Ann Whitefield – all guilty of manipulation of an unsuspecting male for their own ends. The reviewer of *The Adored One* in the *Era* noted the similarities.[35] Shaw and Barrie 'the two great discoverers of the modern woman' unite in their celebration of 'the triumph of femininity'. 'It is this very woman that rules the world. For her man will put aside all laws, will perjure himself, will count himself blessed to be allowed to die for her.' The difference is that while Barrie tolerates, even indulges, these 'embodiments of femininity', Shaw's heroines are, to a greater or lesser extent, delineated as knowingly 'monstrous' by their creator. Unwittingly, perhaps, the American actor, Hilda Spong, hits the mark: 'I find Barrie's women are women I have always known, and I find Shaw's cleverer than most women.'[36] However, Barrie proved that, in the right context, Frohman's Repertory Season, he was able to produce a play about a New Woman that satisfied the critics and met the principles of the New Drama movement, *The Twelve-Pound Look* (1910).

The Campaign for a Repertory Theatre[37]
After the financial failure of the Barker/Vedrenne management at the Savoy Theatre in 1908, progress towards the achievement of the repertory ideal was foundering. Barker wrote to Gilbert Murray: 'All our lot of dramatists are slacking off in production because they can't be sure of anything but matinee audiences. Repertory is our salvation.'[38]

Barrie had shown an interest in the repertory idea, when he became a member of the Council of the Incorporated Stage Society in 1904, whose remit included a commitment to establish a Repertory Theatre in London. In his Lecture to the Playgoers' Club in the same year, he expressed 'a passionate belief in a repertory theatre', and if one such existed he 'would send the plays he should write in future to it'.[39] In 1909, he approached Charles Frohman, his friend and long term producer, suggesting that he mount a repertory season at his London base, the Duke of York's Theatre. Edward Garnett, citing Archer, Shaw, Barrie, Granville Barker and Galsworthy, as 'the main links in the historical chain of the repertory theatre movement', affirms 'that Mr. Frohman's repertory theatre would not have come into being without Mr. Barrie's own inspiring example and striking dramatic success'.[40]

The Repertory Theatre project produced two masterpieces, Barker's *The Madras House* and Galsworthy's *Justice*. (It was Barrie's happy suggestion to include this in place of *The Eldest Son*, the author's original proposal.) Barrie contributed three one-act plays of varying quality, but each in its own way was appropriate to the repertory experiment. *Old Friends* was a pallid reflection of Ibsen's *Ghosts* in addressing the subject of inherited illness, in this case, alcoholism. *A Slice of Life*, a late addition to the season, was a light-hearted spoof on what the *Times* reviewer described as 'the absurdities and self-conscious tricks of the modern play' (2 July 1910). By far the most successful and certainly the most accomplished was *The Twelve-Pound Look*. The play's message that self-fulfilment for women lay in acquiring marketable skills, such as typewriting, rather than in being the unpaid helpmeet of a wealthy, pompous and self-regarding partner, fits well with the philosophy of the contemporary women's movement. Shaw's Vivie Warren, with no less determination but more rhetoric, rejected her mother's sleazy partner, Croft, to work in Honoria Fraser's chambers, and in *The Madras House* Barker's Miss Yates, a single parent, will work to support her child rather than become dependent on the morally corrupt Constantine. Barker, who directed, was quick to praise Barrie's play as 'the best of its kind', demonstrating the 'moral purpose of a woman of spirit'. He staged a revival with his wife, Lillah McCarthy, at the Kingsway in October 1911. *The Twelve-Pound Look* was one of the most successful productions of the repertory season in terms of attendances with twenty-five performances.

In financial terms, the Duke of York's repertory season has to be dismissed as one of the many fruitful failures with which the rise of the New Drama is littered, but, although Barker had come to the conclusion that the future of repertory lay in the 'Provinces', he recognised that '[w]hatever has been done or left undone, gained or lost, at the Duke of York's Theatre […] the practicability of modern repertory has been proved, and the public now knows by demonstration what a Repertory Theatre is. That is a definite step forward' – a step enabled to a large extent by Barrie's enthusiasm and influence.[41]

The Campaign against Stage Censorship

For much of the nineteenth century the Lord Chamberlain's Reader of Plays had caused only minimal disruption, but the period between 1890 and 1910 saw the banning of works such as Ibsen's *Ghosts,* Shaw's *Mrs Warren's Profession,* Granville Barker's *Waste,* Edward Garnett's *The Breaking Point,* Maeterlinck's *Monna Vanna,* and Brieux's *Damaged Goods.* All of these were privately performed by one or other of the theatre societies created 'to be free of the shackles of the censor'.[42] The banning of Barker's *Waste* in 1907 galvanised the playwrights into action, and although neither Barrie nor Galsworthy had ever been troubled by the Censor, they were leaders in the campaign for reform, together with those who *had* suffered, Barker and Shaw.

Galsworthy and Gilbert Murray persuaded Barrie to join a provisional committee for the advancement of the movement. Together they sent a letter to 'every dramatist of the day', urging them to sign a protest against this 'slight on our Profession'. Replies were to be sent to Barrie's address.[43] Seventy-one signatories supported the petition published in the *Times* and the Committee for the Abolition of the Office of Dramatic Censorship was formed. At Barrie's suggestion they prepared a memorial to the Prime Minister and collected signatures of distinguished writers who were not dramatists and of other celebrated persons from outside the theatre. William Archer's amusing fantasy about a possible next step shows Barrie's central role in the enterprise:

> The Dramatic Authors of England are to assemble in Trafalgar Square. Barrie will address them from the base of Nelson's column, and the Savoy orchestra will play 'Britons never will be slaves!' The procession will then form, and will be headed by Pinero and Shaw walking arm in arm. Immediately behind them will come Garnett and Galsworthy, each bearing the pole of a red banner with the inscription 'Down with the Censor'. An effigy of Redford, which is being prepared by the Savoy property man, will be carried by Frederick Harrison and W B Yeats; and over its head will wave a banner, carried by Gilbert Murray.[44]

In February 1908, Barrie led a deputation to meet with the Home Secretary, Herbert Gladstone, standing in for the Prime Minister who was ill. That meeting produced no immediate result, and it was not until July 1909 that a Joint Select Committee on the Stage Plays (Censorship), chaired by Herbert Samuel, Chancellor of the Duchy of Lancaster, was established. Forty-nine witnesses were examined, including Archer, Shaw, Barker (who read a submission from Frohman, possibly ghosted by Barrie), Galsworthy, and Barrie, despite his reluctance to make a personal appearance – 'to assist from the background is my passion'.[45]

In his testimony Barrie affirmed his view that the Censor had an adverse effect on the drama: 'I feel strongly that it makes our drama a more puerile thing in the life of the nation than it ought to be, and is a stigma on all writing plays.' It also discouraged non-dramatic writers from turning to the theatre, and existing playwrights from writing according to their consciences. 'The great thing is that you should try to say what is in you to say. There are a number of dramatists who have serious views which they want to express in a dramatic form [...] they are doing it against all their own commercial interests.' He was anxious to define the difference between 'the well-intentioned play of a rebel character' and the 'play of low intention'.[46] All the New Dramatists in their evidence sought to stress the distinction between an indecent play and one that responsibly challenged contemporary orthodoxies, but Barker believed that Barrie's testimony made the case with the greatest clarity:

> When J. M. Barrie, giving his evidence before the Censorship Committee, was asked how he would distinguish a sincerely unconventional play from a catch-penny piece of riskiness, he answered that you could always tell whether a thing was well meant or not. For days everyone had been exhausting their wits to define and re-define and define again the difference between what might be medicinal and what was merely noxious. But this answer was accepted; one felt the truth of it. By cultivating an artistic as well as a moral conscience – a clean palate – good taste in fact, one can distinguish well enough between a normal work of art and an abnormal.[47]

Despite good definitions, sound arguments, and distinguished petitioners, the outcome of the Select Committee's deliberations changed little in practice. Barrie, as was his wont, turned to the theatre to parody the issue. *The*

Dramatists Get What They Want (1912) – American title, *The Dramatists and the Censor* – was included in the revue *Hullo, Ragtime!* at the London Hippodrome. The farce ridiculed the incompetence of the censorship, but also, in true Barrie fashion, gently satirised the 'decadent' dramas that were the victims of the blue pencil.

Conclusions

William Archer asserted that Barrie was 'not part of the intellectual movement' and 'raised no critical question'. Generally 'lacking in philosophic insight, in one or two of his plays he seems to be feeling around for a philosophy but he never quite finds it'. (*Mary Rose* and *Crichton* are given as examples.) He concludes: '[Barrie's] strength lies in observation and fantasy, not in thought.'[48] Shaw agreed: 'When you review his series of plays – all charming – you can't with justice say there is any strong purpose behind the charm.'[49]

Rather than deny Barrie a 'philosophy' or a 'purpose', it is fairer to say that Barrie's 'philosophy' was not that of Archer, or for that matter of Shaw, or Galsworthy, or even of Barker. Their belief in socio-economic reform as the key to the salvation of humankind was indicative of an essentially optimistic world view. Barrie was not an optimist. Shaw's obituary was entitled: 'Barrie: the man with Hell in his soul'. It continued: 'His plays were terrifying. Behind all the tenderness and playfulness there is a sense of inexorable destiny. He was a Calvinist to the marrow.'[50] Andrew E. Malone agreed that '[Barrie's] pity is as deep as that of John Galsworthy, his social sense is as lively as that of Bernard Shaw; but he has none of the faith in the perfectability of mankind which distinguishes these dramatists.'[51] As a determinist, Barrie was also a pessimist. For him, better social conditions are not a solution to 'inexorable destiny'.

Granville Barker understood Barrie's dramaturgy better than most. 'Into the dominant dramatic movement of the time he did not [...] fit very well. Realism was in the ascendant, and to try poetry or fantasy was to risk being labelled amateur or crank.'[52] Barker himself showed some inclination towards 'fantasy', evidenced in his collaborative play with Laurence Housman, *Prunella* (1904), and his interest in directing the plays of Maeterlinck and Schnitzler. He drew attention to Barrie's affinity with the Elizabethan Masque, referring particularly to *Peter Pan* (1904) and *A Kiss for Cinderella* (1905).

But throughout his dramatic works, the spirit of masquerade is omnipresent. His characters readily assume masks or secret 'fictional' roles, for example, the anti-hero of *Walker, London,* Phoebe in *Quality Street* (1902), Maggie in *What Every Woman Knows,* Mrs Dowey in *The Old Lady Shows her Medals* (1917), Peter Pan and Wendy, Leonora, and the characters in *Dear Brutus* (1917) who act out what they might have been in the magic wood. This pervasive performative element links with his use of metatheatricality as a vessel for his commentary on current theatrical practice.

Barker also acknowledged Barrie's constant attempts to adapt his individual style of writing to the exigencies and demands of the commercial stage, but in the last analysis, Barker believed, it was to these demands that he invariably bowed. Barrie and the New Dramatists were united in seeking a measure of change in the contemporary theatre, but they had differing views as to the extent, or the precise nature, of the changes and how they might be effected. Their dramatic interests were often parallel, but sometimes overlapped – a delicate distinction.

Notes

1   William Archer, *The Old Drama and the New* (London: Heinemann, 1923), p. 31.
2   J. C. Trewin, *The Edwardian Theatre* (Oxford: Blackwell, 1976), p. 60.
3   Sheldon Chaney, 'The New English Dramatists', *Theatre Magazine (NY)*, 19 February 1914, p.81. Quoted in Carl Markgraf, *J. M. Barrie: An Annotated Secondary Bibliography* (Greensboro, N. C.: ELT Press, 1989), p. 13.
4   Thomas H. Dickinson, *Contemporary Drama of England* (Boston: Little Brown, 1931), p. 230.
5   Jean Chothia, *English Drama of the Early Modern Period (1890–1914)* (London: Longmans, 1996), pp. 83–84.
6   Desmond MacCarthy, *The Court Theatre* (London: A. H. Bullen, 1907), p. 15.
7   G. B. Shaw, 'Barrie: "The Man with Hell in his Soul"', *Sunday Graphic*, 20 June 1937. Reprinted in *Shaw*, 13 (1993), pp. 151–53.
8   H. V. Marrot, *The Life and Letters of John Galsworthy* (London: William Heinemann, 1935), pp. 77–79.
9   Denis Mackail, *The Story of J. M. B.* (London: Peter Davies, 1941), p. 397.
10 Shaw, 'Barrie', p. 152.
11 Mackail, pp.468–70. See also Luke McKernan's webpage **thebioscope.net/2008/05/30/ pen-and-pictures-no-3-jm-barrie** (Accessed 18 January 2012).
12 Granville Barker, 'J. M. Barrie as a Dramatist', *Bookman* (October 1910), pp. 13–21.
13 William Archer, 'Ghosts and Gibberings', *Pall Mall Gazette* (8 April 1891).
14 J. M. Barrie, *Ibsen's Ghost. A Play in One Act*, ed. Penelope Griffin (London: Cecil Woolf, 1975).
15 G. B. Shaw, *The Quintessence of Ibsenism* (London: Walter Scott, 1891).

16 *World*, 3 June 1891. See *Ibsen's Ghost*, ed. Griffin, p. 67.
17 *Illustrated London News* , 6 June 1891. *Ibsen's Ghost*, ed. Griffin, p. 66.
18 *Ibsen's Ghost*, ed. Griffin, p. 13.
19 Mackail, p. 178.
20 *Ibsen's Ghost*, ed. Griffin, p. 13.
21 For example, G. B. Shaw, *Our Theatre in the Nineties*, 3 vols (London: Constable, 1931); H. Granville Barker, *The Exemplary Theatre* (London: Chatto and Windus, 1922).
22 'The Theatre', *World*, 11 April 1905, p. 622.
23 *Graphic*, 27 March 1915, p. 412.
24 See Leon H. Hugo, 'Punch: J. M. Barrie's Gentle Swipe at "Supershaw"', *Shaw* (1990), pp. 60–72.
25 *Times*, 26 June 1909.
26 See R. D. S. Jack, 'Barrie and the Extreme Heroine', in *Gendering the Nation*, ed. Christopher Whyte (Edinburgh: Edinburgh University Press, 1995), pp. 137–67.
27 *New Statesman*, 59 (23 April 1960).
28 Jack, 'Barrie and the Extreme Heroine', p. 137.
29 Letter to R. Golding Bright, 9 April 1923, *Letters of J. M. Barrie*, ed. Violet Meynell (London: Peter Davies, 1942), p. 63.
30 *Illustrated London News* (13 September 1913).
31 11 March 1914. Quoted in Markgraf, p. 102.
32 H. M. Walbrook, *Barrie and the Theatre* (London: Peter Davies, 1922), p. 125.
33 Jack, 'Barrie and the Extreme Heroine', p. 160. Jack also writes convincingly on Barrie's celebration of women's manipulative strengths in his adaptation of *The Taming of the Shrew* in *The Ladies Shakespeare* (1914).
34 *Bellman*, 25 (26 October 1918). Quoted in Markgraf, p. 290.
35 10 September 1913. Quoted in Markgraf, p. 103.
36 'Working with Pinero, Barrie and Shaw', *Theatre (NY)*, (1920), pp. 32–34. Quoted in Markgraf, p. 51.
37 See P. P. Howe, *The Repertory Theatre: A Record and a Criticism* (London: Martin Secker, 1910).
38 C. B. Purdom, *Harley Granville Barker* (London: Rockcliff, 1955), p. 98.
39 'Papers Past', *Star*, 25 April 1904.
40 Edward Garnett, 'The Repertory Theatre in England', *Nation (NY)*, 89 (5 August 1909), pp.125–26. Quoted in Markgraf, p. 225.
41 Granville Barker, 'The Theatre-the Next Phase', *English Review* (July 1910), p. 639.
42 J. T. Grein and C. W. Jarvis, 'A British Theatre Libre. A Suggestion.' *The Weekly Comedy* (7 December 1889). N. H. G. Schooderwoerd, *J. T. Grein, Ambassador of the Theatre* (Assen: Van Gorcum, 1962), p. 191.
43 Janet Dunbar, *J. M. Barrie: The Man Behind the Image* (Boston: Houghton Mifflin, 1970), pp 165–66.
44 Letter to Lady Mary Murray (1 November 1907). C. Archer, *William Archer: Life, Work and Friendships* (London: Allen and Unwin, 1931), p. 321.
45 Purdom, p. 93.
46 John Palmer, *The Censor and the Theatres* (New York: Michael Kennerley, 1913), pp. 219–21. See also Steve Nicholson, *The Censorship of British Drama. 1900–1968, Vol. 1: 1900–1932* (Exeter: University of Exeter Press, 2003).

47 Barker, 'The Theatre; the Next Phase', p. 640.
48 Archer, *The Old Drama and the New*, pp. 336–37.
49 Shaw, 'Barrie'.
50 Ibid.
51 Arthur E. Malone, 'The Conservatism of J. M. Barrie', *Fortnightly Review*, February 1927, pp. 210–21. Quoted in Markgraf, p. 350.
52 H. G. B[arker], 'Preface to *The Boy David*', *The Plays of J. M. Barrie* (London: Peter Davies, 1938), pp. ii–xxxii.

2. 'The odd, odd triangle': Barrie's Metatheatrical Critique of the Victorian Dramatic Tradition

ANNA FARKAS

When Max Beerbohm reviewed J. M. Barrie's latest play, *Little Mary*, in the *Saturday Review* in October 1903, he wrote: 'The critics have paid Mr. Barrie many handsome compliments on "Little Mary", and the handsomest of all is the general demur that, however delightful it may be as an entertainment, "Little Mary" can scarcely be regarded as a play. This is but another way of telling Mr. Barrie that he is now perfect master of the medium in which he works.'[1] The idiosyncrasy of Barrie's style has long led critics, both contemporary and modern, to consider his drama as somehow divorced from the theatrical tradition he worked in. Thus Beerbohm could claim, for example, that a Barrie play at its best transcended its form because it 'must, seeming so unlike other plays, seem to be hardly a play at all.'[2] For Beerbohm and many of his contemporaries this was a mark of Barrie's genius, but it has since led to his marginalisation in theatre history. As the author of *Peter Pan* (1904), he has been manoeuvred into the narrow niche of whimsical fantastical comedy. As a result, the important role played in the upheavals of the British stage in the early twentieth century by the playwright to whom George Bernard Shaw ascribed 'the final relegation of the Nineteenth Century London theatre to the dust-bin'[3] has been largely forgotten by modern scholarship. In order to fully appreciate J. M. Barrie's modernity as a playwright, we first need to consider his relationship to the past.

This chapter will focus on Barrie's engagement with the Victorian dramatic tradition through his use of metatheatrical satire in a series of plays written between 1900 and 1915.

When *The Wedding Guest* premiered in London at the end of September 1900, reviewers immediately recognised 'an ancient and familiar story'.[4] 'The theme of the play is the one to which all our dramatists seem to have at the moment condemned themselves', the *Speaker* commented.[5] Other publications located the play's provenance more precisely. The *Birmingham Daily Post* wrote that 'the trail of the "problem play" was over it all' and

The County Gentleman concluded that 'it really seems as if the era of the problem play had returned once again, for our leading dramatists are tumbling over one another in their eagerness to solve the eternal problem of two women and a man', noting that in *The Wedding Guest*, 'there is much that is conventional'.[6] The *Athenaeum* suggested as a likely model Arthur Wing Pinero's *The Profligate* (1889), from the first 'surge' of problem plays a decade before. At the same time, like the majority of the reviews, it pointed to a number of close contemporaries that followed the same pattern and all opened in the West End in the same season as *The Wedding Guest*: Sydney Grundy's *A Debt of Honour*, Lucy Clifford's *The Likeness of the Night*, Henry Arthur Jones's *Mrs. Dane's Defense* and Frank Harris's *Mr. and Mrs. Daventry*.[7] These plays all focus on 'the so-called sexual problem' as the *Fortnightly Review* described it,[8] the sexual double standard, which sanctioned premarital sex in men, but stigmatised unmarried women who were not virgins as fallen women.[9] Although technically only a subcategory of a type of play that examines social questions, the sexual problem play was by far the most popular incarnation of the problem play in the late-Victorian theatre and, therefore, became synonymous with the general term.[10]

According to Michael Booth, 'the immediate father of the problem play in England is Ibsen',[11] but the sexual problem play of fin-de-siècle Britain owes at least as much to the French tradition of the well-made play; especially fallen-woman plays by Victorien Sardou and Alexandre Dumas *fils*, as Kerry Powell and Sos Eltis have demonstrated in relation to Oscar Wilde's society drama.[12] The tradition Barrie was drawing on in *The Wedding Guest* included Wilde, but was represented most prominently by Arthur Wing Pinero and Henry Arthur Jones, who had both written important plays in the early 1890s about the sexual double standard – Pinero's *The Second Mrs Tanqueray* (1893) and Jones's *The Case of Rebellious Susan* (1894) stand out – and were still actively contributing to the genre when Barrie attempted it, as the productions of Jones's *Mrs Dane's Defence* in the same year and Pinero's *Iris* the year after demonstrate.[13] This renewed interest in the problem play at the turn of the century provoked a detailed assessment of the genre in the *Fortnightly Review*. There the author attributed its continued popularity to the influence of 'the Scandinavian hypnotist' Ibsen, 'which, like the distressing question of pauperism, is always with us'.[14] The author also criticised drama as a vehicle for such a topic, however, as the conventions of the well-made play prevented a comprehensive assessment of the problem on the stage, resulting in an extremely formulaic pattern:

> Let A stand for the husband, and B for his wife. Then C will represent the other woman. How are you to solve the problem of the man's position? There are only three possible methods: either B, the wife, disappears [...] or C disappears, usually by suicide. The last alternative, the disappearance of some cowardly A, the husband who has been the cause of all this precious coil, is more rare, though it, too, is a conceivable hypothesis.[15]

This scenario is exactly reproduced in *The Wedding Guest*. Set in Scotland, the first act of the play shows the preparations for the wedding of the painter Paul Digby to Margaret Fairbairn, a young woman, who was raised to be especially innocent – or ignorant, Barrie suggests this synonym early on – by a father who kept her in a childish state. Margaret is not aware that Paul had a previous relationship with Kate Ommaney, an artist's model, whom he lived with in London. She makes her appearance at the ceremony and eventually reveals their affair and its result, their infant daughter. The contrast between the 'good' and the 'bad' woman is built up in a conventional fashion. Wide-eyed, eighteen-year-old Margaret enjoyed a privileged, sheltered upbringing while world-weary Kate, who is older, had to fend for herself working as a seamstress and a model. Margaret's initially rigid notions of sexual morality, which give way to greater tolerance in the course of the play, reflect a similar development in theatrical precursors like the convent-educated Ellean Tanqueray in *The Second Mrs Tanqueray* and the American Puritan Hester Worsley in Wilde's *A Woman of No Importance* (1893). Meanwhile, Kate was identified by *The Times* as 'the usual "other woman", the tempestuous foil to serene innocence'.[16] The critics recognised the play's most conventional element in the 'melodramatic figure'[17] of the fallen woman, who had haunted page and stage in England and France for at least half a century before the premiere of *The Wedding Guest*.[18] When reading the play, this identification is very plausible in the first three acts, where Kate provides the most sensational effects; in the final act, however, she introduces a different note.

The conventional impasse in the plot is reached when Margaret finally learns of her new husband's disreputable past and returns to her father, threatening to break up the marriage. So, who is to go, A, B or C? Barrie has all the main characters sit down together in the last act to thrash it out between them. Margaret's father, Mr Fairbairn, is exposed as a hypocritical and deeply conventional humbug. Paul told him about the affair before the wedding, but Mr Fairbairn refused to pay too much attention to it: 'My rule, Janet—look on the bright side, you know. Let sleeping dogs lie. I dislike painful subjects—' (*DE* 263). When Margaret appeals to his wisdom, and asks for his advice: 'Do you see any bright side now?', he replies: 'The servants don't know' (*DE* 264) and makes Kate a proposal:

> MR FAIRBAIRN. [...] I happen to know a farmer – a widower – who is in need of a housekeeper—
> [...]
> MRS OMMANEY. [...] I think I know what is coming, Mr. Fairbairn. Your farmer lives in Australia, doesn't he?
> MR FAIRBAIRN. How did you know?
> MRS OMMANEY. Oh, I have read them also.
> MR FAIRBAIRN (*puzzled*). Read them? Read what? I know the man – a splendid climate.
> MRS OMMANEY. Where I should be out of your way. [...] You were to say, I think, that I could write to them once a year?
> MR FAIRBAIRN. At Christmas time.
> MRS OMMANEY. Saying what a beautiful peace had come into my life, and baby is such a comfort, and that sweet-smelling flowers are growing up the porch of my rustic home!
> MR FAIRBAIRN (*delighted*). Yes, yes!
> MRS OMMANEY. Honeysuckle?
> MR FAIRBAIRN. Anything you like.
> MRS OMMANEY. I should prefer honeysuckle. It is usually honey-suckle. Do let it be honeysuckle. (*DE* 265)

The fallen woman, who had seemed so thoroughly predictable up to this point, now reveals herself to be well-read in her own genre. She deftly unmasks the absurdity of another plan, this time proposed by Margaret, that she and Paul raise his and Kate's illegitimate child so Kate can return to her father's Cornish fishing village: 'Oh, you baby, trying to do what is right! Your father is a selfish old man, you are a generous girl, but you tell the same fairy tale. You have brought the honeysuckle from Australia and planted it at my father's door.' (*DE* 269)

In the typical sexual problem play, the dramatic exit of the fallen woman at this point – often by suicide, as the *Fortnightly Review* reminded its readers – indicted the sexual double standard in principle, but not in practice; the fallen woman still ended up dead in most cases. Although these plays acknowledged that her ostracism was not fair, there was still no place for her in the world of the play. Here, Kate's metatextual knowingness disrupts the illusion, exposing the artificiality of the genre to the audience, and forcing the characters themselves to question their outlook. Margaret angrily confronts her father: 'What I thought your fine philosophy, it was only an avoidance of disagreeable truths. Do you think—but you don't think, you have shirked the trouble of thinking for so long that now, when you must, you can't. And I am in the same plight.' (*DE* 266) Barrie critiques the problem play from within by having the heroine herself point out the shortcomings of her type, and suddenly the underlying value-system of the entire genre, Victorian idealism, is under fire, as it can only provide contrived, 'fairy tale' solutions to the problem at hand. The resonance with Shaw, whose *Plays Unpleasant* from the 1890s were meant to 'force the spectator to face unpleasant facts,' is evident.[19] But Barrie does not really go that far. He merely observes that the traditional sexual problem play is unwilling and unable to deal adequately with 'disagreeable truths'. Unlike Shaw, he does not use the stage as a pulpit; his criticism is directed at the shortcomings of his chosen medium, not at society at large.[20] Overall, *The Wedding Guest* remains within the constraints of the genre. In the end, Kate voluntarily gives up her claim and announces that she will return to her father after all, and Paul and Margaret reconcile when Paul solemnly promises to 'atone'. (*DE* 269)

In *The Wedding Guest,* Kate Ommaney's startling metatextual awareness remains a fleeting moment in an otherwise serious attempt at the sexual problem play, which was received by the critics on those terms. But when Barrie returned to the theme five years later in *Alice Sit-By-the-Fire* (1905), the metatheatrical current was too prominent to ignore. In his review in the *Manchester Guardian*, William Archer called the play 'a burlesque, and a ruthless one. It will give a death-blow to an already moribund form of art – the French drama of intrigue and self-sacrifice.'[21] Reginald Farrer applied the same label in the *Speaker*, but identified 'the more obvious absurdities of the Oscar Wilde school of polite melodrama' as the target.[22] The term 'burlesque' is used here to denote metatheatrical satire in a general sense, rather than the more specifically defined genre of the theatrical burlesque, a highly topical parody of a particular play or production, which was very popular in the English theatre in the eighteenth and the earlier part of the nineteenth century.[23] Barrie's own first success on the stage, *Ibsen's Ghost* (1891), a spoof of the string of productions of Ibsen plays that agitated London in the 1891 season, was an exercise in that genre; but the scope of *Alice Sit-By-the-Fire* is broader.[24] Here the satire is both less topical and less domineering than in a traditional burlesque. The play satirises the contemporary theatre's on-going preoccupation with aberrant female sexuality from within the framework of a domestic comedy. Barrie chooses the same approach as Jane Austen in *Northanger Abbey* (pub. 1818) and Richard Brinsley Sheridan in *The Rivals* (1775), as the critics for *The Times* and the *Athenaeum* pointed out in their reviews.[25] He adopts the perspective of a young girl who has become so enamoured by the theatre that she is no longer able to differentiate between fact and fiction.

Seventeen-year-old Amy Grey and her best friend Ginevra have been to the theatre five times in a week and all the plays were very similar, as Ginevra comments: 'Real plays are always about a lady and two men; and alas, only one of them is her husband. That is Life, you know. It is called the odd, odd triangle.' (*DE* 601) When Amy's parents, the eponymous Alice and Colonel Grey, return home from a long absence in India, the girls quickly detect suspicious signs in Alice's behaviour towards Stephen Rollo, an old family friend and suspect 'an assignation' (*DE* 624) when he asks Alice to visit him at home. Here the familiar script takes over. Amy knows from the plays she has seen that she must go to the man's house in evening dress, to get back the compromising letters; 'There are always letters', observes Ginevra (*DE* 624). If necessary, Amy will have to sacrifice herself to save her mother's reputation. Complications ensue when both parents arrive at the lodgings of their bachelor friend – they had both been invited, of course – and all parties are temporarily confused as to who, if anyone, has been compromised. In *Alice Sit-by-the-Fire*, the metatheatrical satire takes the shape of a play-within-a-play, which 'play-deluded'[26] Amy is determined to act out in spite of the discouragement she meets with in the person of the unlikely villain Stephen Rollo. Barrie demonstrates in this play how easily the complicated stage business of well-made melodrama can be adapted to generate laughter, rather than suspense, if the rigidity of the pattern is exposed. And although the traditional dichotomy of the good and the bad woman is retained on the surface, it quickly begins to unravel.

Barrie had already begun to deflate the type of the good woman in *The Wedding Guest* by refusing simply to accept her characteristic 'innocence' as the inevitable result of youth and virginity. Margaret's upbringing, as it is described by her aunt, sounds more like a behavioural experiment, 'You were ten when your mother died, and your father has kept you at that – like a stopped clock.' (*DE* 221) Barrie also refused to endorse the genre's habitual reverence for innocence in that earlier play. Mr Fairbairn's 'theory' of child-rearing, which attempted to keep all deviation from rigid principles of morality a secret, is dismissed as mere 'laziness' (*DE* 221) and Margaret herself eventually identifies her upbringing as a handicap, as has been shown above. In *Alice Sit-by-the-Fire*, Amy's innocence is a fact, but it also is not especially noteworthy, as she is a very unusual thing for the time: a seventeen-year-old in a play who is not the romantic lead and is therefore not sexualised. Rather, she is a child playing a game. Her innocence manifests itself in her naive belief in the reality of what she has seen on stage, making her the butt of the joke. The heroine of this play is the older woman, 'the belle of the Punjaub' (*DE* 622), who knows 'the world' (*DE* 620) – the usual euphemism for sexual experience – without having done more than flirt. Both Alice's respectability and her sexual power are asserted repeatedly. The Colonel recalls, for example, how 'when for one month in the twelve we went to—to—where the boys were, it was like turning you loose in a sweet-stuff shop. [. . .] But I knew my dear, and could trust her' (*DE* 610). Her own daughter casts Alice as the fallen woman, but Barrie makes sure that the audience understands that she is no such thing, without, however, diminishing the character's confident sexuality. As a result, *Alice Sit-by-the-Fire* issues a powerful challenge to the madonna/whore dichotomy of the fallen woman play. This effect was underscored by the casting of Ellen Terry – then fifty-eight years old – whose enormous popularity was not noticeably affected by her irregular private life.[27]

The expansion of the metatextual element from *The Wedding Guest* to *Alice Sit-by-the-Fire* demonstrates how Barrie grew more confident in the use of this method for 'sustained critical commentary on [. . .] theatrical forms', as Richard Schoch writes about burlesque proper.[28] And although one might have suspected that the parody in *Alice Sit-by-the-Fire* was exhaustive, Barrie revisited both the approach and the subject matter within a few years. In November 1903, around the same time he was developing the scenario for *Alice*, he sketched an outline in one of his notebooks that was simply titled 'Problem Play'. This consists of a list of numbered notes, the second and the third of which lay out the situation of the proposed play, while the last one makes a suggestion how the parts are to be interpreted:

> 2) Husband dramatist – wife actress – married because each pretended
> to have had a past.
> 3) Secret sorrow neither had a past.
> [. . .]
> 25) Man might mimic Tree, woman Mrs Campbell.[29]

Mrs Patrick Campbell had famously created the role of Paula Tanqueray in *The Second Mrs Tanqueray*, while Herbert Beerbohm Tree put on plays by Henry Arthur Jones and Oscar Wilde at the Haymarket theatre, including Wilde's sexual problem play, *A Woman of No Importance* (1893). It is likely that some of the parodic energy that inspired the author at that moment eventually went into the next play on this topic to be realised, *Alice Sit-by-the-Fire*, but Barrie did not completely discard the scenario. He returned to it in 1910, when a repertory season he was involved in at the Duke of York's theatre was foundering.[30]

The resulting short play, *A Slice of Life* (1910), was very well received in the press. *The Times* called it 'a masterpiece of most delicate and searching dramatic criticism' after its premiere at a charity matinee in London in July 1910, while the audience at the first American production in January 1912 reportedly 'roared' with laughter.[31] Barrie retained the parody of the conventions of the problem play as he had outlined it in 1903. Mr and Mrs Hyphen-Brown, a married couple of theatre professionals, are troubled by the 'double life' they have been leading.[32] The climax is reached when they confess to each other that neither had a past before they married. Mr Hyphen-Brown has always been 'an absolutely moral man' and Mrs Hyphen Brown 'was a good woman even before' she met her husband (133). The author also updated the piece, however, by adding a second layer of meta-theatrical satire. This is directed at the altered rules of communication in 'the new drama' (131). The maid knows that she would lose her position 'if missus were to catch me soliloquizing in a modern play' (127), the telephone is employed for the exposition and Mr Hyphen-Brown apologises when his wife catches him trying to use an aside: 'I beg your pardon. But it is so infernally difficult to make things clear without them.' (129) Having only recently participated in one of the decisive events in the development of the modern theatre in Britain, the repertory season at the Duke of York's Theatre, Barrie broadened the range of his satire in this skit by drawing attention to the emerging orthodoxies of the realist 'New Drama'.

He revisited the plot of sexual intrigue once more after that, but only to finally announce its demise. In *Rosy Rapture: The Pride of the Beauty Chorus* (1915), which was variously called a revue or a burlesque,[33] Lord Lillian addresses the audience:

> You see before you the celebrated three who have been in every thoughtful play since it was first discovered that all the Drama needs is two bores and a passion. (*Indicating himself and James*) the bores, (*indicating Rosy*) the passion. In other words the husband (*he bows*), the wife (*Rosy curtseys*), the lover (*James scowls and bobs*). In short, the triangle.[34]

However, 'there's no living to be made out of being a lover nowadays,' so James decides to 'try poultry farming' instead.[35] Both *A Slice of Life* and *Rosy Rapture* return to the satirical method of the traditional burlesque as Barrie had already realised it in *Ibsen's Ghost*. The plot is barely there, the characters are mere ciphers, and the play consists of a quick succession of physical and verbal comedy which targets either well-known commonplaces of the stage – like the conventions of the problem play – or particular productions – like the 'imitations of popular players', which the critic for the *Observer* observed at a performance of *A Slice of Life* in November 1910.[36] And although they therefore necessarily lack the complexity of Barrie's earlier treatments of this theme, they are revealing both as a sign of the persistence of Barrie's interest in this particular genre and his contempt for it.

J. M. Barrie's experiments with the fallen woman play illustrate his critical engagement with the Victorian tradition, regarding both form and content. His playful dismantling of the genre's formulaic plots also undermine its traditional conservative content in relation to the representation of women on stage. Although female-centric, the sexual problem play and its precursor, the melodrama of sexual intrigue – the 'triangle' plays, as Barrie called them – reduce female characters to their status on the sexual marketplace. The only roles available to them are those of desirable virgin or tainted fallen woman; women *are* the problem in these plays. By turning this pattern inside out through the use of metatheatrical satire and exposing its artificiality and fundamental moral bankruptcy in *The Wedding Guest*, *Alice-Sit-by-the-Fire* and *A Slice of Life*, Barrie prepared the stage for a new type of heroine and a different kind of play about gender relations. This is already apparent in *Alice Sit-by-the-Fire*, which unites a heroine, whose vibrant sexuality we are told explicitly is *not* a problem, with a portrayal of a remarkably harmonious and equitable marriage. It becomes more pronounced in the plays Barrie wrote between 1905 and the outbreak of the First World War, the majority of which are variations on the theme of the strength and diversity of the female character. Taken together, they are a systematic rebuttal of the conventional dramatic heroine. The ageing actress in *Rosalind* (1912) is not young, Maggie Wylie in *What Every Woman Knows* (1908) is not beautiful, Kate in *The Twelve-Pound Look* (1910) rejects romance by choosing paid work over marriage, and Leonora in *The Adored One* (1913), which later became *Seven Women* (1917), is 'a politician [...] a mother [...] a coquette [...] a murderess,' (*DE* 949–50) and much more. Barrie's modern heroines match – if they do not trump – the complexity of his male characters, a considerable achievement in face of the paradigms of the dramatic tradition of the Victorian theatre.

Notes

1 Max Beerbohm, 'Little Mary', *Saturday Review*, 3 October 1903, pp. 423–24, p. 423.
2 Beerbohm, p. 423.
3 See J. T. Grein, *The World of the Theatre: Impressions and Memoirs, March 1920–1921* (London: William Heinemann, 1921), p. vii.
4 '"The Wedding Guest," at the Garrick', *Pall Mall Gazette*, 28 September 1900, pp. 1–2, p. 1.
5 P. C., 'The Theatre: The Wedding Guest', *Speaker*, 6 October 1900, pp. 17–19, p. 18.
6 'Mr. J. M. Barrie's New Play', *Birmingham Daily Post*, 28 September 1900, p. 5; 'A Problem in Scotch', *County Gentleman*, 6 October 1900, p. 1256.
7 'Drama: The Week', *Athenaeum*, 6 October 1900, p. 451. See also, P. C., p. 18, and especially, ZYX, 'Problems and Playwrights', *Fortnightly Review*, November 1900, pp. 858–66.
8 ZYX, p. 859.
9 R. D. S. Jack recognises *The Wedding Guest*'s roots in this tradition, which he describes as the 'limited English dramatic tradition relating to *Lady Audley's Secret*', but chooses to focus on Ibsen's influence instead, which he traces in the play's mythic and symbolic structure. See *The Road to the Never Land: A Reassessment of J. M. Barrie's Dramatic Art* (Aberdeen: Aberdeen University Press, 1991; repr. Glasgow: Humming Earth, 2010), p. 64). For a thorough assessment of the representation of the fallen woman in the British theatre, see Sos Eltis, 'The Fallen Woman on the Stage: Maidens, Magdalens and the Emancipated Female', in *The Cambridge Companion to the Victorian and Edwardian Theatre*, ed. Kerry Powell (Cambridge: Cambridge University Press, 2004), pp. 222–36; Sos Eltis, *Acts of Desire: Women and Sex on Stage, 1800–1930* (Oxford: Oxford University Press, 2013).
10 The broader definition of the genre, which George Bernard Shaw identified as the definitive mode of the modern drama, has also been applied to Barrie's work. (see George Bernard Shaw, 'The Author's Apology', in *Plays Unpleasant* [London: Penguin, 2000], p. 197). Marty Gould recently described *The Admirable Crichton* as a 'problem play [which] exposes what really lurks beneath the polished veneer of turn-of-the-century high society'. (original italics). See Marty Gould, 'Emblems of Authority in *The Admirable Crichton*', *Modern Drama*, 54.2 (2011), pp. 141–60, p. 142. Eliott Simon included Barrie in a study of the problem play between 1890 and 1914. He does not mention *The Wedding Guest*, but also discusses *The Admirable Crichton*, as well as *Peter Pan* and *Dear Brutus*. See Eliott M. Simon, *The Problem Play in British Drama 1890–1914*, Salzburg Studies in English Literature: Poetic Drama and Poetic Theory, 40 (Salzburg: Universität Salzburg, 1978), pp. 197–241.
11 Michael R. Booth, *Theatre in the Victorian Age* (Cambridge: Cambridge University Press, 1991), p. 177.
12 See, for example, their respective discussions of Wilde's sources for *Lady Windermere's Fan*: Kerry Powell, *Oscar Wilde and the Theatre of the 1890s* (Cambridge: Cambridge University Press, 1990), pp. 14–32; Sos Eltis, *Revising Wilde: Society and Subversion in the Plays of Oscar Wilde* (Oxford: Clarendon Press, 1996), pp. 55–94.
13 For Pinero's and Jones's contribution to the development of the well-made play in the British theatre, see John Russell Taylor, *The Rise and Fall of the Well-Made Play* (London: Methuen, 1967), pp. 35–80.

14 ZYX, p. 859.

15 ZYX, pp. 859–60.

16 'Garrick Theatre', *Times*, 28 September 1900, p. 4.

17 ZYX, p. 863.

18 See Eltis, 'Fallen Woman on Stage', pp. 222–24.

19 Shaw, *Plays Unpleasant*, p. 25.

20 By contrast, Shaw's own variation of the sexual problem play, *Mrs Warren's Profession* (1893), one of the *Plays Unpleasant*, deals with the real problem of the socio-economic causes of prostitution in late-Victorian England.

21 W[illiam] A[rcher], 'Mr Barrie's New Plays', *Manchester Guardian*, 6 April 1905, p. 5.

22 Reginald Farrer, 'The Tragedy of Time', *Speaker*, 8 April 1905, pp. 34–35, p. 35.

23 I draw on Richard W. Schoch's description of the characteristic form of the burlesque in the second half of the nineteenth century here. See Richard W. Schoch (ed.), *Victorian Theatrical Burlesques*, (Aldershot: Ashgate, 2003), pp. xx–xxi. For the history of the burlesque in the English theatre, see V. C. Clinton-Baddeley, *The Burlesque Tradition in the English Theatre after 1660* (New York: Benjamin Blom, 1971); Robert F. Wilson, Jr., *'Their Form Confounded': Studies in the Burlesque Play from Udall to Sheridan* (The Hague: Mouton, 1975).

24 For a detailed assessment of Barrie's attempt at 'classical' burlesque, see Penelope Griffin's introduction and appendices to her edition of the play, *Ibsen's Ghost: A Play in One Act* by J. M. Barrie, ed. Penelope Griffin (London: Cecil Woolf, 1975), and Tracy Davis's commentary in the play's most recent edition in Tracy C. Davis (ed.), *The Broadview Anthology of Nineteenth Century Performance*, (Peterborough, Ont.: Broadview Press, 2012).

25 'Duke of York's Theatre', *Times*, 6 April 1905, p. 10; 'Drama', *Athenaeum*, 15 April 1905, p. 474.

26 'Duke of York's Theatre', *Times*.

27 Terry married three times and had two illegitimate children.

28 Schoch, p. xii.

29 Beinecke Library, Yale University, Barrie Vault Shelves, A2/5, fols 3–5.

30 For a detailed account of this experiment, for whose financial backing Barrie had enlisted his long-term friend and business partner, the American theatre producer Charles Frohman, see Jan McDonald, *The 'New Drama' 1900–1914* (Basingstoke: Macmillan, 1986), pp. 37–44.

31 'St. James's Theatre', *Times*, 2 July 1910, p. 8; 'Miss Barrymore's Surprise', *New York Times*, 30 January 1912, p. 7.

32 'A Slice of Life', in *The Works of J. M. Barrie*, Peter Pan Edition, 18 vols (New York: Charles Scribner's Sons, 1929–41; repr. New York: AMS Press, 1975), XVIII, p. 132. Further references are given parenthetically in the text.

33 *The Times* announced it as 'Sir James Barrie's New Burlesque' in a first notice before the premiere, and then referred to it as a 'revue' in the actual review that appeared two weeks later. See 'Sir James Barrie's New Burlesque' and 'The Barrie Revue', *Times*, 10 and 23 March, both p. 7. Len Platt lists it as an example of the emerging genre of musical comedy. See Len Platt, *Musical Comedy on the West End Stage, 1890–1939* (Basingstoke: Palgrave Macmillan, 2004), p. 22. *Rosy Rapture* was a failure on stage, which is not surprising given its absurd plot and manifold other weaknesses. It is, however, a fascinating example

of writing for the theatre that is both experimental and geared towards popularity. Its cocktail of metatheatrical references to nearly all forms of performance that had currency at the time – music hall, ballet, early cinema, serious drama etc. – makes it a valuable resource for further research on Barrie's experiments with dramatic form.

34 Beinecke, R 68/1, Scene 2, p. 1.
35 Ibid., Scene 7, p. 4.
36 'At the Play', *Observer*, 27 November 1910, p. 9.

3. Barrie's Later Dramas: The Shakespearean Romances

R. D. S. JACK

A Difficult Case?

In this study, I shall use Barrie's major Shakespearean Romances – *Quality Street* (1902), *The Admirable Crichton* (1902), *Peter Pan* (1904), *Dear Brutus* (1917) and *Mary Rose* (1920) – as a conservative focus for arguing that *all* his post-Victorian drama deserves to be reassessed on his own terms. The evidence behind this claim will be drawn largely from Barrie's own evidence in his journalism, academic criticism and (retrospectively) in *The Greenwood Hat*. The quotation – in fact, misquotation – from Abraham Cowley in *Margaret Ogilvy*, where Barrie recalls identifying with the lines of the Cavalier poet, illustrates how soon the desire 'to be for ever known/And make the age to come my own' (*MO* 41) possessed him.[1] The thirteen prose works, thirteen dramas and one opera of his Victorian apprenticeship demonstrate how hard he worked at preparing himself for the role of literary genius.

However, as Hollindale noted in 1995, Barrie endured a particularly severe fall in critical esteem after his death. From being unquestioned master of the London stage and 'so obviously an original and delightful genius'[2] that most followed William Archer's lead in being 'content to treat him shortly because he raises no critical question,[3] he fell victim to Oedipal interpretations which turned attention away from his dramas to his early prose and the Pan myth.[4] This view coincided with a determined attempt to assess him against realistic criteria. Barrie might plead that he was an imaginative writer who should not be judged by 'the dull historian' (*ST* 10) or wish 'God to blast'[5] biographers but he did so in vain.

Hollindale traces the early stages of that belated critical reaction which not only opposed this view but did so in an exactly polarised manner. Far from being childish, in love with his mother and simply read on the surface, that group argued that Barrie had a complex mind, that he was only in love with art and that his layered texts had to be understood on a variety of levels.

Since then new voices have urged the positive case. The contribution of gender critics is particularly important. From that perspective Humphrey Carpenter and Eve Kosofsky Sedgwick see the Thrums tales as juvenilia and correctly focus their assessment on the more ambitious Tommy novels.[6] Our understanding of Barrie's prose has also moved from George Blake's sophistic condemnation of it on realistic criteria to the subtler, more informed vision of Andrew Nash's work.[7]

In the face of this, the tenacity of the dismissive, Oedipal/Kailyard view is surprising. Nor are those who wish to continue the myth the only ones who remain influenced by simplistic views inculcated over a long period by critics and reinforced by the media. Even at the three successful 150th Anniversary conferences held in Kirriemuir, Dumfries and Madrid in 2010 and 2011 that power remained. The distance we have come was reflected in the subtle analyses offered but the focus was still on Pan, Thrums and Mrs Barrie. Plays other than *Peter Pan* scarcely featured.

My own position in the polarised debate needs explanation. Hollindale argued that my study *The Road to the Never Land* set a new level for criticism. He also made the just reservation that my claims needed fuller support. *Myths and the Mythmaker* was, in this context, my own attempt to provide it.[8] It concentrated on Barrie's Victorian apprenticeship and tried to fill the many factual and influential gaps which were particularly noticeable for Barrie. Yet, as T. S. Eliot claimed, closing gaps is an indispensable requirement if one wants to step outside competing critical opinions and initiate a new approach – 'It is fairly certain that "interpretation" is only legitimate when it is not interpretation at all but merely putting the reader in possession of facts which he would otherwise have missed.'[9] The range of evidence provided will emerge in this article but a full account exists in Chapter 2 of *Myths and the Mythmaker*.

Any detailed study of Barrie's Victorian apprenticeship reveals him self-consciously testing the limits of his artistic strengths and weaknesses across a wide variety of forms. 1900 emerges as the key transitional year which saw two ambitious works that met with mixed receptions and failed to meet Barrie's perfectionist aims. Seen accurately by Ormond as 'the last play of Barrie's *apprenticeship*', his Ibsenite play, *The Wedding Guest*, was the least comic of his dramas since the failure of *Richard Savage*, while arguably the most ambitious of his novels, *Tommy and Grizel*, puzzled readers and led its author to turn increasingly to the tighter, enacted form of drama in preference to the looser, narrative structure of the novel with its concomitant temptation to introduce autobiographical material into his essentially imaginative world.[10]

Barrie was convinced at this time that the theatre's tighter form and limitation to the voices of its characters would cut out those autobiographical tendencies which the looser novel mode permitted. The opening direction to *Alice Sit-by-the-Fire* (1905), for example, makes the case exactly. His character, Amy, as onstage writer of a prose diary, may have more freedom than he has as playwright but his is the greater artistic challenge as '[i]n a play you can keep yourself out more easily as the characters have to do it all themselves.' (*DE* 597). In 1935, in a letter to Cynthia Asquith, his position has not changed: 'In a play you can keep yourself out much more easily as the characters have it all to do themselves.'[11]

The Rhetorical Way

(1) Guides and Guidance

To counterbalance those realistic criteria popularly imposed upon Barrie with a more sympathetic approach I shall use the Christian Humanist rhetorical method which formed the introduction to Professor David Masson's course of 'Rhetoric and Belles Lettres' which Barrie attended at Edinburgh University and adapted in his own academic criticism.[12] This implies following the Aristotelian causal line. In practice, I shall consider the first effective cause (author) and the last (audience) before advancing to close analysis (formal and material causes).

Relating the *Alice Sit-by-the-Fire* quotation to Barrie's personal views on drama, confirms another important line in his literary theory. Masson's opening lectures covered figures and modes. The wide variety of translations from one mode to another which Barrie practised in the Victorian period proves his mastery of those skills. The fullest proof of the method's later development comes with his ten different modal treatments of the Pan myth.[13]

Barrie's claim that he wishes to emphasise those theatrical strengths which are not shared by prose is the other side of the modal coin. He discusses this quintessential theatre in his journalism and in his criticism. In academic terms it stems from Professor Campbell Fraser's championing of Berkeley's theory that our understanding of ideas and the 'real' is sensually based.[14] Dramatic confirmation of this view begins as early as *Walker, London* (1892). *Peter Pan* and Tinker Bell – a character who exists in stage effects alone – again prove continuation and development.

The questions raised 'finally' involve assessing how well a writer or orator has persuaded the particular audience he is addressing. The *Alice* evidence is again helpful. The 'teamwork' side of Barrie's essentialist drama implied constant attendance at rehearsals and a readiness to re-write when actors or directors could convince him. Yet again *Pan*, with its many endings and strange rituals yet demarcated lines beyond which he would not go, offers the fullest proof of that position.[15]

The second and third causes involve analysis of a text's form and meaning. Barrie's extreme fall from literary grace poses a difficult question here. If the evidence of Barrie's serious intentions is so obvious, how can critics have missed it for so long? This is an understandable position only partly answered by Archer's argument that his genius was so obvious that it was assumed rather than explained. It is here that Toril Moi's *Ibsen and the Birth of Modernism* provides complementary evidence. Barrie is on record saying that he valued Ibsen as 'the greatest author of his age.'[16] As Moi explains, Ibsen also suffered an extremely negative reaction at the hands of those who wished to succeed and replace him.[17] Simplistic, disparaging definitions of his work 'such as realism, naturalism, melodrama and romantic drama' were inappropriately applied to the Norwegian playwright as well.[18] Only much later, when 'acceptance unseen' ended and his plays were re-assessed against more subtle, apposite criteria did he regain his reputation.

This account at every stage anticipates Barrie's position. The similarities begin with acceptance that both have to be read on two levels. Ibsen, as Haakonsen saw, makes an immediate realistic appeal but 'On a deeper level the action has a different, deeper and freer ideality, or constantly tends towards it.'[19] They continue with Moi's contention that he developed this approach within a specifically theatrical kind of modernism where 'the work is its own norm.'[20] Barrie's quintessential, radical vision of theatre has already been noted but he also asks to be read on two levels. First, in his academic essays, which are part of his proposed study of *The Early Satirical Poetry of Great Britain*, he argues that the finest comic writers of genius *must be* satiric – that is, use wit for serious ends. How difficult that might be he wistfully notes in his Nash essay, saying that an Englishman would rather 'seek reputation at the cannon's mouth' than support a cause at which people laughed.[21] Two audiences, the popular and the learned, are also implied if a playwright is to earn a living yet aim at impressing 'the world to come'. (GH, 152). Crucially, the same method is advocated by the activities of his Imp who not only counterpoints one level against another but may subversively let them contradict each other.

His journalism on its own disproves the popular view that he was not interested in the serious problems of the day. His Nottingham Journal leaders prove his expertise over a range of topics from the Industrial Revolution and the Napoleonic Wars to a view of the 'New Woman' which Ibsen would have applauded. Other popular myths are contradicted by that evidence. Far from rejecting Darwinism he accepts its major conclusions, a position he also attributes to the rustics in Thrums at the start of his earliest collection, Auld Licht Idylls (1888). Far from ignoring the theological challenges it presented, his enthusiasm for Frazer and Bergson, Ibsen and Strindberg indicates his acceptance of the 'uncertainty principle' underlying modernism.[22] If further proof were needed that Barrie, like Ibsen, was a unique modernist sophistically assessed on conservative criteria then his first solo play on the London stage provides it. Ibsen's Ghost (1891) not only showed his critical awareness of four Ibsen plays, it ended in Pirandellian fashion with the characters desperately consulting different translations to see if any allowed them to escape death!

Napoleon and Revolution also emerge as strong leitmotivs, while his diligent research into why actresses were underpaid is only one practical piece of evidence which draws him closer to Ibsen's radical views on woman's power.[23] Barrie's feminist bias derives from his belief that woman's multi-mind makes her the natural leader in this new, more competitive world.[24] Further parallels between Ibsen's art and world view will be considered proving that they do not inhabit entirely different worlds but share many views and techniques. At this point, however, the fact that Ibsen was critically resurrected from the same depths as Barrie is the main, hopeful conclusion.

If this gave his Kirriemuir student hope, Barrie's consistent appeals to be judged on two levels, satirically and quasi-allegorically, can profitably be used to explain why those who read the opening acts of Barrie's Romances on one level comically fail to understand the art of the man whom Hugh

Walpole nicely described as knowingly tricking those who 'have taken him at his surface-word.'[25]

(2) Light Fantastic Openings?

On these premises, only one final comment on Barrie's sources is needed as an introduction to a more detailed discussion of form and meaning. Masson's Shakespeare lectures are clearly the major influence on Barrie's Romances. Rather than being despised by a pupil anxious to escape from academe, the usual biographical conclusion, Barrie found Masson's approach a sympathetic one. His teacher had, for example, a high view of comedy, his pupil's natural mode. This was couched in Bergsonian, idealist terms. Thus Dickens and Cervantes stand at the top of his prose hierarchy while Shakespeare transcends all other dramatists. Those views, coupled with a biographical account of the Bard's rise to genius from rustic oblivion which shadowed the origins and aspirations of his student, encouraged Barrie to follow and adapt his professor's views. 'How did Barrie adapt and modernise these ideas?' would therefore be an appropriate question to pose when considering how these plays open. But the popular view denies its premise. For George Blake and the Kailyard critics there are no ideas beyond self-analysis.[26] Light comedy goes hand in hand with fanciful escapism.

All five Romances *do* open comically. In *Quality Street*, Phoebe Throssel's naïve views of Napoleon and the world of warfare are farcically revealed in her meeting with the Recruiting Sergeant on the newspaper provided for him. In *The Admirable Crichton*, the irony of a servant apparently arguing for the continuation of his servitude against a master who proposes democracy is also comically presented. *Peter Pan*, whose surface comedy is designed for a children's audience, offers a different kind of humorous appeal with one astonishing spectacle following another in the weird Darling world. The later Romances are darker but farcical and comic episodes precede the movement to wood (*Dear Brutus*) and island (*Mary Rose*).

Masson's definitions of key critical terms must also be understood as Barrie's usage almost always follows his teacher's. 'Sentimental' for example covers a wider range of application than its modern equivalent, including the creation through imagination of noble ideas, while the realistic line in Shakespeare's pastoral or, as Masson calls them, his 'sylvan' dramas is of the imaginative, poetic kind appropriate to the Romance mode.[27]

The 'double' text in these openings is easy to read but easier to *see*. It also highlights dramatically the major topic to be examined in this way. For example, the first Act in *Quality Street* uses metaphorical and nominal methods to highlight a current source of debate – the role of women in a condescending paternalistic society. The room in which the spinsters sit conveys their irrelevance visually as it only obliquely views the outside world. Poetically it becomes a 'cage' in which genteel women are imprisoned like birds (e.g. Phoebe Throssel). At a time when social change is near, Barrie dramatises a situation which faces the most heroic of these women with the wider challenge of warfare using the Sergeant as a representative of those wars. Phoebe's comical misconceptions about warfare are, however, counterpointed against her natural bravery as the sergeant, sanitised by standing on a newspaper, recognises. In this, Barrie's most overtly poetic Romance, he adapts Shakespeare's methods to Victorian preoccupations. 'Miss Livvy's' metaphoric claim in Act 3 that the potentially beautiful garden of Phoebe's life has been 'choked' by the 'weeds' (*DE* 323) of male paternalism especially recalls the techniques Shakespeare employs in *Richard II*, as does Phoebe's fourth act protestation (*in propria persona*) that women's 'little' battles are a microcosm of men's 'great' ones (*DE* 328).

Barrie's interest in modal variety would suggest that *The Admirable Crichton* would offer both similarities and differences. The latter begins with the generative development of the plays from Barrie's Notebooks onwards. *Quality Street* develops slowly in the Notebooks and is itself a modal translation from Barrie's earlier prose: the sisters, the blue room and their romantic stories had first appeared in the *Tommy* novels. By contrast, the idea for *The Admirable Crichton* came quickly and inspired a play with no obvious sources. In it we move from female potential imprisoned to another kind of social deprivation – that of the Victorian servant. Crichton, like Phoebe, is a hero in waiting. But the new topic – whether Nature favours equality or hierarchy? – adds a time dimension and poses two additional questions. 'How can hierarchy logically be advocated by one of its heroic victims?' and 'Does Nature confirm hierarchy in different societies and times?' Like *Quality Street* and consistent with Barrie's views on layered composition *Crichton* is popularly grounded. His audience knew of the recent democratic experiments currently being practised in radical aristocratic houses. It is the hypocrisy of these experiments which is revealed in

Lord Loam's unconsciously hypocritical embracing of democracy one afternoon a month.

If *Crichton* is less poetic than *Quality Street*, in it Barrie continues to explore the aural and visual powers of theatre. A cameo in which the lethargy of the Loam ladies invites comparison with *Sleeping Beauty* opens a play which regularly signs its characters' personalities and moods visually, aurally and nominally – Crichton rubbing his hands when in servile mode, Lady Mary whistling; Lord *Loam's* earthiness. Indeed, so extreme were Barrie's stage demands – especially for the cameo which ends Act II – that the carpenters and lighting crew went on strike.

But even *Crichton's* theatrical effects pale before those proposed for *Peter Pan*. To understand how radical the proposed script was one need only remember that a cast of over fifty was originally intended and that one London producer declared Barrie to be insane in producing this strange hybrid of 'circus and extravaganza' complete with flying children and clock-devouring crocodiles.[28] This reaction repays closer critical scrutiny. *Peter Pan* has the same basic form as *Quality Street* and *The Admirable Crichton*. Their dramatic action had followed a circular pattern where 'real' Edwardian settings had enclosed the ideally fanciful retreats of fairy-tale ball and desert island respectively. The precise definition of this 'reality' is not naturalistic but, as Masson explains it, one in which 'the poetic or imaginative faculty produc[es] a new or artificial concrete'.[29] It is in that sense with the methods of Shakespeare's 'sylvan' dramas in mind that Barrie shaped those plays. *Peter Pan* follows a similar pattern, opening in a recognisable Edwardian setting, that of the night nursery complete with mother, children and night lights. After the fantasy of Peter's Island it is to that setting we return. So why, apart from the more extreme practical and financial demands it made, was *Peter Pan* so vehemently rejected by the impresarios of Barrie's day?

The influence of Masson's teaching will later provide a more detailed answer to this question. But the current focus of argument is on the guidance offered in the first acts of Barrie's Romances. *Quality Street* and *Crichton* had signed their form and meaning early on. Any differences proposed in *Pan* should, therefore, be similarly evident. And, as the curtain rises, two variations at once impress themselves on the audience. The Darlings may live in the recognisably Edwardian world described above but fantasy has already invaded it in the shape of a Newfoundland Dog-Nanny. That this change in balance was consciously made is apparent in Barrie's opening stage directions to Arthur Lupino, who played Nana in the first production. He is advised to act as normally as possible! This advice is then applied to the entire cast via the motto 'The little the less and how much it is.' (*PP* 88).

The second difference concerns the topic chosen. As in the earlier Romances, the nature of the question to be explored and the means of dramatising it is made patently clear. As the opening dialogue demonstrates a childish vision is to be the medium and birth the topic:

> JOHN (*histrionically*) We are doing an act; we are playing at being you and father. (*He imitates the only father who has come under his special notice.*) A little less noise there.
> WENDY Now let us pretend to have a baby.
> JOHN (*good-naturedly*) I am happy to inform you, Mrs. Darling, that you are now a mother. (*Wendy gives way to ecstasy.*) (*PP* 89)

While the vehicle of childish game-playing helps to explain the more strongly fanciful opening, the nature of the topic introduces a new artistic challenge. The freedom of children's vision is not directed to social and political problems in the manner of *Quality Street* and *Crichton*. John's game touches on the first of life's mysteries, that of birth.

Barrie might have chosen to go beyond time while focusing on birth alone. Instead, he expands beyond the first act and the nursery into the Never Land. And there, just as clearly, copulation and death are viewed in childish terms. In Act Two, the sexual act is represented by the arrow Tootle fires at Wendy. Her subsequent 'illness' and confinement in the toy house then translate pregnancy and allow her to claim motherhood on emerging from it. The lagoon scene at the end of Act Three shadows the 'game' of death. On the game level Peter takes for himself the role of altruistic hero. By giving Wendy the kite as their only means of escape from the rising waters he would appear to be sacrificing himself for her. But, of course, the fact and fear of human death are not for a weightless immortal boy. For him death remains just 'an awfully big adventure.' (*PP* 125).

The only other Romance to address a world beyond time is *Mary Rose*. Like *Pan*, it adapts the basic pattern of *Crichton* to mirror that change formally. In broad structural terms both end as well as begin in a manner suited to that more ambitious frame of reference. *Pan* ends with a return to the Never Land rather than the nursery, while the mystery of Mary Rose's imprisonment within and beyond time is signed by enclosing the faery island within three time dimensions rather than one. The play opens and ends after the First World War. The second scene of Act 1 and the opening scene of Act 3 offer retrospective visions of Mary's engagement and her return as wife and mother from the island. The fantasy of the faery island is again centrally placed but within *three* different time perspectives.

Mary Rose's opening also confirms that aural and visual effects were as important for Barrie in 1920 as in 1902. The alterations in the rehearsal scripts bear witness to the latter. The play also had a musical director and placed more emphasis on singing than any work since *Jane Annie*. Barrie confesses that the same tensions arose as in the opera in a letter to Cynthia Asquith of 5 January 1926, where he admits retaining one singing section as the cut 'looked like breaking the composer's heart'.[30] Visually, the apple tree which appears in every act, shadows natural growth and so highlights both the timely and untimely phases of Mary's life. The thirty years which separate the first scene of Act 1 from the second allow it to start in death (its roots described beyond the sight of the audience) then dominate the window with its youthful greenery. Dramatically, the young tree also offers the springboard for Mary's first leap down to the stage. Theatrical time thus provides a sad preface to Mary's joyful youth.

The opening act to *Dear Brutus* is much lighter but offers a wide range of comic tones and styles. Purdie and Joanna's parodic re-visiting of earlier 'other woman' comedies, the stock comedy of class centred on Matey and the Elizabethan wit of Lob re-confirm the play's sources as does its title. Barrie's interest in the origins of art can again be traced back to his Victorian period. They are also found in *Pan*, but as the scenes in which he traced drama back to the *commedia dell'arte* and had Hook imitate the style of past actors were excised after the first performance, *Dear Brutus's* dramatic translation of Cassius's *Julius Caesar* contention into a modern *Midsummer Night's Dream* setting can claim to be his fullest exploration of this modernist pre-occupation.

Allegorically Cassius's philosophical opinions stand above the social and political concerns of the earlier Romances but below the mysteries of *Pan* and *Mary Rose*. 'Are we free or determined by our genetic make-up?' is a perennial question but one which Darwin's theories had thrown into relief. The controversy over Ibsen's *Ghosts* had also given that theme a particular, theatrical focus. Add the play's virtuosic comedy and the enduring importance of the question explored in *Dear Brutus* provides a fitting end to this 'opening' review.

(3) Escapism at the Centre?

If the openings to Barrie's Romances dramatise serious questions in a layered text, it is difficult to sustain the popular view that the 'magic' islands and woods which follow are signs of his desire to escape reality. Indeed, can a surface reading validly deny the existence of ideas while refusing to admit the level at which they are presented? The range of Barrie's political and philosophical views has already been discussed. This is also the area in which Masson's teaching most obviously influences him. To illustrate this a closer examination of Masson's theory and particularly his definition of Realism and Idealism is needed. Interestingly, that focus returns us to the parallels with Ibsen. As Moi argues, European criticism in Ibsen's day was vitally concerned with the concepts of Realism and Idealism, how to define them and whether they were mutually exclusive. Ibsen's return to fame was itself dependent on the recognition that both approaches were combined in his work. Once that model had been established critics found it easier to re-discover the poetic and mythic sides to his art.[31]

The same considerations and solutions apply to Barrie. Masson's philosophical and rhetorical publications use Realism and Idealism as a major means of organising his argument. His account is a subtle one as his introduction to the question in *British Novelists and their Style* reveals. 'The question with the Realist author with respect to what he conceives is "How would this actually be in Nature?" The question with the Idealist artist is "What can be made out of this? With what human conclusions, ends and aspirations can it imaginatively be interwoven?"'[32] On these grounds Masson reserved a high position for what he called the 'Sylvan Romances' (e.g. *As You Like It*) as their modal definition involved transitions from one approach to the other.[33]

Masson's views on the Real have been shown to have their 'poetic' and 'artificial' roots in the Renaissance. His definition of the Ideal also discriminates nicely between the concept as Platonic Idea and as Coleridge's secondary Imagination, that creative faculty which goes beyond the scope of historian or philosopher to explore the wider range of possibility and potentiality.[34] How do these ideas affect our view of Barrie's modernised Sylvan Romances – *Quality Street, Crichton* and *Dear Brutus*? In Masson's terms they are not escapes from the real but movements from the Real to the Ideal, being 'the willing and avowed transference of the poet himself into a kind of existence which, as being one of the few elementary conditions, was therefore the best suited for certain exercises of pure phantasy in which the poet delights.'[35] As such they combine the Real and Ideal as re-defined rather than viewing them as irreconcilable opposites. Masson stresses that 'Never was a world so pictorially real, so visually distinct as that of Shakespeare's plays.'[36] The more the bias favours the idealistic side, however, the better. It is on these grounds Masson prefers Dickens's world of 'ideal phantasy' to Thackeray's more realistic vision. Barrie academically favours Skelton over Nash on the same principles.[37]

Major structural and topical differences were detected in the 'mysterious' Romances, *Peter Pan* and *Mary Rose*. These should also be mirrored in Masson's teaching if he is indeed Barrie's major influence. The lectures Barrie attended confirm this division. Only in Shakespeare's late Romances, Masson explains, do Realism and Idealism interplay mysteriously to convey a 'final mood of masterly and contemplative calmness'. Only in that group, typified by *The Tempest*, does he show us 'That intensely real world joining with that interpretation of the mysterious as forming part of it' which is his version of Coleridge's Primary Imagination.[38]

Both these questions were addressed by Ibsen.[39] Indeed, once Barrie's sharing of Ibsen's artistic ideals is understood, his reasons for idealising the Norwegian dramatist become even clearer. The difference is one of timing. Ibsen has been returned to the ranks of dramatic genius because his own criteria for judgment have at last been re-instated. Regrettably, Barrie has not yet made the leap from simplistic detraction to nicely formulated praise. Awaiting that development, the current definition of their inter-relationship in histories of criticism remains one parody, *Ibsen's Ghost*. Refine his critical position and the list lengthens to include, minimally, *Walker, London, The Wedding Guest*, the death of Tommy Sandys, the topic of *Dear Brutus* and the original Norwegian setting for *Mary Rose*.

(4) The Non-sense of an Ending?

Those who only read the surface of Barrie's plays have one last concern. The endings, they believe, are unsatisfactory. That reaction is understandable. I have read eighteen different endings to *The Admirable Crichton,* some of which are radical. The last movement in *Quality Street,* on the other hand, is only subject to minor alterations but nonetheless evokes a confused audience reaction. Even *Dear Brutus,* which has the most direct story line, refuses to give a clear answer to Cassius's claim for personal freedom. All, however, demonstrate a close relationship between form and meaning while highlighting specifically theatrical devices and celebrating the artificiality of the mode.

Peter Pan offers the most radical 'theatrical' challenge of all. The 1929 Dedication explicitly claims multi-authorship as the outcome of one of his theories – theatrical teamwork. Barrie also argues for Wendy's power as creative force and so confirms two major elements in his world view. The same contrast between the unchanging mythic world and ever-changing human imperfection is reflected in the rituals he introduced. The scripts the first cast received containing only their own lines and the measuring each year of the lost boys were meant to mirror the uncertainty and cruelty of Darwinian Nature respectively. The play as mirror of life had also to be seen as running continuously with each production a new, unforeseeable experience.[40]

Diachronic evidence and acknowledgement of a layered text combine to challenge assumptions of authorial insecurity. This is apparently strong as the eighteen endings of *Crichton* and the twenty-five I have read for *Pan* confirm. But Barrie's apprenticeship reveals his early interest in open endings as accurate mirrors of a doubtful age. Many of his Victorian dramas, e.g. *The Little Minister* (1897), 'Becky Sharp' (1893) as well as his opera, *Jane Annie* (1893), end on questions. As neat endings remained the Victorian norm, these signs of incipient modernism were misunderstood and criticised in his own day.

Barrie's rhetorical criticism and the quintessential approach to the theatre it supports clarify another area of concern. When asking why apparently similar topics such as the heroism-in-waiting of Phoebe and Crichton are so differently 'ended', Barrie's critical practice focuses on the relationship between form and meaning. 'How do these topics relate to the chosen dramatic structure and the generative evidence available?' thus becomes the first critical question. *Quality Street* raises the issue of female heroism frustrated within a specific moment in time and place. The spinsters exist in England before women's rights are established. Barrie's final cameo signs doubt within that framework. Audiences come out wondering why this comedy's happy marital conclusion leaves them sad. The answer is that they haven't *seen* any such thing. The silent ending focuses on three figures not two. Miss Susan in her quaker cap (the symbol of continued imprisonment) stands on one side of the nominally ordinary lover who has been Phoebe's necessary passport beyond the cage of Quality Street. In that street we know Susan has many companions. Phoebe's heroism, her self-dramatising and her literal re-inventing of herself have all been necessary to make her the single exception to the rules which still define women's fate.

The topic in *Crichton* is more generally posed and raises more complex issues. Its different endings therefore accord with different views of the hierarchy/democracy debate as refracted through the lens of time and social change. Most of the endings I have read are associated with the first, pre-war London run. They accurately reflect the social limits within which Crichton's heroic potential is defined in English society at that time. They offer slight variations on an unchanging theme – Crichton may choose to depart the stage with or without Tweeny, to a public house or an unidentified location but he always distances himself from the Loams and the hereditary hierarchy they represent in order to wait. Here Barrie's faithful enacting of his thesis does imply the dramatic anti-climax which was the object of criticism.

The texts which offer Crichton heroic hope and give the play a more powerful conclusion fall into two categories. These are the New York productions of 1904 and 1931 and the English revival texts of 1916 and 1920. When William Gillette played Crichton to an American audience Barrie returned to the more tragic vision of the early drafts allowing Gillette to play the part with 'brooding menace'. This audience had undergone its revolution and chosen democracy. That the younger Gillette continued this more tragic interpretation in the post-war revivals is confirmed by the critic who wondered why this 'lucubration of the woes of the world' was called a comedy.[41]

For London audiences the new society which Crichton awaited arrived later. In the post-war revivals of 1916 and 1920 the butler could logically hope for a return to the leadership role he had enjoyed on the island. As that formulation implies, it is society and with it the original topical premises which change, not Crichton. The butler's initial championing of hierarchy seemed to guarantee that Nature only offered variations on that principle. With warfare the antithetical opposition – hierarchy or democracy – becomes blurred. What had seemed a 'solved' case in favour of hierarchy is now returned to the doubts of the American 'Case.' Now the London audience leaves the theatre wondering whether Nature ordains democracy and/or a new hierarchy based on merit.

Dear Brutus and *Mary Rose* post-date the time of Darwinian *angst* and belong to a period when many of women's political aims have been achieved. In reflecting that time, Barrie still enacts woman's greater potential but a different tone and other topics enter the equation. In *Dear Brutus*, for example, Mrs Coade's uniqueness in self-possession makes her the only one who does not need to enter the magic wood. But within the wood women do not notably learn more than men. Indeed, it is a male – Dearth – whose personal fate is most sympathetically treated and most poignantly challenges the title's assumption that we act freely. While this is also the Romance whose open ending is most evident on the surface of the drama, its overt advertising of its Shakespearean sources highlights the metafictional line in Barrie's critical theory. This is consistent with his practice of highlighting, against an unchanging mythic background, now one line in his dramatic theory, now another.

Characteristically, given his essentially melancholy view of the world, only a few find their midsummer experience a positive one. Patrick Braybrooke sums up the open yet predominantly sad conclusion well when he sees 'the glow of mournfulness' resulting from 'Barrie['s] genius, that genius which makes us sob when we feel we ought to laugh, to laugh when we feel we ought to cry'.[42]

This study has focused on the principle of modal variation which Barrie uses in his Romances. One last example links earliest to latest. Barrie had become interested in the new cinematic form and applied his quintessential formula to it. As a result his cinema scripts emphasised the differences between film and drama and were regarded as ahead of their time. His script for *Peter Pan*, for example, with its time-lapse photography and ambitious spatial effects was returned by Hollywood and a much more conservative film produced.[43] In 1936 he produced another radical film script which looked back to his earliest, 'sylvan' sources. His version of *As You Like It* was produced in 1937 with Laurence Olivier and Elisabeth Bergner in the major roles.[44]

If one looks in the same spirit for the 'beginnings' of *Mary Rose* and those features which distinguish it, the early date at which the concept occurred provides a surprise. In Notebook 16 Barrie records, '*Saddest – Sight in World*. A mother who has lost her child sleeping hugging, her arms hugging the child she thinks is there.'[45] That places it in 1904 when he was preparing for *Peter Pan*, its closest structural and topical companion.

Measured against that quintessential norm, the variations and developments to be found in the metaphysical Romances, *Peter Pan* and *Mary Rose* become more understandable. Their maximal use of aural and visual effects was noted earlier and the range of these experiments in *Pan* discussed. Their ambitiousness was shown to derive heterogeneously from the demands of the plot itself. In *Mary Rose* the relationship between consciously theatrical form and the 'double' meaning of the Imp is analytically conceived and practised from the outset. Barrie's early scripts use the triple-time structure and in particular the parallel cameo scenes in Acts II and III to compare and contrast Mary's two returns to the timeless island. In the *Definitive* edition the stage crew are alerted to the effect desired: 'The call is again heard but there is this time in it no unholy sound.' (*DE* 1148). As in *Dear Brutus*, hope within a surrounding gloom is the balanced if unresolved conclusion.

In the original manuscript, Barrie's consciousness of the variations with *Peter Pan* itself are clearly evident. To end by analysing this 'beginning' is also appropriate for an argument which has worked diachronically and concentrated on circular structures and open endings. As in the 'Definitive' text, the gradual transition from 'modern' to eternal is mirrored in the lighting effects: 'The part of the stage occupied by the room remains dark till the fall of the curtains but beyond the scene begins to clear.'[46] That an ending which will make explicit the play's close links with *Pan* is proposed at once becomes evident as 'the Tinker Bell light' is the first to break the darkness which has descended. Barrie's only character defined entirely by stage effects heralds an equally ambitious, wordless structural experiment.

To convey the mystery which is about to be revealed, the use of gauze to veil the island part of the stage is suggested. As a further guide for the audience, only the part of the island revealed in Act II is to be shown at first. As light increasingly floods the stage and the mysterious sound of the waves is first heard, the stage directions make its identity clear. 'As the island clears we see part of a pine tree removed from inside so that it is like the trees of Peter Pan.' Peter enters, sits on the trunk and plays his pipes. Joanna (the name of the play's heroine at this time) then arrives 'from a boat if this can be organised'. She meets Peter joyfully and he puts berries in her hair 'so that she looks like Wendy.' The general direction – 'Mysterious lights/music/the still sad music of humanity' follows accompanied by the clear suggestion, that she, unlike Wendy, is trapped for ever. 'When they have gone we hear the plop, plop, plop, meaning that the island *has got her again*.'[47]

The manuscript also highlights dramatic sources more thoroughly than later versions. Barrie first set the drama in the fjords of Norway 'in honour of Ibsen' thus making his two dramatic idols the respective sources for his own late Romances.[48] Even when that setting-source is deleted, the ambitious use of the unique sensual powers of the theatre combine to underline Barrie's mythic world in which the origins of nature and artistry are vitally inter-related. As *Mary Rose's* immediate predecessor, *Dear Brutus*, had already taken Barrie's ideas on the origins and powers of art to a new stage of development, that consideration may have contributed to his decision to move away from a manuscript which shows real promise.

To end by raising new questions and opening up new areas of enquiry was Barrie's way in the Romances. To look at the other mature dramas and reassess the European influences on him are only the most obvious of the ways forward suggested here, once his sadly comic art is again valued on its own terms.

Notes

1 Barrie misquotes the first line of the couplet 'What shall I do …' as 'What can I do …'
2 See Peter Hollindale (ed.) *J. M. Barrie: Peter Pan and other Plays* (Oxford: OUP, 1995), pp. xxx–xxxiv.
3 William Archer, *The Old Drama and the New* (London: Heinemann, 1923), p. 331.
4 See Harry M. Geduld, *Sir James Barrie* (New York: Twayne, 1971).
5 Cited in Andrew Birkin, *J. M. Barrie and the Lost Boys* (London: Constable, 1979), p. 9.
6 Humphrey Carpenter, *Secret Gardens: A Study of the Golden Age of Children's Literature*

(London: Allen & Unwin, 1985); Eve Kosofsky Sedgwick, *Epistemology of the Closet* (Hemel Hempstead: Harvester Wheatsheaf, 1991).

7   Andrew Nash, *Kailyard and Scottish Literature* (Amsterdam & New York: Rodopi, 2007).

8   R. D. S. Jack, *The Road to the Never Land: A Reassessment of J. M. Barrie's Dramatic Art* (Aberdeen: Aberdeen University Press, 1991); Jack, *Myths and the Mythmaker: A Literary Account of J. M. Barrie's Formative Years* (Amsterdam & New York: Rodopi, 2010).

9   T. S. Eliot, 'The Function of Criticism', in *Selected Essays* (London: Faber & Faber, 1932), p. 32.

10 Leonee Ormond, *J. M. Barrie* (Edinburgh: Scottish Academic Press, 1970), p. 84. My italics.

11 Beinecke Library, Yale University, Barrie Vault Shelves A3/4.

12 Barrie's lecture notes (National Library of Scotland, ADV MSS 1878–82, 6648–57 [6652: 1–57]) and essays (Beinecke, S354 [Skelton]; T83 [Nash]).

13 Jack, *The Road to the Never Land*, p. 164.

14 See Alexander Campbell Fraser (ed.), *Selections from Berkeley* 2nd edn (Oxford: Clarendon Press, 1878), pp.v–xlv; NLS, ADV MS 6650, Lectures 1–5.

15 See R. D. S. Jack, 'Peter Pan as Darwinian Creation Myth', *Literature and Theology* 8:2 (June, 1994), pp. 155–73.

16 Barrie's high opinion of Ibsen is in a letter to Cynthia Asquith enclosed with his 1931 revised edition of *Ibsen's Ghost*. Beinecke, Ib 6/2.

17 Toril Moi, *Henrik Ibsen and the Birth of Modernism* (Oxford: Oxford University Press, 2005).

18 Moi, p. 30.

19 Daniel Haakonsen, *Henrik Ibsens Realisme* (Oslo: Aschehoug, 1957), p. 31, cited in Moi, p. 35.

20 Moi, p. 35.

21 Beinecke, T63 f.44.

22 Steven Matthews (ed.), *Modernism: A Sourcebook* (New York: Palgrave Macmillan, 2008), p. 118.

23 Beinecke, W67. Statistical proof that actresses were underpaid.

24 See Jack, *Myths and the Mythmaker*, pp. 38–46.

25 Barrie, *McConnachie and J. M. B.*, ed. Horace Walpole (London: Peter Davies, 1938), p. 3.

26 George Blake, *Barrie and the Kailyard School* (London: Arthur Barker, 1951).

27 For Masson's views on sentiment and imaginative realism, see his *Recent British Philosophy* (London: Macmillan, 1865); for their earliest expression in a literary context, see 'The Scottish Influence in British Literature', and 'Theories of Poetry', in Masson, *Essays Biographical and Critical* (Cambridge: Macmillan, 1856), pp. 394–402; 415–59.

28 The impresario was Beerbohm Tree.

29 Masson, 'Theories of Poetry' p. 421.

30 Beinecke, A3.

31 Moi, pp. 67–91.

32 Masson, *British Novelists and their Style* (Cambridge: Macmillan, 1859), p. 250.

33 Masson, *Shakespeare Personally*, ed. Rosemary Masson (London: Smith, Elder, 1914), p. 134. (The book is a publication of Masson's Shakespeare lectures.)

34 Coleridge placed the secondary Imagination which half created and half perceived

between the simple kaleidoscopic power of Fancy (re-arranging but not re-creating) and the primary Imagination as 'Agent of all human perception' and 'repetition in the human mind of the eternal act of creation.' *The Collected Works of Samuel Taylor Coleridge* VII.1, ed. James Engell and W. Jackson Bate (Princeton, NJ: Princeton University Press, 1983), pp. 304–5.

35   Masson, *British Novelists and their Style*, p. 8; Beinecke BVS, S354 f.66.

36   Masson, *Shakespeare Personally*, pp. 137, 155.

37   Beinecke, S354 f.6, 66; T63 f.70; Masson, *British Novelists and their Style*, p. 251.

38   Masson, *Shakespeare Personally*, pp. 134, 155, 137.

39   On Barrie and Ibsen, see Jan McDonald's chapter in the present volume.

40   Jack, *Myths and the Mythmaker*, pp. 319–22; Roger Lancelyn Green, *Fifty Years of Peter Pan* (London: Peter Davies, 1954), p. 22.

41   *New York Times*, 10 March 1931.

42   Patrick Braybrooke, *J. M. Barrie: A Study in Fairies and Mortals* (London: Drane's, 1924), p. 158.

43   R. D. S. Jack, 'From Drama to Silent Film,' *International Journal of Scottish Theatre*, 2:2 (2001), pp. 1–17.

44   Beinecke, A85.

45   Beinecke, M37/1.

46   Beinecke, M37/1, III, 30.

47   My italics. See Leonee Ormond, 'J. M. Barrie's Mary Rose,' *Yale University Library Gazette*, 58 (1983), pp. 59–63.

48   Beinecke, M37/1, I. 1–37.

4. The Boy Who Never Grew Up? J. M. Barrie and Cinema

JONATHAN MURRAY

Were it ever to be pitched as a film project itself, the story of J. M. Barrie's relationship with cinema might be justly described as a tale blessed with a little bit of everything: an abundance of amusing and intriguing incident, abrupt and unlooked-for reversals of fortune, and a cast list comprising some of the most famous names in film history. A wealth of silver-screen adaptations past and present demonstrates the significant, and still on-going, nature of Barrie's contribution to the life of the cinematic medium. But it is also true that cinema made a notable contribution to the life of J. M. Barrie. What follows here thus takes the form of a double bill, with any intermission solely at the reader's discretion. Part one of the discussion provides a summary overview of Barrie's personal excursions, whether playful or professional, into moving image production. It also enumerates some of the varied artistic responses made by a diverse range of filmmakers to the author's extensive oeuvre. Part two then investigates the terms of Barrie's continuing appeal to twenty-first-century film artists and audiences alike. It does so by analysing the two most prominent Barrie-themed movies of the past decade. The first is the most recent feature-length adaptation of *Peter Pan* (P. J. Hogan, Aus/USA/GB, 2003), a special-effects-laden extrava-ganza with a reputed production budget of some $100,000,000 – an eye-watering sum that suggests just how contemporarily marketable hard-nosed commercial film producers still believe Barrie's celebrated literary creation to be. The second is the Oscar-nominated biopic *Finding Neverland* (Marc Forster, USA/GB, 2004). This film underscores Barrie's enduring cultural resonance in a different way, showing how popular interest in the author remains intense enough to draw viewers not only to his most famous story, but also to the story of that story itself – the complex personal and professional background to its genesis more than a century ago.

Barrie's enthusiastic engagement with the infant medium of cinema is a matter of historical record. So, too, is the fact that this passion touched both his personal and professional lives. The author turned his hand to amateur writing, producing, and directing duties on at least two occasions, the best known of these perhaps being *The Yellow Week at Stanway* (GB, 1923), a self-produced proto-home movie that documents a house party hosted by Barrie in the Cotswolds during the late summer of 1923.[1] Yet he first stepped behind a film camera nearly a decade earlier, to make the now-lost short *How Men Love* (GB, 1914). A comic parody of the Western genre, the work in question was performed by an illustrious cast list drawn from the ranks of the great and the good, including fellow writers G. K. Chesterton and George Bernard Shaw. *How Men Love* received its only documented public screening in October 1916, as part of a fundraising evening held at the London Coliseum in aid of a war hospital charity.[2] That same year, Barrie also scripted another now-lost short, *The Real Thing At Last* (L. C. MacBean, GB, 1916). Although these two films are today unavailable, certain characteristics they seem to have shared offer a tantalising suggestion of the intensity of Barrie's interest in cinema, an emergent popular narrative medium that he appears to have wished not just to take part in, but also to take apart. From what we know of them, *How Men Love* and *The Real Thing At Last* were not simply movies, but movies about the movies, satirical culture-clash comedies that pre-empted postmodernism's subsequent interest in the self-referential aspects of artistic and popular cultural production. Both projects sought to comment upon the strangeness, from a British cultural perspective, of contemporary Hollywood's cultural mythologising (*How Men Love*) and its early attempts to transfer the plays of William Shakespeare to the big screen (*The Real Thing At Last*).[3]

Barrie gained first-hand personal and professional knowledge of the rapidly evolving American studio system in the years that followed these early forays into film. During 1917 and 1918, he became personally acquainted with the great US silent cinema director D. W. Griffith. The latter spent a significant part of those years in Britain, researching and shooting the Westminster government-supported, pro-British war propaganda movie *Hearts of the World* (USA, 1918). Griffith even went so far as to credit his original scenario for that project to one Gaston de Tolignac, an individual who was, the director claimed, an intimate of Barrie's.[4] Several years later, Barrie himself wrote the scenario for a high-profile Hollywood undertaking, the first screen adaptation of *Peter Pan* (Herbert Brenon, USA, 1924).[5] The author seemed notably enthused by the prospect that cinema's distinctive formal and technical properties might expand the cultural reach and resonance of his original literary vision, 'do[ing] things for *Peter Pan* which the ordinary stage cannot do [...] strik[ing] a note of wonder [...] whet[ting] the appetite for marvels'.[6] In the end, however, Barrie's scenario was largely discarded for the purposes of the final production, despite that document including several new scenes (a flashback to the duel in which Peter cuts off Hook's hand, for instance) not present in his original play. The spurned scribe complained that the finished film thus constituted a missed opportunity, 'only repeating what is done on the stage, and the only reason for a film should be that it does the things the stage can't do'.[7]

Yet even the disappointment that Barrie expressed here serves as an indication of just how high his hopes for cinema's cultural impact appear to have been: dismissal of one specific film (the 1924 *Peter Pan*) is couched in a way that simultaneously allows the author to assert his personal belief in the new creative possibilities that film as a popular narrative medium was enabling. Indeed, Barrie's links with film production persisted right up until his death in 1937. The author's final play, *The Boy David* (1936), was written as a star vehicle for the actress Elisabeth Bergner, wife of the Austro-Hungarian filmmaker Paul Czinner. Barrie first met the couple in 1934 after they relocated to London, fleeing the rise of Fascism on the European continent. In a letter of 1 February 1934, he enthusiastically recounted his first experience of seeing the 'remarkable' Bergner perform onstage.[8] Some two years later, the opening credits for Czinner's screen version of Shakespeare's *As You Like It* (GB, 1936), a film starring Laurence Olivier as Orlando alongside Bergner's Rosalind, advertised the project as based upon a 'treatment suggested by J. M. Barrie'. As Samuel Crowl notes, however, the precise extent and nature of Barrie's creative input into this film has not been clearly documented, although suggestive affinities between it and the author's plays and novels are anything but impossible to find.[9]

But Barrie's notable enthusiasm for film during the twentieth century's early decades represents only half the story of the author's relationship with cinema during the period. Early-twentieth-century filmmakers were comparably drawn to Barrie, plundering all corners of his extensive oeuvre for screenplay material between 1900 and the early 1950s. The silent cinema historian Luke McKernan, for instance, identifies no fewer than twenty-one short or feature-length Barrie adaptations produced during the silent era (i.e., between 1896 and 1928).[10] The author's popularity during that time was such that two of the then-major Hollywood production studios, Paramount and Vitagraph, released competing film adaptations of the 1897 stage version of *The Little Minister* – (Penrhyn Stanlaws, USA, 1921), (David Smith, USA, 1922) – almost simultaneously.[11] Moreover, by that point in time the Barrie story in question had already been subject to two prior screen adaptations, in 1913 and 1915 respectively, while its most famous cinematic incarnation, the Katherine Hepburn star vehicle directed by Richard Wallace in 1934 (and based on Barrie's original 1891 novel), was still to come. Hepburn also starred in director George Stevens' 1937 adaptation of Barrie's 1902 play *Quality Street*, the second screen version of that text after the 1927 silent work directed by Sidney Franklin. Yet another of Barrie's most famous theatrical creations, *The Admirable Crichton* (1902), was repeatedly adapted for the big screen, twice directly – *The Admirable Crichton* (G. B. Samuelson, GB, 1918) and *The Admirable Crichton* (Lewis Gilbert, GB, 1957) – and several more times indirectly, including *The Man of Her Choice* (Francis Ford, USA, 1914), *Male and Female* (Cecil B. DeMille, USA, 1919), and *We're Not Dressing* (Norman Taurog, USA, 1934).

Yet both the nature and scope of popular cinema's engagement with Barrie changed radically as the twentieth century reached its mid-point. A final flurry of high-profile adaptations of the author's work appeared in cinemas during the early 1950s. The 1912 play *Rosalind* became a 1953 Ginger Rogers comedy, *Forever Female* (Irving Rapper, USA). Another of Barrie's lesser-known stage works, *Alice Sit-By-The-Fire* (1905), a play dismissed by its creator as 'old-fashioned and little more than a charade',[12] constituted the starting point for *Rendezvous* (Mitchell Leisen, USA, 1951), a film starring Joan Fontaine that is sometimes known by its alternative title, *Darling, How Could You!*. After this point in time, however, the greater part of Barrie's oeuvre abruptly disappears from the silver screen. Emblematic of the author's fate in this regard was Alfred Hitchcock's repeated failure to realise a long-cherished ambition to make a film version of Barrie's play *Mary Rose* (1920). The great director saw that work during its first run on the London stage, and it had a profound impact on him. *Vertigo* (USA, 1958), perhaps Hitchcock's most critically acclaimed film, shares with *Mary Rose* the central plot device of a beautiful young woman's uncanny return from the dead. During *Vertigo*'s development, Hitchcock had the only surviving recording of composer Norman O'Neill's score for the original theatrical production of *Mary Rose* shipped to America. Once in possession of that soundtrack, the director gave it to Bernard Herrmann, his long-term composer of choice, to act as a point of creative reference during the completion of *Vertigo*'s haunting and subsequently much-celebrated score. Hitchcock's most concerted effort to bring *Mary Rose* to the cinema screen then came several years later. Around the time he was working on *Marnie* (USA, 1964), the director collaborated with screenwriter Jay Presson Allen on a script for the Barrie work that fascinated him so.[13] Although Hitchcock's *Mary Rose* project would never see the light of day, the director always refused to concede defeat. Towards the end of his life, he confided to interviewers that the opening scene of his final film, *Family Plot* (USA, 1976), should be seen as a surreptitious tribute to Barrie's play.[14]

In sharp contrast to the first half of the twentieth century, the vast majority of Barrie's novels and plays have played little or no part in popular film culture over the last sixty years. But despite that fact, the author remains a significant presence in the minds of modern-day filmmakers and filmgoers alike. This apparent irony can be explained with reference to the most famous feature film dating from the last major round of Barrie adaptations in the early 1950s. Walt Disney Studios' animated version of *Peter Pan* (Clyde Geronimi/Wilfred Jackson/Hamilton Luske/Jack Kinney, USA, 1953) ought to be seen as a harbinger of things to come in the six decades following that film's production and theatrical release. During the period in question, Barrie's continuing cinematic profile came to rest on a literary base that shrank relentlessly with the passing of time, not unlike the water-bound rock upon which Wendy and Peter are perilously stranded in the author's most famous work. For, if Barrie's oeuvre has been adapted by modern filmmakers less and less, one text within that corpus has been revisited by them more and more. A veritable slew of *Peter Pan* adaptations and spin-off projects has seen the author's contemporary reputation increasingly defined by one of his literary works, as opposed to his life's work in literature. As a result, one notable trend within recent Barrie scholarship has been to trace *Peter Pan*'s exuberantly diverse popular cultural iterations and incarnations in exhaustive detail.[15]

Post-Disney feature adaptations of *Peter Pan* span both mainstream and alternative traditions of film production. In addition to director

P. J. Hogan's version discussed below, writer/director Damion Dietz's low-budget American Independent feature *Neverland* (USA, 2003) transforms Barrie's original narrative into a story of present-day queer identity and initiation: Peter, Tinker Bell, and the Lost Boys become drink-and-drug-addled young adults pursued around the darkest corners of a dilapidated funfair by a sexually predatory Hook. Stage musical versions of *Peter Pan* abound, including the 1950 version composed by Leonard Bernstein and that written by Leslie Bricusse and Anthony Newley in 1976. Three such productions have been turned into feature-length television movies – (Vincent J. Donehue, USA, 1960), (Dwight Hemion, USA/GB, 1976), (Glenn Casale and Gary Halvorson, USA, 2000) – starring, among other performers, Mia Farrow, Danny Kaye, Mary Martin, and Cathy Rigby. Indeed, musical theatre-based attempts to combine stage and screen technologies in retelling the *Peter Pan* story continue up to the present day. The technically ambitious 2008 Mexican project *Sueña* choreographed live theatrical performance against a projected screen backdrop of 2-D motion graphics animation,[16] while a lavish 2009 stage musical version of *Peter Pan*, starring the actor Jonathan Pryce as Captain Hook, mixed live performance with computer-generated, 360° back projection during its initial London stage run and subsequent US tour.[17]

In addition, the last quarter-of-a-century has also witnessed a proliferation of *Peter Pan* spin-off film and television works. Firstly (and most famously), director Steven Spielberg's *Hook* (USA, 1991) imagines the story of a now-adult Peter (Robin Williams), an unattractive corporate hatchet man forced to recover the repressed memory of who (and what) he once was, when Hook (Dustin Hoffman) reappears from the past to kidnap Peter's young children. In contemporary promotional interviews, Spielberg acknowledged the profound influence that Barrie's most famous creation had exerted on him. The director noted, for example, the crucial thematic importance within his films of scenes depicting flight. Spielberg traced this authorial preoccupation back to his childhood exposure to Barrie: 'to me, anytime anything flies, whether it's Superman, Batman or E.T., it's got to be a tip of the hat to *Peter Pan* […] my first memory of anyone flying is in *Peter Pan* […] it's a big deal in all of my movies […] to me, flying is synonymous with freedom and unlimited imagination.'[18] A decade later, Walt Disney Studios revived and extended its longstanding creative and commercial interests in the *Peter Pan* story. The animated feature *Return to Neverland* (Robin Budd and Donovan Cook, USA/Can/Aus, 2002) echoed the plot premise of Spielberg's movie in telling the story of Wendy's daughter Jane, a young girl carried away from Second World War London to Neverland by a still-vengeful Hook.[19] Then, between 2008 and 2012, Disney used the character of Tinker Bell as the basis for no fewer than four feature-length spin-offs from the studio's original 1953 adaptation of *Peter Pan*: *Tinker Bell* (Bradley Raymond, USA, 2008), *Tinker Bell and the Lost Treasure* (Klay Hall, USA, 2009), *Tinker Bell and the Great Fairy Rescue* (Bradley Raymond, USA, 2010), and *Tinker Bell and the Secret of the Wings* (Roberts Gannaway and Peggy Holmes, USA, 2012); a fifth entry in the series, *Tinker Bell and the Pirate Fairy* (Peggy Holmes, USA), is currently slated for theatrical release in early 2014. Elsewhere, the 2011 television mini-series *Neverland* (Nick Willing, GB) offered an alternative account of Peter's pre-Neverland years to that outlined in Barrie's *The Little White Bird* (1902) and *Peter Pan in Kensington Gardens* (1906). This project might be best described as *Peter Pan* with an (Oliver) Twist: in Willing's work, Peter and the Lost Boys are a gang of young London pickpockets who operate under Hook's Fagin-like control before being magically transported to Neverland.[20]

Thus, if Peter Pan has always been the boy who never grew up, today he also appears to be a fictional child who never goes away. In a real-life echo of the exceptional status and fantastical powers that Barrie afforded his character within the realms of fiction, Peter continues to soar effortlessly above the inexorable decline of his creator's other books and plays into cinematic desuetude. This cultural phenomenon cries out for analysis as well as acknowledgement. For that reason, the rest of the discussion here examines in detail the two most prominent Barrie-themed films of the past decade, P. J. Hogan's adaptation of *Peter Pan* and Marc Forster's Barrie biopic *Finding Neverland*. The fact of modern-day audiences' enduring collective fascination with Barrie's most famous creation is obvious; but the knot of socio-cultural aspirations and anxieties that underpins that interest is, as we shall see, a complex one to disentangle.

Remarkably enough, Australian director P. J. Hogan's *Peter Pan* was the first live-action feature-length adaptation of Barrie's original texts made for theatrical distribution since Herbert Brenon's 1924 silent film. It is also a work that makes its revisionist intent clear from the very outset. An introductory inter-title rearranges the opening sentence of Barrie's 1911 novel *Peter and Wendy*. The latter text's celebrated assertion that 'All children, except one, grow up' (*PW* 69) is recast to read: 'All children grow up – except one'. In this way, Hogan and co-screenwriter Michael Goldenberg announce their primary interest in exploring the general rule of human physical and psychological maturation, the process that 'all children' go through, rather than the fantastical exception that Barrie's titular boy-hero personifies. Their version of *Peter Pan* therefore concentrates its energies on telling the story of Wendy (Rachel Hurd-Wood) instead of that of Peter (Jeremy Sumpter), and thus on narrating a story of willing entry into adulthood, rather than wilful escape from it. As Todd McCarthy notes, 'an undeniable cusp-of-adolescence romantic/sexual subcurrent' clearly differentiates this film from previous small- and silver-screen versions of Barrie's original story, 'undeniably bring[ing] a new component to the debate over whether or not to remain a child'[21] within critical responses to the author's literary texts and subsequent film and television adaptations of them.

The central way in which Hogan's *Peter Pan* foregrounds Wendy's story is by underscoring that teenage girl's ardent desire to tell it for herself. The film's opening shot, for instance, offers a breath-taking computer-generated aerial panorama of snow-covered, early-twentieth-century London. On one obvious level, the image in question suggests the as-yet-unseen Peter's physical point of view as he flies to the attic nursery window of the Darling residence: indeed, his shadow briefly flits across one of the rooftops shown by the rapidly moving camera. But on another, young Wendy's simultaneous voiceover narration emphasises the alternative idea of an adolescent female perspective on events. What viewers see at this juncture is thus coded as the product of her maturing imagination, as well as (or even instead of) that of Peter's magical elevation. 'Cinderella', the girl is heard telling her younger brothers John (Harry Newell) and Michael (Freddie Popplewell), 'flew through the air, far from all things ugly and ordinary'. As Wendy continues narrating, her fairy-tale heroine arrives at the ball to find herself, not consorted by Prince Charming, but confronted by a gaggle of pirates led by the simultaneously scary and seductive figure of Captain Hook, 'with eyes blue as forget-me-nots'. The film never explains the source of Wendy's prior knowledge of Barrie's villainous ensemble. Instead, its primary concern is to suggest that the place and people of Neverland as viewers subsequently witness them should be understood as Wendy's authorial appropriation of the raw materials of story and setting with which Barrie provides her, rather than a reverent attempt on the filmmakers' part to replicate the terms of the latter's original literary vision. More pointedly yet, in an immediately succeeding scene with no antecedent in Barrie's original play or books, Wendy announces an 'unfulfilled ambition' to her family: 'to write a great novel in three parts about my adventures'. The film goes on to imply that this adolescent aspiration is to some extent achieved in later years. An unseen adult female narrator (revealed, in the movie's final scene, to be the grown-up Wendy) imposes her presence and perspective repeatedly throughout the course of the work. At the film's end, she retrospectively claims everything that viewers have seen and heard as an audio-visualisation of the tale that she tells 'to my children'. The latter narrative is not so much Barrie's early-twentieth-century story of a Victorian girl, but rather the subsequent story of herself which that Victorian girl-become-woman has created and recounted for the benefit of a later generation of infants.

Hogan's *Peter Pan* signals a fascination with the transitional period between adolescence and adulthood in other ways, too. As well as ascribing imaginative ownership of its narrative to the character of Wendy within it, the film repeatedly draws attention to the sexually charged nature of the story-worlds which that young woman moulds. From the work's very first scene, Wendy is presented as a protagonist more interested in things physical than things faerie. Her overheated descriptions of Hook and his minions speak of an inchoate fascination-cum-repulsion with the male body: Alf Mason is 'so ugly, his mother sold him for a bottle of Muscat', while 'every inch' of Bill Dukes is 'tattooed'. Wendy's prudish schoolteacher (Kerry Walker) – a minor character sketched in, significantly enough, as a dismissive caricature of post-menopausal female sexual inactivity – is later scandalised by her precocious pupil's ambiguous drawing of Peter's nocturnal visitations to the Darling nursery. The image in question appears to show a young man lowering himself onto a willing female form lying prone upon a bed. Moreover, the febrile atmosphere that Wendy conjures during the film's early moments survives the narrative shift from reality (London) to fantasy (Neverland) intact. The heroine's breathless approbation of the pirates' ship when she first sees it upon arrival in Peter's domain ('forty gunner, she must do twelve knots under full sail') displaces motifs of physical potency from the frame of a lover onto that of a schooner. And the vessel's captain is no less virile (and, therefore, seductive) in Wendy's eyes. Hook as played by Jason Isaacs is a significantly younger and more physically attractive figure than that presented by previous cinematic and televisual imaginings of Barrie's villain. Indeed, viewers first see the character topless, muscular and tattooed, with no attempt to conceal his amputated stump. Later in the narrative, the adult Wendy's voiceover narration singles out the grown-up pirate, rather than his eternal boy nemesis, as 'the dark figure who haunted her stories', and remembers how her younger self 'was not afraid, but entranced' by her first close-quarters encounter with dissolute adult masculinity. The point-of-view shot accompanying these words shows a medium close-up of Hook in profile, as seen from adolescent Wendy's concealed vantage point. The cropped framing of the image in question turns the loaded musket that the pirate holds in front of him into a decidedly phallic-looking erect protuberance.

All the examples described above indicate the extent to which Hogan's *Peter Pan* attempts to align Barrie's original story with a wider tradition of children's literature within which fantastical narratives act as a means to prepare prepubescent and adolescent human beings for their imminent initiation into adult sexuality. In the words of the Darling siblings' Aunt Millicent (Lynn Redgrave) – the film's most significant new addition to Barrie's traditional cast of characters, and the protagonist who first draws explicit attention to Wendy's liminal state – the exploration of physical and emotional intimacy in adulthood is 'the greatest adventure of all: they that find it have slipped in and out of Heaven'. The adolescent Wendy instinctually knows this to be true, even if she as yet lacks direct verifying experience of it. Immediately before the climactic duel between Peter and Hook, Wendy explains to the latter that the former 'needed a Wendy' because 'he liked my stories: Cinderella, Snow White, Sleeping Beauty'. Thus enlightened, the Captain salaciously identifies the vital common factor that links these traditional tales: they 'all end in a kiss' between desiring lovers. On one hand, then, the movie suggests that teenage Wendy's eagerness to narrate stories has its roots in her increasingly urgent desire to attain sexual maturity. But on the other, the film also acknowledges the fact that grown-up Wendy is able to narrate only because her successful achievement of that goal has provided her with an audience for those tales: her own biological offspring.

In other words, if the state of adolescence is what first gives Wendy something to tell others, it is the state of adulthood which subsequently gives her others to tell something to. This seems a quite different concluding emphasis to those struck by Barrie in his 1904 play and 1911 novel. The theatrical *When Wendy Grew Up: An Afterthought* ends with the now-adult heroine asserting that the story of Peter Pan will endure 'so long as children are young and innocent' (*PP* 163), while the omniscient narrator of *Peter and Wendy* argues that the titular hero's story will continue 'so long as children are gay and innocent and heartless' (*PW* 226). But Hogan's adult Wendy speculates differently: to her mind, 'so it will go on: for all children grow up, except one'. In other words, the longevity of the characters and story world created by Barrie is predicated upon the fact that most children do *not* stay innocent or heartless – for if they did, they would and could not sire children in their own turn. Cultural (re-)creation and physical procreation are thus figured as symbiotic human acts. The lesson proffered by this retelling of the story of the boy who wouldn't grow up is that boys who will not grow up are by definition incapable of telling stories.

In a sign of just how diverse contemporary cinematic adaptations and appropriations of Barrie's *Peter Pan* texts are, this essay's second case study develops a very different set of creative ideas and emphases from those expounded within Hogan's *Peter Pan*. Adapted for the screen from American playwright Allan Knee's 1998 play *The Man Who Was Peter Pan*,[22] director Marc Forster's *Finding Neverland* offers an ostensibly sympathetic account of the most famous period within Barrie's public and private lives: the remarkably intense relationship he formed with the Llewelyn Davies family during the first years of the twentieth century, and the consequent impetus which that bond gave to the writing of the *Peter Pan* stories. The film's thematic project thus involves the systematic recuperation of an individual human reputation. In promotional interviews, lead actor Johnny Depp went out of his way to dismiss 'the rumour, the hearsay' surrounding the nature of Barrie's relationship with the Llewelyn Davies children, focusing instead upon 'what I believe to be the truth […] Barrie was being a child himself – he wasn't using people'.[23] It is certainly the case that *Finding Neverland* exonerates the author from any significant portion of blame for the eventual failure of his marriage to Mary Ansell (Radha Mitchell), and, as Depp suggests, the film also explicitly refutes the imputation of predatory desires, whether psychological or physical, to Barrie's remarkable attachment to the Llewelyn Davies boys. In these ways, *Finding Neverland*'s portrait of the artist as a perpetually young man clearly differentiates itself from the much more sceptical account of this period in Barrie's life outlined in the work of Andrew Birkin: *The Lost Boys*, a three-part BBC television drama first broadcast in 1978, and *J. M. Barrie and the Lost Boys* (1979), a detailed biographical study.

More generally, *Finding Neverland* also strives to construct Barrie as not simply an angelic figure, but also an allegorical one. Director Forster identified his film's central theme as 'the power of a man's creativity to take people to another world [...] the transformative power of the imagination – being able to transform yourself into something greater than you are'.[24] Screenwriter David Magee concurred, foregrounding his script's 'interest in exploring [how] one's own life inspires art and how art in turn informs our lives'.[25] Thus, *Finding Neverland*'s version of Barrie never misses an opportunity to encourage the bereaved infant Peter Llewelyn Davies (Freddie Highmore) to simultaneously exploit and ameliorate personal pain by turning it into the stuff of stories: 'write about anything [...] write about the talking whale [...] that's trapped inside your imagination and desperate to get out'. Such tear-jerking idealism indicates the extent to which the film frames itself as two things at once: the story of a specific literary creation on one hand, and a story about the nature of (and need for) literary creation *per se* on the other.[26] But the work also proves to be a far more conflicted and contradictory text than my introductory summary of it might initially suggest. Firstly, while *Finding Neverland* repeatedly utilises metaphors derived from the idea of the theatrical backstage in order to present its narrative as a plausible/reliable explanation of how and why Barrie wrote *Peter Pan*, the work is simultaneously riddled with glaring historical inaccuracies. Secondly, it is also the case that the movie's account of its central characters' respective personal histories works to present childhood as a place of intense psychic hurt, a state to be escaped from, rather than, as Johnny Depp's Barrie repeatedly suggests, an Arcadian domain within which one should struggle to remain for as long as possible.

Finding Neverland presents itself as an insider account of literary genius right from the work's opening scene. Much of the sequence in question unfolds in the backstage area of London's Wyndham Theatre in 1903, where the opening night performance of Barrie's new play *Little Mary* is about to commence. A range of theatrical devices and conventions – lighting rigs, rainmaking machines, actors' marks, cue calls, painted scenery – are carefully emphasised. In this way, the film begins with a suggestion that all works of literature come with two distinct stories attached to them. On one hand, there is the publicly available narrative that any published text itself contains; but on the other, there is also a less easily accessible counterpart, the tale of the writer's successful conception, completion, and circulation of their art. Although this scene takes up a mere five minutes of *Finding Neverland*'s ninety-three-minute running time, it provides the movie's audience with an important cue to guide their subsequent interpretation of the film's extended depiction of Barrie's failing marriage, the cementing of his new (platonic) relationship with the recently widowed Sylvia Llewelyn Davies (Kate Winslet) and her four young sons, and the author's confessional account of his own unhappy childhood. These events are framed as the biographical backstage motivation and machination necessary to bring *Peter Pan* into being: 'without that family', Mary tells her former husband during the film's closing moments, 'you could never have written anything like this'. Another sense of just how important the idea of laying bare the backstage to individual human lives and achievements is to *Finding Neverland*'s thematic project can be gauged from the fact that this motif surfaces within more than one of the film's subplots. The first three scenes depicting the deterioration of Barrie's home life, for instance, all begin with close-up shots of domestic servants fulfilling their duties: cutting out press reviews of the author's work, bringing tureens of food to the dining room, and so on. The normally unseen labour – if not quite backstage, then certainly below stairs – that underpins the public performance of bourgeois Victorian matrimony is given its own brief moment centre stage.

But *Finding Neverland*'s account of *Peter Pan*'s genesis is in fact a wilfully unreliable one, notwithstanding the film's vocal claims to behind-the-scenes-style accuracy and authenticity. Indeed, a painstakingly phrased, litigation-aware opening inter-title ('Inspired by True Events') acts as an early warning that terms and conditions apply to the movie's account of its central protagonist's private tribulations and public triumphs. *Finding Neverland*'s co-producer, Richard N. Gladstein, openly acknowledged the film's manifold deviations from the historical record, arguing that 'a story about the making of art' by definition had the right to exercise poetic licence, and so produce a quasi-biographical narrative containing 'as much fiction as fact'.[27] For instance, *Finding Neverland* brings the death of Arthur, the father of the Llewelyn Davies household, forward by some five years in time, to a point before the movie's narrative even begins; Sylvia's demise is similarly relocated, taking place in early 1905 rather than, as was the case, in 1910; the unfortunate couple are given four male sons, rather than the five they had in real life; Charles Frohman (Dustin Hoffman), Barrie's long-term theatrical producer, is located in London for *Peter Pan*'s opening night, when the impresario was in fact on the other side of the Atlantic, in New York.[28] Viewed neutrally, changes such as these simply entail that the terms of dying Sylvia's lionisation of Barrie ('you brought pretending into this family: you showed us we can change things by simply believing them to be different') are as applicable to the characters' creators as they are to the characters themselves. A more sceptical response, however, might judge *Finding Neverland*'s blithe manipulations of documented fact as a symptomatic example of the self-serving deceit which the remarkably perspicacious young Peter Llewelyn Davies sees as the fatal flaw scarring all acts of fiction, 'grown-ups lying [...] stupid stories [that] pretend that things aren't happening'. Vicky Wilson echoes the unhappy boy's protestations in a perceptive review of the film, noting the (perhaps counterintuitive) extent to which *Finding Neverland* celebrates, but 'also challenges the transcendent power of make-believe: Sylvia [...] and Barrie acknowledge their true feelings for each other only when it is arguably too late; all the family's clapping to save the fading Tinkerbell can't keep their mother from death'.[29]

On one hand, then, *Finding Neverland*'s narrative actively seeks to offer a consolatory vision of innocent childhood pleasures and Barrie's selfless care for the vulnerable Llewelyn Davies children. But on the other, the film cannot prevent itself from simultaneously offering up ample evidence to support Peter's angry infant questioning of the murky consequences attendant upon the human impulse to create fictional dramas in response to the disappointments of lived experience. In stark contrast to popular understandings of Barrie's *Peter Pan*, many of the events within *Finding Neverland* depict childhood as a place of misery, rather than magic. They also suggest that the traumatising impossibility gnawing at the heart of many human lives relates to the idea of the pre-adult as a prison that one is never able to escape, rather than an Eden to which one is never able to return. The film's introduction of Michael (Luke Spill), the first of the Llewelyn Davies boys whom Barrie meets, is suggestive in this regard. Viewers first see that child trapped within a state of imaginary incarceration, lying obediently beneath a park bench to which he has been banished by his elder brother George (Nick Roud) in the course of a roleplaying game. Barrie seeks to intercede on Michael's behalf, but when he discovers that the 'crime' for which the boy is being punished is simply that of being George's younger sibling, he concedes that 'I cannot free you'. Played for gentle humour though this vignette is, it assumes much more disquieting retrospective implications after Barrie's later confession to Sylvia that his own boyhood was irredeemably scarred by the sudden death of his elder brother and his mother's undisguised, emotionally unbalanced favouring of her deceased offspring. The author's facetious description of George as 'the horrible tyrant' who shackles Michael in passing and for fun could just as easily apply to the parent who has bound him throughout life and for real.

The nagging suspicion that many childhoods are more haunted than happy manifests itself repeatedly within *Finding Neverland*'s visual imagery as well as through the film's storyline. Logically unmotivated floor-level camera positions, suggestive of an infant's physical (and psychological) vantage point on an inexplicable and uncontrollable surrounding adult world, repeatedly appear within scenes of imminent or unfolding emotional trauma. A tightly framed shot of Barrie's feet come together with those of the doctor who examines Sylvia after the first significant manifestation of her terminal illness; viewers see the author's shoes in close-up once more as he climbs the staircase at home to discover that his wife has left him; a similar composition, albeit framed at greater distance, stresses, briefly but acutely, the vulnerability of the three waiting Llewelyn Davies boys as a hospital doctor ushers Barrie (but not the children) through to see Sylvia and George in a private consulting room. More formally ostentatious yet is the series of shots at different points in the narrative where the camera defies gravity, placing itself outside a window that viewers know to be located well above ground level. On one hand, the intended implication of this motif seems to be that Barrie's imaginative creation of *Peter Pan* was an extended process that predated the author's actual completion of the play bearing that fictional boy's name. But on the other, many of the images in question also place viewers in the position of powerless witnesses to the actions of adults who endure, share, or inflict private pain upon each other. Barrie is intermittently shot through a window during the scene in which he tells Sylvia the story of his own unhappy childhood; his lonely wife is briefly seen through a first-floor window collecting press cuttings that document her increasingly absent husband's illustrious literary career; a similar shot of the exterior of the Barrie household introduces the scene during which James and Mary exchange painful home truths in what both know to be a vain attempt to rescue their marriage.

Finally in this regard, we might also note the challenging ambiguity that structures *Finding Neverland*'s seemingly sentimental narrative bookending device. The film depicts two opening night parties: an excruciating one at its beginning (*Little Mary*) and a euphoric one at its end (*Peter Pan*). During both, Barrie converses with a beneficent elderly woman, Mrs Snow (Eileen Essell). In the course of the *Little Mary* soiree, the old woman is accompanied by her comparably aged husband (Jimmy Gardner). At the *Peter Pan* reception, however, she informs Barrie that her spouse has recently passed away. On one immediately obvious level, the dignified sincerity and simplicity of Mrs Snow's manners on both occasions clearly supports *Finding Neverland*'s central thematic contention that, in director Marc Forster's words, 'we all don't want to grow up [...] once we lose the child within us, we lose all creativity'.[30] Mrs Snow notes lovingly of her deceased husband that 'he was really just a boy himself, you know: to the very end'. Her own first name, moreover, is belatedly revealed to be Rose. This (quite literally) flowery metaphor suggests that different seasons of human consciousness coexist within any life that is truly well lived. But given the frequently distressing content of *Finding Neverland*'s narrative, other interpretations of the old couple's symbolic significance are equally plausible. In the respective cases of Barrie and the Llewelyn Davies boys, for instance, the prospect of inhabiting the emotional landscape of boyhood 'until the very end' represents the promise of a lifetime marred by significant psychological suffering. Moreover, the image of a rose in snow is equally amenable to optimistic or pessimistic interpretation: the inspirational persistence of childhood innocence and beauty long after the physical state of youth departs vies with the chilling thought of defenceless infant fragility cruelly exposed in an inhospitable adult world. On one hand, the narrative of *Finding Neverland*, like many of its makers' public pronouncements about the film, strives to follow the example set by stereotypical popular understandings of Barrie's original *Peter Pan* story. The result is a conscious and conspicuous celebration of a notion of 'Childhood' conceived in universal and profoundly idealised terms. But on the other, and despite the film's strategic massaging of the historical record in order to support its preferred thematic agenda, the account offered of the genesis of Barrie's most famous literary work also gives semi- and/or subconscious expression to a range of deep social and cultural anxieties that constellate around the figure of the child.

Viewed from the vantage point of the early twenty-first century, J. M. Barrie's relationship with cinema fascinates precisely because of its fractured nature. Extensive early-twentieth-century engagement with large sections of the author's output – not to mention Barrie's enthusiastic, forward-looking experimentations with cinema as an emergent narrative medium during the same period – was supplanted in the century's second half by a mono-maniacal fascination with the figure and story of Peter Pan alone. Moreover, as the two film analyses presented here suggest, the roots of enduring interest in Barrie and his eternal boy might plausibly be traced to the profound capacity of both figures to disturb, as well as to delight, us. Unlike many other writers in the first rank of nineteenth- and early-twentieth-century British literature (the Brontës, Dickens, and Hardy all spring immediately to mind here), it is at present hard to envisage any imminent re-engagement by contemporary filmmakers with the full breadth of Barrie's prodigious literary achievements. Yet so long as Peter remains capable of tempting artists and audiences to assume a position akin to that of the Darling children – for the silver screen is nothing if not a window that opens out onto different ways of seeing and experiencing the world – then the precise terms of his creator's cinematic future are impossible to predict.

Notes

1   See Luke McKernan, 'Pen and pictures no. 3 – J. M. Barrie' (2008), **www.thebioscope. net/2008/05/30/pen-and-pictures-no-3-jm-barrie** (Accessed 29 March 2013); Cynthia Asquith, *Portrait of Barrie* (London: Greenwood-Heinemann Publishing, 1971), pp. 132–148, 156–59; Denis Mackail, *The Story of J. M. B.* (London: Peter Davies, 1941), pp. 584–85.

2   For further details, see McKernan, 'Pen and pictures no. 3 – J. M. Barrie'; 'Barrie Conceit for Charity: His Film Play Shows Shaw and Chesterton in "Thrillers"', *New York Times*, 10 June 1916; G. K. Chesterton, *The Autobiography of G. K. Chesterton* (New York: Sheed & Ward, 1936), pp. 238–40.

3   Laurence Raw, 'Early Shakespeare', *Literature/Film Quarterly*, 39.2 (2011), pp. 160–61.

4   Arthur Lennig, 'Hearts of the World', *Film History: An International Journal*, 23.4 (2011), pp. 428–58, pp. 431, 434.

5   For further details, see Jacqueline Rose, 'Writing as Auto-Visualisation: Notes on A Scenario and Film of Peter Pan', *Screen*, 16.3 (1975), pp. 29–53. Barrie's scenario for that project is reproduced in its entirety as an appendix in Roger Lancelyn Green, *Fifty Years of Peter Pan* (London: Peter Davies, 1954).

6   Frederick C. Szebin, 'Peter Pan escapes cinematic Neverland', *American Cinematographer*, 76.10 (1995), pp. 97–101, p. 98.

7   Quoted in Donald Grafton, 'The Last Night in the Nursery: Walt Disney's Peter Pan', *The Velvet Light Trap*, 24 (1989), pp. 33–52, p. 33.

8   Viola Meynell (ed.), *Letters of J. M. Barrie* (London: Peter Davies, 1942), p. 104.

9   Samuel Crowl, 'Babes in the Woods: Or The Lost Boys', *Literature/Film Quarterly*, 11.3 (1983), pp. 185–89.

10 See McKernan, 'Pen and pictures no. 3 – J. M. Barrie'.

11 David Pearce, 'Forgotten faces: why some of our cinema heritage is part of the public domain', *Film History: An International Journal*, 19.2 (2007), pp. 125–43, p. 131.

12 *Letters of J. M. Barrie*, p. 200.

13 Joseph McBride, 'Alfred Hitchcock's Mary Rose: An Old Master's Unheard Cri de Coeur', *Cineaste*, 26.2 (2001), pp. 24–28.

14 David Lubin, 'Buts and rebuts – Hitchcock: a defense and an update', *Film Comment*, 15.3 (1979), pp. 66–68.

15 See, for instance, Bruce K. Hanson, *Peter Pan on Stage and Screen, 1904–2010*, second edition (Jefferson NC: McFarland, 2011); Alfonso Muñoz Corcuera and Elisa T. Di Biase (eds.), *Barrie, Hook, and Peter Pan: Studies in Contemporary Myth* (Newcastle: Cambridge Scholars Publishing, 2012); Kirsten Stirling, *Peter Pan's Shadows in the Literary Imagination* (New York and London: Routledge, 2012).

16 James Young, 'Stage show, amid a toon', *Variety*, 15 September 2008, p. 7.

17 Karen Fricker, 'Peter Pan', *Variety*, 12 September 2009, p. 5.

18 Quoted in Ana Maria Bahiana, 'Hook: interview with Steven Spielberg', *Cinema Papers*, 87 (1992), pp. 12–16, p. 15; see also the director's comments in Graham Fuller, 'Hook, line, and Spielberg', *Interview*, 21 December 1991, pp. 6, 8, 70.

19 For more details, see Andrew Osmond, 'Return to Neverland', *Cinefantastique*, 34.1 (2002), pp. 50–51.

20 Willing explains his approach to the Neverland project in contemporary promotional interviews: see Christina Radish, 'Director Nick Willing NEVERLAND Interview' (30 November 2011), **collider.com/nick-willing-neverland-interview** (Accessed 29 March 2013); Maj Canton, 'NEVERLAND: Interviews with Writer Nick Willing & Cast' (4 December 2011), **www.tvtango.com/news/detail?id=413** (Accessed 29 March 2013).

21 Todd McCarthy, 'Pan flies, but doesn't soar', *Variety*, 14 December 2003, pp. 48, 52.

22 See Mike Goodridge, 'Miss Bellflower lives for another day', *Screen International*, 22 December 2004, p. 12.

23 Quoted in Mike Goodridge, 'This year's Mr Right guys', *Screen International*, 3 January 2005, p. 10.

24 Quoted in Miramax Films, 'Finding Neverland press notes', British Film Institute Library microfiche; see also Forster's comments in Stephen Dalton, 'In search of the inner child', *Times*, 28 October 2004 (T2 section), p. 14.

25 Quoted in Miramax Films, 'Finding Neverland press notes'.

26 This dual focus was commented upon in numerous contemporary reviews of *Finding Neverland*. See, for instance, Mike Goodridge, 'Finding Neverland', *Screen International*, 17 September 2004, p. 25; Glenn Kenny, 'Finding Neverland', *Premiere* (US edition), 18.3 (November 2004), p. 22; Will Self, 'Playing around with Peter Pan's Ghost', *Evening Standard*, 28 October 2004, p. 33.

27 Quoted in Robert Koehler, 'The best years of their lives', *Variety*, 2 January 2005, pp. 6–7; 32, p. 7.

28 Kevin Jackson, 'The Innocents', *Sight and Sound*, 14.11 (2004), pp. 14–17.

29 Vicky Wilson, 'Finding Neverland', *Sight and Sound*, 14.11 (2004), pp. 50–51, p. 51.

30 Quoted in Mark Salisbury, 'The family of Pan', *Premiere* (US edition), 18.2 (October, 2004), pp. 86–88, p. 87.

PART II: BARRIE AND LITERARY TRADITIONS

5. Barrie's Farewells: The Final Story

DOUGLAS GIFFORD

J. M. Barrie's magnificent last story, the novella *Farewell Miss Julie Logan*, has always fascinated me, both as a wonderful example of the classic Scottish supernatural tale, and as leaving unanswered so many questions as to why, so late in his life, Barrie should return to fiction, and more especially to a novella, so apparently unlike anything he had written before.[1] His last major novel, *The Little White Bird*, had appeared almost thirty years before, in 1902, and for the next three decades he was to commit himself to his plays and non-fiction. So why did he return to fiction?

To answer this, a brief outline of Barrie's main fiction is necessary. And from the outset, it is surely long overdue that the overworked description of Barrie as a writer of 'Kailyard' fiction should be laid to rest. *Auld Licht Idylls* (1888) with its accounts of social life in nineteenth century Angus, uses fiction lightly (through the schoolmaster of Glenquharity as teller, and some invented names for remembered locals). Hardly 'Kailyard' or fictional are its substantial descriptions of absolute rural penury, or the bothy system, or the meal riots of the early nineteenth century. It is true that *A Window in Thrums* (1889) and *Margaret Ogilvy* (1896), his non-fictional yet highly creative tribute to his mother, indeed share the sentimentalising ruralism of fellow Scottish writers like 'Ian Maclaren' and S. R. Crockett.[2] In this early period Barrie was clearly trying various voices and topics – as his first fiction, *Better Dead* (published before *Auld Licht Idylls* in 1887), demonstrates. Here, in this quasi-surrealist story of a young Scot new to London, who becomes an assassin of high-ranking political and social figures on behalf of a mysterious secret political association, are echoes of Robert Louis Stevenson's tales of hapless innocents in sophisticated and sinister London in *New Arabian Nights* (1882) and more especially the story of 'The Suicide Club', with its decidedly similar blend of mature London evil and its spider-like attraction to naive youth.

Better Dead, so reminiscent of Stevenson's favourite fiction genre, had thus already shown that Barrie was not to be circumscribed by Thrums and

Kailyard. His next novel, *When a Man's Single* (1888), quickly moved on from its tragic opening setting in Thrums to London, houseboat parties and farce. This was to become the basis of Barrie's first successful play, *Walker, London* (1892). On a surface reading, *The Little Minister* (1891), so apparently full of Kailyard worthies, and often regarded as Barrie's main Kailyard novel, would suggest that he had decided to return to the territory of *Auld Licht Idylls*. R. D. S. Jack, however, argues that, while the novel is unsuccessful, and has much rural sentimentalisation, it marks a turning point for Barrie. Here, he argues convincingly, is where Barrie's future love of the mingling of fantasy and 'realistic' storytelling begins.[3] Part of the novel's failure, Jack argues, lies in its uneasy juxtapositioning of fantasy and reality. In Barrie's presentation of Babbie as a witching spirit of the woods, the romantic yet mythic heroine can dimly be seen as an early anticipation of Peter Pan and Julie Logan, in representing 'natural' freedom and protean instability, mocking the dour realities of Thrums and its would-be authoritative little minister.

That said, the 1890s saw two novels which cannot fairly be described as apprentice work. *Sentimental Tommy* (1896) and its sequel, *Tommy and Grizel* (1900), have begun to assert themselves as fictions which were radically groundbreaking in their time, with their psychological anatomisation of the mind of a creative genius whose tragedy lies in his inability to distinguish between empathetic imagination and unacceptable realities. The very title of the first, with its ironic use of 'sentimental', is an indication that the novel will wreak havoc with the Kailyard world, manipulating its iconographies of ministers, worthy doctors, grotesque elders and colourful locals, through the machinations of Tommy, as much a London guttersnipe as a Thrums boy. Barrie's best fiction is understood most fully if recognised as playing complex imaginative games with variant forms of himself as principal actor. Here he appears as Tommy Sandys, with his dual London and Thrums background, unlike Barrie in physical and other characteristics, but preoccupied with many of Barrie's issues – the nature and possibility of love; the attraction of the use of the 'magerful' (masterful) will to power over women and children as superior to sexual consummation; the preference for pretend sensations and roles over genuine experience and search for identity.

If these two novels reveal much of the author's self-criticism, then *The Little White Bird* (1902) likewise can be understood in terms of Barrie, like

Tommy, adopting yet another *dramatis persona* to explore in fiction personal issues which would appear to draw from his relationships with Mary Ansell and the Llewelyn Davies family. With his fiction's typical playing with names drawn from actuality, Barrie seems almost to be signalling to us this clue to his meanings, so that events in life become, as in dreams, rearranged and yet recognisable as expressing yet again his will to power: in *The Little White Bird* his retired army Captain W— manipulates marriages, children and fortunes with that mixture of sentiment and cruelty, compassion and masterfulness, in ways which might well have been Tommy's had he survived to play his games in London.

This brief discussion of Barrie's major fiction cannot proceed into any real consideration of his drama. R. D. S. Jack's revelatory *The Road to the Never Land* argues convincingly for the development of huge and largely unrecognised subtlety in the major plays, demonstrating that Barrie was working with Darwinian and Nietzschean ideas of power and survival in a world devoid of final meaning or God – other than the elusive and ambiguous meanings of art and the creator, Barrie himself. Jack traces the development of Barrie's creation myth, showing how he disguises a final darkness of vision behind the fantastic escapism in *Peter Pan* (1904), and follows this with what Barrie termed his 'sinister' period: the dark supernatural plays, *Dear Brutus* (1917) and *Mary Rose* (1920).[4]

This briefest of outlines must suffice as setting a background to *Farewell Miss Julie Logan*, which represents Barrie, now over seventy, creating a literally wonderful *finale* in storytelling which appears to look back in two distinct perspectives. The first, I argue, is a sly leave-taking of his novels and stories, as well as a farewell to the glens and people of his youth. I speculate that Barrie, that endless player of metafictional games, who re-threaded character after character and situation after situation, indicating consistently that he was drawing on his own life and relationships, knew well what he was doing, and was now looking back over the range of his work, and taking leave of it. Arguably, from his lonely Adelphi Street flat in London, he was taking leave of Scotland itself, in returning for a last time to the territory of his early novels, to the homely ministers, dominies and their quirky communities in their often snow-bound Highland glens. The slyness, however, lies in so far as the full subtleties of Barrie's apparently innocent if complex tale are only to be found by those familiar with the early fiction, the *Tommy* novels, *The Little White Bird*, and *Peter Pan*, as well as plays such as *The Admirable Crichton* (1902), *Little Mary* (1903), *Dear Brutus,* and *Mary Rose.*

To briefly summarise the novella: a young minister, Adam Yestreen, has come to a Highland parish (probably around Glen Clova, north of Barrie's Kirriemuir, though for Barrie's purposes the remoteness is emphasised by not placing the action, apart from the vaguest references to a railway line). He is hardly the sharpest of men; he is fascinated by the gaiety of the summer English visitors, who relieve his loneliness, in serious contrast to his winter experience, when the glen can be locked in deep snow, cut off, the unrelieved whiteness prone to cause delusions. Challenged by the English to keep a diary, he begins on December 1, 1860. The diary runs till December 31 – the dark turning of the year. (Is there significance in the fact that 1860 is the year of Barrie's birth?). We learn that Adam is disciplining himself. He has abandoned his fiddle as unsuitable for a minister (though he loved it at college); and although 'half a Highlander' (*FMJL* 250), he particularly deplores the old Jacobite tunes. Oddly, he thinks fit to digress to tell us how his predecessor, the Reverend Carluke, cut down the Jargonelle tree outside the manse, because 'it gave the manse the appearance of a light woman' (*FMJL* 251). Just as oddly, he tells us of a squirrel which for long haunted the manse garden but has now gone, since it seems to have taken a dislike to him. The rest of the chapter goes on to introduce his neighbours, and in particular the elderly but spirited aristocratic Mistress Lindinnick of the Grand House, who fascinates and disappoints Adam with her sly tricks and wayward ways. We realise just how much he is under the spell of the vivacious English, who seem to know more of the traditions and tales of the neighbourhood than the locals.

The second chapter goes on to describe Adam's servant, the utterly loyal but ill-favoured Christily (an echo of poor Janet M'Clour of Stevenson's 'Thrawn Janet'), and his close friend Dr John, an overworked endlessly active practitioner, who in staying at the manse tells Adam the local history, and in especial the story of 'Someone who was with him', the legend of the girl who risked all to help the young pretender, Prince Charles, by climbing the huge and formidable rocking stone – the Logan Stone. The legend says that Prince Charles enjoined the neighbourhood 'to feed her and honour her as she had fed and honoured him' (*FMJL* 263).

DOUGLAS GIFFORD

Adam goes on to tell of his 'distant predecessor', the minister Rev. H (no further details are given) of half a century ago. He kept a sinister diary, in which unearthly entries suggest that when the glen was locked he endured visits from a 'Spectrum'. It 'padded' at night in the manse, and tormented him to death: 'his face was in an awful mess' (*FMJL* 266). Dr John thinks that wayward woman and spectrum may be the same thing. Barrie never explicitly links his various suggestive appearances, from that of squirrel and spectrum to Julie herself, but his implications, while subtle, are clear.

The glen becomes locked in snow for Adam, a wonderful description of wintry silence and alienation. Adam begins to hear his fiddle playing itself – and becoming almost animate in a strangely sensual way. But worse is to come; Dr John has struggled through the virtually impassable glens to reach a woman on the point of giving birth, to find that his midwife work has been done by a Stranger, whom Joanna describes as preternaturally gay and wild, almost animal like, a weird mixture of tenderness and cruelty. Adam preaches against his peasant parish's acceptance of such blasphemy; and (perhaps this is the equivalent of the moment in ballads and folk legends where Dark Forces are challenged and awakened) the mysterious and beautiful Julie Logan appears as one of his listeners. Adam falls instantly in love with her. Disturbingly, no-one else has seen Julie Logan.

At this juncture the story most strongly suggests that Adam's sense of reality has been broken by abstinence, loneliness, and desire, accentuated by the utter silence of the snow-packed glen. Barrie has subtly prepared for this psychological reading. The exotic English summer visitors have filled his head with desire for a richer way of life, as well as fascinating him with their 'stories that crawl amongst our hills like mist', just as has Dr John's account of the mysterious spectrum-midwife. Clues, beautifully planted, suggest that Adam (who doesn't like his name, signifying the worldly desires of men) is intrinsically a much more sensual and indeed frustrated person than he believes. Tiny details indicate this – his relish for the strange feminine word 'jargonelle', and the hint that he misses the exoticism of the despoliated tree, cut down 'because it gave the manse the appearance of a light woman' (*FMJL* 251); his almost wistful repetition of Dr John's description of the 'wayward woman' who helped Prince Charles escape; or his delight in the delicacy of Joanna's child, the yearning of one who would be a father.

Barrie slyly uses the fiddle, which Adam banished as worldly temptation, as sexual metaphor. It even has the shape of a woman – and as Adam's mind grows more strange (he seems to hear it playing itself), it falls into his arms and seems to cling to him. And this rational reading can be pursued till the end. Adam, not realising that his friends are deeply concerned for his sanity, angrily protests against what he sees as their denial of Julie Logan. He goes to the Grand House to find Julie Logan, whom he believes to be the grand-niece of Mistress Lendinnick, who, attempting to ease him down gently, says that she has packed off the girl to Edinburgh since she does not approve of her. (Her words regarding Julie Logan throughout are deeply ambiguous; in one reading she is humouring the hallucinations of Adam; in another, Barrie suggests that she knows very well that the girl is unearthly, and potentially evil).

The denouement is Barrie at his best. Adam sits by the mirror-like loch which vividly reflects the Grand House and its huge bow window. Looking into the reflection (a fine metaphor for the idea that Adam is looking into his own mind) he witnesses, or creates, the unearthly gathering of ancient Jacobite aristocrats, silently conversing, dancing, until they make way and obeisance to Julie Logan. She accepts their tribute of a basket of food, and emerges to walk with Adam, whom she now seems to regard as her soulmate. In this rational reading, this is the climax of Adam's mental breakdown; she is forbidden to him by the guilt induced by his Protestant upbringing, since she reveals herself to be a Catholic; whereupon she becomes unsustainable in his mind. He collapses and recovers slowly. He leaves the glen by the summer, to work in a Lowland mining parish. When, twenty-five years on, mulling over with Dr John their bizarre experiences, they prefer to blame all on the wintry stillness – with Adam constantly denying the existence of the girl.

But Barrie clearly meant the story to resonate with other possibilities. Why else would he make a subtle change at the end which completely destroyed the possibility of a single interpretation? This is not to say that it destroyed the rational reading; rather, that it set up an opposite pole of possibility, or two mutually exclusive readings in tension with each other, thus generating bewilderment and wonder for the reader. Andrew Nash has shown how the earlier text pointed the emphasis on the psychological reading.[5] He notes, most importantly, the fact that the earlier text had Adam try unsuccessfully to find Julie Logan's tribute-basket, only to hinder his recovery. In the later version however, Adam reveals at the end that he did find the basket. This becomes the crucial revelation that allows a supernatural reading, which could run thus:

Adam is half a Highlander, his very surname now suggesting a throwback to an older Scotland. He can preach in Gaelic. He is thus at least half in tune with the landscape and its legends. Indeed, the very opening conjures up the sinister as he tells us how the December blasts, personified, seems to hunt him down, so that he is close to being 'the conductor of a gey sinister orchestra' (*FMJL* 249). He protests too much against Jacobites, Catholicism (although he wears a gown, which some see as tending towards Roman); he is clearly susceptible to sinister influences, especially after reading his predecessor's diary. He intuitively knows that the vicinity is haunted by something, and that something is a presence which seems to be able to take the form of animals – the strange squirrel which haunts ministers, the padding creature which destroys Mr H, the fox-like spectrum midwife. All this suggests that Adam is tempting fate by publicly challenging local superstition, and thus awakening the spirit of the territory from its lairs around The Eagles Rock and the Logan Stone. In this reading that spirit expels him from its territory by means of his breakdown.

Questions remain: if expulsion is his fate, then why does Adam fall in love with Julie Logan, and, apparently, she with him? Why is he allowed witness to the ritual of subservience by the dead Jacobites to the girl who served their Prince? Barrie has stressed Adam's Highland connection (of Yestreen) – and his guileless simplicity, so that he does not realise how attractive he is to the English ladies. And these, together with the fact that he is in tune with the unseen, are enough to break through the spectrum's cruelty to the underlying goodness of spirit which saved Prince Charles. Barrie implies that it is Adam's essential innocence and spirituality which saves him. Julie Logan's confession that she is a papist releases him from her spell – thrusting him from the glen, but allowing him his second happy life of marriage and children in the southern mining town, with its advances in technology so in contrast with the simple life of the glens. But the story is not finished; it suggests (and Barrie emphatically pointed this way both through the discovery by Adam of the tribute basket, and by our reading through Adam's unconvincing denials of the supernatural a quarter of a century later) that the old Adam of Yestreen, with who knows what ancient history behind his forebears, may well return after death to the glen and Julie Logan. Arguably, too, it is not just Adam but also Barrie who closes the story with the words 'I have a greater drawing to the foolish youth that once I was than I have pretended. When I am gone it may be that he will away back to that glen' (*FMJL* 307).

Clearly Barrie, who himself returned to his glens to be buried in Kirriemuir, invests this story with meanings to do with his own desires, in the period before his death five years later. How, though, can it be argued that *Julie Logan* takes farewell of Barrie's fiction?

I have argued that Barrie continually used his fiction to explore and present himself (and his relationships with children and adults), through personas as diverse as his little minister, Gavin Dishart, to the sophisticated sentimentalist London-Scottish writer Tommy Sandys, and the manipulative man of feeling, Captain W— of *The Little White Bird*, to Peter Pan himself. Is there in *Julie Logan* a final and very personal touch in the way Barrie re-models previous fictions? Slyly, Barrie will here refashion his diminutive early ministers – in particular, *The Little Minister*, so that the elfin Babbie is transformed into the much more sinister Julie, who takes on the role of a 'magerful' woman, and the diminutive Gavin to the tall, handsome yet endearingly innocent Adam Yestreen. It is as though this last story returns to the territory of *The Little Minister* to replay that first rather naive and strained version in much more subtle and disturbing ways, yet in ways which reflect on much older innocence and evil.

The story's title intrigues, suggesting that the author himself is actually thinking or even saying a subtle farewell – but to what? Yes, it could refer to Adam's loss of the mysterious and haunting Julie, and his final thoughts regarding her, expressing a yearning farewell, with an uncanny implication that spiritually he may return to her. Additionally, the title, with its elegiac tone and over-arching sense of an even broader farewell, is hardly in Adam's style or voice. Given the increasing contemporary recognition of Barrie's subtlety in fiction and drama in mixing perspectives and meanings, author and character, in style or voice, might we not be entitled to think that Barrie himself is using his story to express reflections on himself, his feelings about his Angus town and glens, and even the range of his writing from deceptive social realism to deeply personal fantasy and self-satire?

If the novella re-arranges much of the territory and many of the issues of *The Little Minister*, it plays also with the two tragic-comic *Tommy* novels. Central to these and the novella is the power relationship of the two main protagonists, although the pattern of the *Tommy* novels is here reversed. Where Tommy was short, stout and obsessively egotistical and self-conscious, Adam is tall, unlike his creator (Barrie was acutely sensitive to his own short stature), handsome yet vulnerably innocent – Barrie in disguise after disguise? Where Grizel represented vulnerable innocence, this becomes the role of Adam, with Julie taking on much of Tommy's masterful manipulation (while retaining the elusiveness and 'natural' context of Babbie). The novella returns not just to the territory of Thrums and its surrounding glens, but to the central Jacobite games of Tommy and his friends, inspired by Scott's *Waverley* (1814) – vividly real for the youngsters of *Sentimental Tommy*, then later replayed as ghosts of adult memory in the sequel. Now, where Tommy's imagination created Captain Stroke and the Pretender, Adam's fevered imagination creates the Pretender's saviour, Julie Logan. And, while *The Little White Bird* does not have a Scottish setting, here again is the arch-manipulator of imagination and relationship power, whose tragedy is that he creates what must ultimately be forever out of reach, both in terms of the boy David, whose love and loyalty he wishes to steal from his mother Mary, and in terms of the phantom child Timothy, created as rival to David, and allowed to die, since he is an impossible ideal. And, of course, this novel creates another, perhaps not so ideal, impossible literary phantom, the greatest of them all, Peter Pan. Like Peter, Julie Logan is ageless, inhabiting a parallel, unknowable world, akin to that found in *Dear Brutus* and *Mary Rose*. All these have at their heart a sinister sense of the 'temenos' of a specific territory which can exert an unearthly influence on those who awaken it; it is this Jacobite 'temenos' which is awakened in *Julie Logan*.[6]

There remain many more fruitful comparisons of relationships between Barrie's novella and his earlier Scottish fiction which cannot be explored here, but his farewell has another perspective which might begin to explain why, in the years between wars and so late in his misunderstood career, he finishes his storytelling with what seems for him an atypical and very traditional tale, one so reminiscent of the line of Scotland's great supernatural short stories, from Scott, Hogg, Stevenson, Oliphant, Neil Munro, and John Buchan, to name but a few. The penultimate chapter heading, 'The End of a Song', suggests an answer. With the echo in the subtitle of Chancellor Seafield's famous closing words at the end of the life of the Scottish Parliament in 1707, it suggests that Barrie was not just alluding to his own 'song', but to that of the great tradition of the classic Scottish folk-supernatural tale, which requires brief overview.[7]

Arguably, the origins and characteristics of this tradition are to be found in some of the great Scottish ballads like the 'The Demon Lover' or 'The Wife of Usher's Well', with their wonderful movement between worlds and meanings. However, for our purposes, I begin with a poetic fiction in poetry, with Burns's 'Tam o' Shanter', one of Scotland's great supernatural folk stories, hugely influential through the next century, and which would have been familiar to Barrie in his youth. With its blend of traditional lore and contemporary irony, and its juxtaposition of racy Scots and elegant literary English, it establishes the template for so much of what is to follow, from Scott and Hogg to Stevenson and Grassic Gibbon. It can be read as a simple tale of the supernatural, where, after the witching hour, Tam, in the tradition of the ballads, invokes the wrath of supernatural forces. In this, the most accepted reading, Tam barely escapes over the keystane of the brig with his life and soul, pursued by the legions of Hell, irate with his impudence. In a diametrically opposed reading, however, Burns's subtlety, in leaving deeper psychological interpretations available, becomes clear. Tam has yearned for drink, song, human warmth, conviviality and even sexuality; after passing midnight, 'o' night's black arch the keystane', he arguably dreams or hallucinates, creating, in nightmare, a version of the experiences of release for which he wished.[8] In this reading, Tam becomes the archetypal Scotsman, dreaming of holiday and release in ways which, because of his Calvinist upbringing, cannot be allowed. His guilty conscience must surround these wishes with dread of punishment. Burns tells us that pleasure to Scots is suspect, a moment seen then gone forever, vanishing amidst the storm of life. Thus the poem creates what will be the classic ambivalence of so much of nineteenth-century Scottish fiction.

Barrie greatly admired the work of Scott and Hogg – and Stevenson, with whom he had a close epistolary friendship. He would of course know the work of recent and contemporary Scottish creators of Scottish supernatural fiction, such as George MacDonald, Oliphant, Munro, and Buchan. I suggest that, looking nostalgically back over the last century, he sought to place himself not just within a Scottish cultural inheritance, but more explicitly within the tradition of ambivalent Scottish fiction, with its mutual exclusivity of supernatural and rational readings which persisted throughout the nineteenth century, and which must have seemed to him to be coming to an end after the Great War amidst technological and social change – thereby, as Nash has argued, placing himself in 'a visible tradition in Scottish fiction, traceable from James Hogg to Alasdair Gray'.[9] Barrie's novella was a conscious acknowledgement of kinship with that tradition – and a farewell to it.

I have already noted Barrie's acknowledgement of Scott's *Waverley*; and clearly, on the evidence of *Mary Rose,* he was familiar with James Hogg's other-worldly long poem 'Kilmeny' (in *The Queen's Wake* of 1813), with its haunting theme of return after years of mysterious disappearance.[10] And while we do not know if he knew Hogg's *The Private Memoirs and Confessions of A Justified Sinner* (1824), there is all of Burns's and Hogg's ambivalence in his picture of what can be read as either a psychologically disturbed young man whose burden of Calvinist guilt drives him to invent an alter-ego who at first tempts him to forbidden pleasures and then seduces him into suicide, or, on the other hand, allowing the young protagonist to be inter-pretable as one of the many who, in traditional stories and ballads, through pride, arrogance or wicked actions, arouse the wrath of God and the devil (or an outraged natural order) and are thereafter haunted by a demon or manifestation. Hogg was to use this mutual exclusivity of interpretation in many of his stories like 'Rob Dodds', 'George Dobson's Expedition to Hell', 'Tibby Hyslop's Dream', 'Mary Burnet' and 'The Brownie of the Black Haggs'.[11] These can be read as tales of complex psychological and human confronta-tions on the one hand, and as traditional ballad-style invocations of devils and preachers from the other landscape on the other.

Like Burns and Hogg, Scott, in novellas such as *The Two Drovers* and *The Highland Widow* (both 1827), and throughout his early novels especially, continually avails himself of an ambivalence which allows the supernatural possibilities to run in parallel with what could be read as simple superstition and coincidence. It is, however, 'Wandering Willie's Tale', Scott's best-known short story, from *Redgauntlet* (1824), which, together with Stevenson's novella 'Thrawn Janet' (1881), can be read as the strongest link between Burns and Barrie. Central to the story is Willie's guidsire (grandfather) Steenie's brandy assisted toast and challenge to the old laird – 'might he never lie quiet in his grave till he had righted his poor bond-tenant' – followed by a sinister health to 'man's enemy' if Satan would but find his rent, or what had come of it.[12] As with Adam's challenge to superstition, so here the challenge is taken up. Like Tam, Steenie rides through a dark night; he is joined by a mysterious rider who hears his tale and offers to help. The climax comes with the appearance of Redgauntlet castle – but far from where it should be. There are two castles, and one is phantom (Barrie will present two Grand houses in his novella). This castle is an outpost of hell, and Steenie, avoiding all the temptations which would have cost him his soul, collects his receipt from the Laird and his demonic revellers.

The similarities between Burns, Scott and Barrie are striking. All involve a relatively humble protagonist who is cheated of desires or needs; all three are inflamed, through drink or intense desire; all three undergo an apparently supernatural experience brought about either by their guilty desires or by their challenging dark forces; all three are caught up in unearthly celebrations of the damned or doomed; and finally, all three survive their ordeal, with the authorial implication that drink or the destabilising mental effects of thwarted human needs have very possibly created the supernatural experiences.

It is important to distinguish between this line of the traditional supernatural and its descent to Barrie, and the related, rich, but less traditional fantasy and supernatural work of Victorian Scottish writers such as MacDonald, Oliphant and Munro. MacDonald's wonderful gothic and religious fantasy – allegories, such as *Phantastes* (1858) and 'The Golden Key' (1867) – draw on European Romanticism and Transcendental philosophy, basing themselves on writers like Jacob Boehme and Novalis rather than on the traditional supernatural of his home territory, Scotland's northeast. His only tale in the folk-traditional genre, 'The Grey Wolf' (1871), a stark account of a lost student's terror with a werewolf-maiden, set in Shetland, has little ambivalence, and few Scottish folk traditional characteristics. Oliphant has two fine ambivalent psychological/supernatural novellas, exploiting residual folklore, in 'The Open Door' (1882) and 'The Library Window' (1896), but the bulk of her fantasy fiction, such as *A Beleaguered City* (1879) and 'The Land of Darkness' (1887) is complex religious allegory closer to that of MacDonald. Munro's supernatural tales, mainly in *The Lost Pibroch* (1896), are a unique blend of Celtic tradition and allegory, recording Highland cultural and moral decay. I do not think that Barrie had these in mind when writing *Julie Logan*. Instead, the stories of two more recent writers, who also owed a great debt to Scott and Hogg, were probably very much in his mind: his friend Stevenson and John Buchan.

Stevenson's fiction is very much in the tradition of ambivalence of Hogg's *Sinner*. I have argued elsewhere that *The Master of Ballantrae* (1888) is a masterpiece of reversible interpretation, the two brothers capable of being seen in very different moral perspectives according to how the reader views the account of the unreliable teller, the family servant Mackellar.[13] So too with his superb novella 'The Merry Men' (1882). Barrie would know these and more – for example, 'The Tale of Tod Lapraik' from *Catriona* (1893). Particularly inspirational, arguably, was 'Thrawn Janet', with its idealistic young minister, the Reverend Murdo Soulis, and his gossiping superstitious parishioners, and its account of how he was changed through his traumatic experiences with Thrawn Janet and his parishioner – or through the devil himself – into a hellfire preacher.

An unidentified peasant narrator, encouraged by drink, tells in rich Scots how as a young man the new minister was sensitive and idealistic, preaching reason against superstition. He is suspect in the eyes of his congregation for his bookishness, and even more suspect when old Janet McClour, hated for her wild past, is taken in through sympathy as his housekeeper. The folk-voice tells us of the transformation of Janet into the devil's familiar, and the apparently ghastly events of her change into grotesque ugliness, her weird speech, and her impossible hanging; and the story of how the Black Man – clearly the devil – is seen after the hellish storm.

The central satire is disguised by the folk-voice, with its belief that Janet is a witch; the reader needs to see through the camouflage of popular hatred and gossip to view the possibility of another, and entirely explicable reading. Janet has had a stroke, twisting her face and body; she is deprived of proper speech; and in her persecuted loneliness and misery she probably hangs herself. There need be no Black Man; instead, the blackness is that of a warped and cruel community. Stevenson leaves open the possibility that the unnatural weather may have unhinged everybody – but the other victim is the minister, whose character is damaged forever through his loneliness, and the realisation that he cannot change debased human nature. Here, surely, are some inspirations for Barrie; the zealous young minister, the gossiping locals, the central challenge to superstition which results in unearthly events, the life-changing effect on the minister, all of which have to be set against the unreliability of the teller, so that the reader is left with two opposing ways of reading.

The influence of Stevenson, given Barrie's huge affection and respect for his elder, is obvious; less recognised is what I consider the equally significant influence of Barrie's younger contemporary John Buchan. Yet, for all it might have seemed likely that these two pre-eminent London Scots, with so much in common as 'lads of pairts', must inevitably share respect and experience, they were in fact antipathetic to each other, with hardly, if any, recorded contact.[14] Buchan the historical novelist and very modern thriller writer, as well as being man of affairs, was severely critical of Barrie and the Kailyard school, while Barrie was moving towards drama and fantasy in ways unappealing to the politically and socially ambitious Buchan. Yet it would be impossible for the well-read Barrie not to know of the fiction of Buchan, especially the Scottish historical novels and stories, produced from 1895 to 1941. And the relationship may be more complex when we consider that Buchan the anti-Kailyarder was perhaps influenced by *The Little Minister* to the extent that in *Witch Wood* (1927) he re-cast some of its main aspects into what he saw as a serious historical novel.

Buchan produced several volumes of short stories, many of which are supernatural – and some very much in the tradition of Scott, Hogg and Stevenson. Two seem particularly relevant to Barrie's novella; 'A Journey without Profit' (1896) and 'The Outgoing of the Tide' (1902). The first echoes 'Wandering Willie's Tale' and Hogg's 'Mary Burnet' in its devilish tempting of a traveller to a phantom castle, while the second is the tale of a Solway witch and tragic love told by the superstitious Reverend John Dennistoun, author of *Satan's Artifices Against the Elect*, and clearly an echo of Stevenson's Reverend Murdo Soulis, and its unreliable narrator. Both of these would attract Barrie; yet it is Buchan's finest and most ambitious historical novel, *Witch Wood*, which appeared only four years before Barrie's novella, that seems to provide the most immediate and powerful inspiration. Here, similar in characterisation to Barrie, is the new, earnest and zealous minister of Woodilee, David Sempill, whose religious idealism will be destroyed by his arch-enemy, the endlessly wily and justified sinner Ephraim Caird of

Chasehope. The dualisms and hypocrisies of rural Scottish morality are exposed throughout, their ambiguities and complexities symbolised in the novel's varied perceptions of Melanudrigill, the ancient Black Witch Wood of Caledon, a place in which Scotland's ancient secrets persist, in its secret places, in the midsummer orgies of the otherwise church-going peasants which continue the fertility rites of Diana. This is the dark side of Calvinism, which David is pledged, like Adam Yestreen, to combat. Yet to the lover David the woods present another aspect, in which his beloved Katherine Yester becomes the green priestess of Scotland's lost innocence. Here, in David and Katherine, in Caird, and the novel's sense of historical tradition and ancient evil, are not only echoes of Stevenson and 'Thrawn Janet', but more recent possible inspiration for Barrie's novella.

The most obvious shared feature of so many of these stories that arguably inspired Barrie's own is their location within the memory of the great political and social upheavals of the past. In particular, they focus most often on Scotland's religious and Covenanting wars, or its Jacobite rebellions, as though these events have been so violent and dark that they have imprinted themselves on ancestral memory, or even so deeply as to leave 'spectrums', ghostly afterimages which at certain calendar occasions seem to flicker back into a kind of actuality that can be seen and felt by observers. Oral – and thus unreliable? – folk tradition (as in Hogg, Scott and Stevenson) most often bear witness to these. Indeed, the entire Jacobite legend of Julie Logan is kept alive, as a kind of literary spectrum or afterimage, through oral tradition.

Again, these stories warn us to beware the reliability of their tellers, from Wandering Willie as a boy believing his grandfather's account, and telling it when an old man himself, to the credulous peasant account of 'Thrawn Janet'. From Hogg onwards these stories repeatedly cite oral peasant sources. And since Barrie's story (like 'Thrawn Janet') is told from the point of view of a young man denied social intercourse and female companionship by the combination of ministerial loneliness and Calvinist upbringing, we are clearly warned to understand his insecurities and vulnerabilities, and to read his account critically.

As variant on the recurrent unreliability of the teller are the many occasions when written records are cited. The idea of a manuscript source as an authentification of extraordinary and supernatural events is an old trick of Scottish fiction since Scott, and in these stories is usually of a nature which encourages suspicion of bias. Hogg's justified sinner Robert Wringhim left a manuscript behind that juxtaposed his deeply subjective supernatural experiences against an editor's first rational account; and Stevenson's narrators in 'The Merry Men' and 'Tod Lapraik' are equally questionable, just as Buchan's 'The Outgoing of the Tide' relies on the testimony of a credulous minister. Barrie clearly works in the same tradition in presenting his strange events through the eyes of a similarly dubious minister witness, aided in his credulity by the sinister diary of the Rev. H (a previous minister) as support for the existence of an unnatural presence in the manse.

All these stories rely on ancient folk-rules regarding the supernatural. Central is the moment when, through challenge or provocation, the supernatural is awakened, seeking retribution. This offence can be within an ancient and pagan folk tradition, or more historically tied to a Calvinist morality which accepts the demonic as a very real possibility. In the case of Barrie's tale, both traditions are involved. Peasant tradition preserves the idea of Julie Logan's continued supernatural existence as a manifestation of Jacobite heroic loyalty outwith religious tradition, while Adam's Calvinist challenge to superstition awakens what can also be seen as an ancient evil, the spectrum having vampire associations. Yet read rationally, it is Adam's Calvinist commitment which forbids fulfilment, tying indulgence (as with Tam o' Shanter) to guilt and punishment, and as with Burns, allowing the punishment to arise from psychological distortion or the breaking of religious taboos. Burns's Tam and his many heirs create the scenario and personas his thwarted desires long for – and just as Tam must be attended by guilt, so too must Adam create an impossible, forbidden and understandably Papist ideal.

The landscapes and territories of these stories is traditional, in the sense that territory is made animate, as though the supernatural forces are somehow manifesting themselves through the very weather, atmosphere and settings of their stories. From Burns on, almost without exception, the settings are dramatic, with contrasts of darkness and light, calm and storm, interior and exterior, together with a sense of a living awareness in the very glens, woods and ancient buildings in which the events unfold. Barrie's opening personification of the blustering winds which seem to attack the manse with unknowable malevolence, skirling through rooms as though they wish 'to seize the venturesome Scots minister who [...] is ready to impeach all wraiths and warlocks' (*FMJL* 249) immediately sets a sinister scene. *Julie Logan* is an outstanding example of a Scottish tradition in which landscape is not just a vivid background to narrative, but an active and living contributor to it, with an almost overwhelming sense on the one hand of claustrophobic winter whiteout, and on the other the sense that the very glen, with its rocking stones, deceptive loch and sinister Grand House, are conspiring in the re-enactment of events of centuries ago.

The role of women in the stories is striking. They are so often witches, carriers of an ancient secret, or simply scapegoats and victims. Julie Logan is descended from Scott's Janet of Tomahourich, Hogg's Lady Wheelhope, Stevenson's Thrawn Janet, Buchan's evil Alison Sempill of 'The Outgoing of the Tide'. Conversely, the women protagonists are recurrently innocents, accorded a kind of special grace, like Alison's daughter Ailie Sempill, and outstandingly, Katherine Yester of *Witch Wood*. Thus these women once again draw on two folk traditions – the predominant locating them as evil, either pagan or Calvinist, but also allowing them an even older and more natural innocence. Julie Logan exemplifies both possibilities, since she has her origins in acts of selflessness and sacrifice, in saving the Pretender, and in her crucial assistance at the snowbound birth of Joanna Minch's baby. Yet she is also vampire-like towards the new-born child in the aftermath of the birth, and it is she who is suspected as the tormentor and killer of the Rev. H. Her actions towards Adam may be said to begin with the desire to punish his challenge to her existence, giving way to a long pent-up realisation that he is her potential soulmate, a fulfilment not disallowed by the story's ending.

These stories also exploit folk traditions of transmogrification, as in Macdonald's lycanthropic 'The Grey Wolf', or Stevenson's identification of Tod Lapraik with a murderous solan goose. Barrie is subtle here; an earlier remark regarding the squirrel which used to haunt previous ministers but which has deserted the manse takes on new significance when Joanna Minch likens her mysterious midwife (Julie Logan) to a squirrel (and was concerned that the stranger might bite her child) – and we recall that the Rev. H's face was horribly attacked by something which 'padded'. Barrie surely hints here at Julie Logan's survival through centuries in non-human yet deeply natural form.

But of course we must finally remember that Julie Logan may simply be a projection of Adam's fevered and suppressed desires. This in turn reminds us that the predominant characteristic of these tales, and of so many of the finest Scottish novels of the nineteenth century, is that of their mutually exclusive readings – in short, their opposing interpretations, read as genuinely supernatural or rationally explicable and emerging from psychological deformation.

Finally, a shared characteristic which is so obvious and rich, and on that very account too substantial to allow more than acceptance here, is that of their rich use of Scots language, once again reinforcing the sense of a vivid oral tradition. It is a truism that one of the great strengths of Scottish nineteenth century fiction is its recurrent mastery of the voices of ordinary and peasant folk. Every story I have mentioned carries this distinction, and Barrie's superbly fulfils its place in the tradition.

Although I have suggested that Barrie was in a sense using his tale as elegy for the classic Scottish supernatural tale, almost at the same time Lewis Grassic Gibbon produced another example in 'Clay' (1934), his magnificent and similarly elegiac account of a crofter who may or may not have fallen under the spell of an ancient Pictish predecessor who thousands of years before had farmed the same farm. Gibbon's *Sunset Song* (1932) also has an ambivalent use of the traditional supernatural but, like 'Clay', the novel's title shares Barrie's sense of cultural leave-taking. With hindsight, however, we can see that the early 1930s marked a watershed in Scottish fiction, and in Scotland's awareness of its older rural and folk traditions. And where the Scottish novel had ignored the huge rise of industrialisation and urbanisation in the nineteenth and early twentieth century, with Grassic Gibbon's *Grey Granite* (1934) the decade would see a focus with a vengeance on urban life and its human degeneration. The novels of George Blake, James Barke and many others, followed after the war with the bleakly urban tragedies of Robin Jenkins and his followers, would dominate. That said, while Barrie sensed the passing of an older culture, reports of its demise were premature, as Naomi Mitchison's novella *Five Men and a Swan* (1957), and Eric Linklater's 'Sealskin Trousers' and *The Goose Girl* (1947) demonstrate. These stories may of course reflect survival of the older culture in peripheral West Highland and Orkney memory, as with the outstanding supernatural stories of George Mackay Brown. Nevertheless, *Farewell Miss Julie Logan* can be seen as a memorial and tribute to a fine tradition in Scottish literature – and as arguably Barrie's finest fiction. Its intriguing conclusion, with its short and contrasting movement to the mining town 'with its enterprise and modern improvements, including gas and carts [...] far superior to my first charge' (*FMJL* 307), acknowledges the huge shift in Scottish social life and culture. Together with the tale's recycling of Kailyard icons, such as the indefatigable doctor, the worthy minister, and the colourful locals, it offers a kind of benedictory farewell to, and gentle satire on, the Kailyard fiction of Maclaren and Crockett and Barrie's earlier self.

Notes

1   I refer throughout to *Julie Logan*, with its ten short chapters, as a novella, just as with similar chaptered stories such as Scott's *The Two Drovers* or Stevenson's 'The Merry Men'. Intriguingly, this form, used often by Scott and Stevenson, is also a favourite of other Scottish authors of supernatural stories, such as George MacDonald and Margaret Oliphant (in 'The Open Door' and 'The Library Window'), suggesting that a form somewhere between short story and novel is best suited to the development of the supernatural–psychological ambivalence of these stories.

2   Maclaren (John Watson) (*Beside the Bonnie Brier Bush*, 1894), Crockett (*The Stickit Minister*, 1893), and Barrie (in his early fiction) were seen as the major proponents of the Kailyard, a fiction of sentimental ruralism, with its archetypal and iconic figures of minister, doctor, and assorted worthies, seen as representative of sterling Scottish worth. Contemporary criticism has challenged the views of critics like George Blake (*Barrie and the Kailyard School*, 1951); and Crockett's output also includes fine historical novels in the tradition of Scott and Stevenson, notably *The Men of the Moss Hags* (1895) and *The Grey Man* (1896). See Andrew Nash, *Kailyard and Scottish Literature* (Amsterdam & New York: Rodopi, 2007).

3   R. D. S. Jack, *The Road to the Never Land: a Reassessment of J. M. Barrie's Dramatic Art*, (Aberdeen: Aberdeen University Press, 1991), pp. 55–56. See also Andrew Nash, 'From Realism to Romance: Gender and Narrative Technique in J. M. Barrie's *The Little Minister*, *Scottish Literary Journal*, 26:1 (1999), pp. 77–92.

4   The 'sinister' period refers both to the time when Barrie's arthritis caused him to write with his left hand, as well to the fact that his work from this point took on the darker cast shown in the later supernatural and war-themed plays, and *Julie Logan*. See Janet Dunbar, *J. M. Barrie: The Man Behind The Image* (London: Collins, 1971), pp. 247–48.

5   *Farewell Miss Julie Logan* was published in 1931 as a free supplement Christmas story in *The Times*. Its popularity led to republication – and with significant changes, as Andrew Nash has noted, perceptively singling out the way in which Barrie, with a single dramatic change, deepened the ambiguity of his story, from an intense psychological study to something far more mysterious. See 'Ghostly Endings: the Evolution of J. M. Barrie's *Farewell Miss Julie Logan*', *Studies in Scottish Literature*, XXXIII–XXXIV (2004), pp. 124–37. (Arguably, Barrie's Scottish successor in drama, James Bridie, had this sly

ending in mind when he likewise threw his play *Mr Bolfry* (1943) towards a supernatural reading with his last-minute ending in which the devil's umbrella gets up and walks off-stage).

6   'Temenos' is the term which John Buchan used in his supernatural stories to describe the sense of a living (supernatural) spirit or entity inhabiting a place.

7   For fuller treatment of the tradition of the supernatural in Scottish literature, see Douglas Gifford, 'Nathaniel Gow's Toddy' in *Fantastical Imaginations: The Supernatural in Scottish History and Culture*, ed. Lizanne Henderson (Edinburgh: John Donald, 2009).

8   *The Poems and Songs of Robert Burns*, ed. James Kinsley, 3 vols (Oxford: OUP, 1968), II, 559.

9   'Introduction', *FMJL*, p. xix.

10   Dennis Mackail notes Barrie's reference to Hogg's unearthly poem, and that the idea of a young woman returning after an unearthly disappearance of seven years can be seen as a possible source for *Mary Rose*. See *The Story of J. M. B.* (London: Peter Davies, 1941), p. 374.

11   Virtually all these tales appeared in *Blackwood's Magazine* between 1823 and 1828, and were then collected in *The Shepherd's Calendar* (1829).

12   Sir Walter Scott, *Redgauntlet*, ed. Kathryn Sutherland (Oxford: Oxford World's Classics, 2011), p. 110.

13   For a fuller discussion, see Douglas Gifford, '*The Master of Ballantrae* and Scottish Fiction', in *Stevenson and Victorian Scotland*, ed. Jenni Calder (Edinburgh: Edinburgh University Press, 1981), pp. 62–87.

14   Barrie went to London in 1885; Buchan, fifteen years later, in 1903. None of Barrie's biographers mention Buchan or any meeting.

6. 'Frae Anither Window in Thrums': Hugh MacDiarmid and J. M. Barrie

MARGERY PALMER McCULLOCH

At first sight, Sir James Barrie would not appear to have been one of Hugh MacDiarmid's favourite authors. In his provocative *Contemporary Scottish Studies* (1926), MacDiarmid brought Barrie together with Neil Munro as writers whose only relevance was in the 'restricted field of Scottish letters', but gave Munro the higher place in this lowly canon by adding that 'no writer worth his salt would not rather have "failed" with Neil Munro than "succeeded" with Barrie'.[1] In 1931, in a discussion on the way forward for the new Scottish literary revival movement, he again denigrated the contribution of Barrie, commenting that 'it is grotesque that an R. L. Stevenson or a J. M. Barrie should "stand for Scotland" instead of a Norman Douglas or a Cunninghame-Graham'.[2] This essay will explore what may have lain behind such criticism of Barrie as a writer, but will also suggest that MacDiarmid's attitude to him was perhaps not so negative as these public statements would appear to communicate. It will also discuss how Barrie inspired one of MacDiarmid's most witty and self-mocking accounts of the frustrations and harassments that beset him in his attempts to revitalise Scotland's literary culture.

In a chapter on Barrie in the *Edinburgh History of Scottish Literature* (2007), R. D. S. Jack comments that 'Barrie is a critical conundrum' – terminology that might well be applied to MacDiarmid also if not for precisely the same reasons. Jack points to the esteem in which Barrie was held by his fellow authors and by the public in his own time: elected President of the Society of Authors and so following Thomas Hardy in that role; in receipt of honorary degrees from several universities and becoming Chancellor of Edinburgh University; and awarded the Order of Merit. Yet, instead of his reputation being raised with the development of Scottish literary studies, it conversely continues to be linked with that of the rejected Kailyard School of writers.[3] MacDiarmid himself had occasions on which he acknowledged Barrie's national status and generosity, if not his literary qualities. In a

Northern Review editorial in September 1924, for example, when he was clearly in need of support for his third and final little magazine of the 1920s, he included as epigraph a generous tribute from Barrie to the magazine, making clear his own appreciation of that tribute. Barrie wrote: 'All good fortune to *The Northern Review*. The first two numbers make excellent reading and a credit to Scotland, which surely ought to have such a monthly'.[4] The grateful editor commented (with perhaps some exaggeration):

> At times like these a little generous word of praise is like a tonic, but when it comes from someone like Sir J. M. Barrie, to whom we look up as one on a great height, and who being a Scot is naturally economical of praise, its effects are only comparable to those of the draught of fire which the gods handed to Tithonus when they cursed him with immortality.[5]

Two decades later, in his autobiography *Lucky Poet*, he placed 'Sir James Barrie' at the head of a group of significant British and Irish *literati* acknowledged as having presented a signed testimonial to him in 1936 for 'the great services you have rendered to Scots letters and to literature in general': a testimonial written at a time when MacDiarmid and his family were living in straitened circumstances on the small Shetland island of Whalsay.[6] There is therefore something of a 'critical conundrum' to be explored regarding MacDiarmid's responses to Barrie, in addition to the contradictory reception the work of each has received from the public.

In the case of Barrie, the timing of his birth may have some bearing on his later literary career and reputation. Barrie was born in 1860, approximately twenty to thirty years earlier than the significant group of Anglophone modernist writers who include not only the more internationally recognised Eliot, Pound, Lawrence, Joyce, and Woolf (who were all born between 1882 and 1888), but also the Scottish Edwin Muir, born in 1887, Neil Gunn in 1891, MacDiarmid in 1892, and Lewis Grassic Gibbon a decade later in 1901. Barrie was therefore much closer in time and literary influence to Victorian small-town fiction, to the Scottish work of Margaret Oliphant which he admired, as she did his; and to the English novels of his contemporary, Thomas Hardy, than to the philosophical and aesthetic ideas of the new century which inspired and influenced MacDiarmid when he attempted to redirect the course of Scottish writing in the years immediately after the First World War. The Irish Yeats was also close to Barrie in age, having been born in 1865, but he came from a family background that was already pushing at artistic boundaries through his father, a portrait painter, and his brother Jack Yeats, a modernist expressionist painter. Yeats's upbringing and his Anglo-Irish social and cultural context therefore offered greater scope for imaginative development and interaction with a new intellectual and artistic elite than did Barrie's small-town Scottish family milieu with its conservative religious and social mores.

It was to this inward-looking small-town context that Barrie initially turned for the material of his early fiction such as *Auld Licht Idylls* of 1888, followed the next year by *A Window in Thrums*. The name 'Thrums' was itself taken from the fiction of Margaret Oliphant, and the stories of life in this hermetic little community (sometimes physically as well as ideologically shut off in severe winter weather from contact with the outside world) came not from their author's own imaginative response to his immediate environment, but from tales told him by his mother, and relating to an earlier period in the century. One noticeable element in both the *Auld Licht* and *Window in Thrums* stories is what might be termed the sense of a remembered or tradition-borne narrative – the creation of a cast list where the characterisation of its limited list of players does not develop beyond the depiction of a set of similar responses to a limited repertoire of events; and a narrative that, although it might at times remind the reader of the religious battles between *Auld Licht* and *New Licht* adherents in Burns's time, is itself without the questioning and explicitly ironical characterisation found in Burns's work, a quality that points forward to the need for social change. Nor do these tales fulfil the purpose of a work about small-town life such as George Eliot's *Middlemarch*, published in 1872 but set in the period of the 1832 Reform Bill, which consciously constructs an historical narrative of social and political change through time. There is a difference in ambition in such comparisons, as well as an absence of first-hand response and reflection; and perhaps Barrie's ambition to make a name for himself in London was initially at least too quickly satisfied by the liking of the capital's periodical press for his small-town Scottish stories. Robert Crawford quotes a comment made to Barrie by the editor of the *St James's Gazette* as early as 1884: 'I liked that Scotch thing – any more of those?'.[7] And Barrie would appear to have been only too happy to oblige, for these Scotch things brought not only fame but also financial gain. This financial success was one of the factors MacDiarmid would later hold against him, for making money in London with *his* modern, and modernist, 'Scotch things' was an ambition the later writer was not able to fulfil.

Recent attempts to restore Barrie to a more positive place in the history of Scottish literature have pointed readers and critics towards the success of his plays. R. D. S. Jack comments: 'No other Scottish dramatist dominated British popular theatre for so long.'[8] And despite the stereotypical nature of the scenarios in the Thrums storytelling, there is also in these tales a quality that points us towards the later playwright. While the nature of the *content* of the dialogue between Barrie's characters may most often be without much imaginative significance, the manner in which that content is delivered is something different, as we hear in the following short example from the early sections of *A Window in Thrums*:

> 'It fair beats me though, Leeby, to guess wha's comin' to them. Ay, but stop a meenute, I wouldna wonder, no, really I would not wonder but what it'll be—'
> 'The very thing 'at was passin' through my head, mother.'
> 'Ye mean 'at the lad Wilkie 'll be to bide wi' the lawyer i'stead o' wi' Sam'l Duthie? Sal, am thinkin' that's it. (*WT* 17–18)

Edwin Muir said that gossip was a form of imagination – even if at a low level of operation.[9] On the other hand, what is of much interest is not the content of the dialogue in the above passage, but the interactive movement of this exchange between characters. If it was in a foreign language, and so not able to be fully understood by its hearers, then such an audience would pick up not the low imaginative level of the speculation, but the rhythmic excitement of the verbal exchange between the speculators. In his poem 'Gairmscoile', MacDiarmid wrote: '*It's soon' no' sense that faddoms the herts o' men*';[10] and in this piece of *Thrums* dialogue (as elsewhere in these stories, especially if read aloud), it's the 'soon', the sound of the exchange that catches our attention and interest; not only the sounds of the words themselves, but the rhythmic movement of the exchanges – the momentary pauses, then the onward rush to build up a point or bring in a contradictory one.

And this is exactly the kind of skill in manipulating dialogue that a successful stage dramatist needs. Perhaps to the London market, the Scots language in Barrie's short stories was to some extent a foreign language, and so readers could enjoy the dexterity and liveliness of the movement of dialogue without being over-preoccupied with its absence of imaginative content. Barrie's later stage success was of course through plays written mostly in English with an occasional Scots-speaking character, especially in the earlier ones, but this fluency of dialogue is again one of their outstanding qualities.

Before leaving Barrie's Thrums for MacDiarmid's later borrowing of its name and implications, it might be of interest to look briefly at the first chapter in *Auld Licht Idylls*, told as an introduction to the Thrums stories which follow in subsequent chapters. This introductory chapter consists of writing of a different kind from that of the ensuing stories, and of *A Window in Thrums*, pointing forward instead to Barrie's late ghost-story *Farewell Miss Julie Logan* of 1932. While the story of Miss Julie Logan is told by a young minister, the speaker in this first chapter of *Auld Licht Idylls* is a schoolmaster, unmarried, and 'alone in the schoolhouse' in the early stages of winter. There is fine observation of nature in this prose writing, unsentimental, yet intimate and knowledgeable in the way that someone living alone begins to watch and interact with the wild-life around: in the opening description of the sparrow 'shivering [...] against the frosted glass' of the window, and the struggle between a weasel and a terrified water-hen on the river bank, creatures who needed 'no professor to teach them the doctrine of the survival of the fittest' (*ALI* 5). And as in *Julie Logan*, there is the almost total subjection of human control over the life of the community to control by the weather:

> Another white blanket has been spread upon the glen since I looked out last night; for over the same wilderness of snow that has met my gaze for a week, I see the steading of Waster Lunny sunk deeper into the waste. The schoolhouse, I suppose, serves similarly as a snowmark for the people at the farm. Unless that is Waster Lunny's grieve foddering the cattle in the snow, not a living thing is visible. The ghostlike hills that pen in the glen have ceased to echo to the sharp crack of the sportsman's gun [...] and only giant Catlaw shows here and there a black ridge, rearing his head at the entrance to the glen

and struggling ineffectually to cast off his shroud. Most wintry sign of all, I think as I close the window hastily, is the open farm-stile, its poles lying embedded in the snow where they were last flung by Waster Lunny's herd. Through the still air comes from a distance a vibration as of a tuning-fork: a robin, perhaps, alighting on the wire of a broken fence. (*ALI* 2–3)

And the chapter ends with the words:

I am alone in the schoolhouse. […] I do not lock the schoolhouse door at nights; for even a highwayman (there is no such luck) would be received with open arms […] Heavy shadows fade into the sky to the north. A flake trembles against the window; but it is too cold for much snow to-night. The shutter bars the outer world from the schoolhouse. (*ALI* 7–8)

With such an opening chapter to this early book, one cannot help wondering what might have happened to Barrie and his writing career had he gone on to write *Miss Julie Logan* at that point instead of succumbing to the temptations of Thrums.

'Frae Anither Window in Thrums'

MacDiarmid, philosophically and psychologically, would appear to have been at the opposite pole from Barrie. Instead of listening to his mother's stories, the boy Christopher Grieve read the 'grown-up' books in the library where his mother worked and which was housed in the building where his family lived. He was a voracious reader, claiming to have read all the library's holdings at an early age. He was also a promising pupil at school, but although he enrolled as a pupil teacher at Broughton Student Centre, he left without taking a qualification. Instead, his post-school education was to a large extent achieved via the influential *New Age* magazine, edited until the mid-1920s by A. R. Orage. Like Edwin Muir, who was similarly educated through Orage's *New Age*, MacDiarmid was therefore brought into contact with the intellectual and aesthetic forces that were creating the movement we now call modernism, including the nineteenth-century philosophical writings of Nietzsche as well as the more immediate early twentieth-century philosophy of Bergson, and the fiction of Dostoevsky which had become readily available through the translations of Constance Garnett. There was also the new work of Pound and Eliot, the founding of Wyndham Lewis's *Blast* as a counterblast to Marinetti's futurism and his popular acclaim in London, the influences coming from French Symbolist poetry. As mentioned earlier, there was an age difference between Barrie and this new group of early twentieth-century writers and cultural activists, and such an age difference, even if only that of a couple of decades, was sufficient to result in very different formative intellectual and artistic experiences and influences. This difference in formative experiences no doubt also contributed to the critical situation where Barrie's early work in particular was scorned by these writers of a 'new age' when they themselves held centre stage in the 1920s.

MacDiarmid was deeply influenced by Orage's belief in the 'expansion of human consciousness' and by his writings on this topic in his book *Consciousness* (1907). *A Drunk Man Looks at the Thistle* (1926) is full of implicit references to this work and its implications in relation to human development.[11] MacDiarmid had high ambitions for his *Drunk Man* poem, writing to his former schoolmaster at Broughton, George Ogilvie, that he had 'set out to give Scotland a poem, perfectly modern in psychology, which could only be compared in the whole length of Scots literature with *Tam O' Shanter* and Dunbar's *Seven Deidly Sins*'.[12] However, the reviews of *A Drunk Man* in the Scottish papers in particular made 'sair reading'. The *Glasgow Evening News* wrote that 'all the worst faults of Mr Grieve's literary ideals will be found fully exemplified in the long poem which he has just published under his mysterious pseudonym of Hugh M'Diarmid'; the Aberdeen *Press and Journal* lamented that 'he seems constitutionally debarred from selecting and cultivating the best of [his] aspirations, debarred, in fact, from anything but constant plangent grieving over his inhibitions.'[13] The London *Times Literary Supplement* was little better, criticising MacDiarmid's use of unfamiliar Scots words and commenting of *A Drunk Man* as a whole that 'it is idle to attempt a coherent account of a poem so deliberately and provocatively incoherent'.[14] MacDiarmid's critics have often found him hubristic and indifferent to any opinions other than his own, but his correspondence with George Ogilvie, especially at this early point in his career, shows how insecure and how sensitive he was to such criticism, and how quickly he could be thrown off course. In that same letter of December 1926, where he mentions both his early ambitions for *A Drunk Man* and the 'sair reading' made by the reviews of the poem when published, we find him already pushing it aside to focus on his next project, the long poem *To Circumjack Cencrastus*: He wrote:

> It will be a much bigger thing than the *Drunk Man* in every way. It is complementary to it really [...] But where the *Drunk Man* is in one sense a reaction from the 'Kailyaird', *Cencrastus* transcends that altogether – the Scotsman gets rid of the thistle, 'the bur o' the world' – and his spirit at last inherits its proper sphere.[15]

He adds that in relation to *A Drunk Man*, this new poem will be 'positive where it is negative, optimistic where it is pessimistic, and constructive where it is destructive'.

Unfortunately, things did not work out as planned. Instead of transcending the intellectual, philosophical, and artistic problems that beset the protagonist of *A Drunk Man*, *To Circumjack Cencrastus* was derailed by the everyday problems besetting its author. Financial problems led to him taking on additional journalistic work and eventually to a move to London in 1929 as editor of Compton Mackenzie's newly established *Vox* magazine. This magazine lasted for only a few months, and its demise left MacDiarmid unemployed and in financial difficulties. Employment in Liverpool was no more successful, and his marriage broke down. *Cencrastus* was published in 1930 in the midst of all these troubles.

To Circumjack Cencrastus is one of the most neglected of MacDiarmid's works and is usually considered to be unsuccessful, although Edwin Muir wrote highly of it when it was first published, finding it 'the full expression of an individual mind'.[16] The poem does not have the structural or thematic coherence of *A Drunk Man*, which is a genuinely continuous long poem, although one that operates by way of a logic of the imagination as opposed to rational thought. *Cencrastus*, on the other hand, is fragmentary, with many of its sections able to stand alone as discrete poems. The philosophically transcendent passages promised in MacDiarmid's letter to Ogilvie are few and far between, and are transitory glimpses of what might be, or perhaps, what might have been. Yet there are many fine poems and poem sequences in the work, including lyrics, explorations of the Irish *aisling* tradition, borrowings such as the translation of Rilke's 'Für eine Freundin'; and many satirical and ironic sections emanating from its author's responses to his own daily experiences. Among the most interesting of the ironical passages is the sequence titled 'Frae Anither Window in Thrums'. This includes no explicit reference to Barrie or his Thrums stories, but details (with much humorous and ironical self-awareness) the speaker's sense of entrapment in a journalistic employment that leaves him no space to develop the intellectually and artistically challenging literary output he feels is within his power, as he sits by the 'winnock [...] here in the hauf licht waitin' till the clock/Chops'. (*CP* 230)

What we have in MacDiarmid's 'Thrums' sequence is a different kind of Scots verse from that of his early lyrics and *A Drunk Man*: more colloquial in language, conversational in form and tone, more subjective, and subjectively self-aware on the part of the speaker, even self-mocking, yet still able to bring an elevated reference without incongruity into the flow of the verse – as, for example, in the lines where the hauf licht from the lozen (window pane) 'skimmers – or goams in upon me/Wan as Dostoevski/Glowered through a wudden dream to find/Stavrogin in the corners o' his mind.' (*CP* 230). This is clever writing, although it seems to flow so effortlessly. In *Lucky Poet*, MacDiarmid took up the question of complaints made against what had been called the 'artificiality – the dictionary-dredged character – of the Scots in which most of my poetry is written'. He continued:

> But the fact is that Scots was my native tongue – I can still speak it as easily as I speak English, and with far greater psychological satisfaction [...] in those days many Scottish papers ran a 'Doric' (i.e. Scots vernacular) column, and the influence of Sir J. M. Barrie (of whom my cousin Bob was a great devotee) and the other writers of the Kailyard school was in the land, and more people spoke Scots – or spoke more (i.e. richer) Scots than do so to-day.[17]

This is an interesting and objective comment by MacDiarmid on Scots language and its use in daily life as well as in his own literary use (and an interesting insight, even if unelaborated, into his view of Barrie's Scots-language writing also). For what makes MacDiarmid's literary and modernistic use of Scots so successful in his early lyrics and *A Drunk Man*, despite in many instances the initial obscurity of the actual meaning of some of the words used, is the fact that behind this literary use of language is his familiarity with the rhythms and sounds of colloquial speech. And from this passage and others in which he makes reference to Barrie, it would appear that MacDiarmid recognised in Barrie that same capacity to use authentically and evocatively the rhythms and sounds of everyday Scots speech. On the other hand, what MacDiarmid could not accept – whether in what has become known as the Kailyard fiction of Crockett and Maclaren, or in the related poor quality verse imitators of Burns – was the low level of ambition in regard to content in much of that work:

> For if it's no' by thocht that Poetry's wrocht
> It's no' by want o' thocht
> The verse that flatters ignorance maun seem
> To ignorant folk supreme
> Sin' nane can read the verse that disna
> The damned thing bides as if it isna! (*CP* 232)

Here we come back to MacDiarmid's preoccupation – obsession, even – with the idea of the expansion of human consciousness, perhaps also an autodidact's obsession with the opportunities for learning he himself did not have. And MacDiarmid was not alone in this, if we think of the various educational and self-help movements that sprang up in the late nineteenth and early twentieth centuries in order to educate the working classes; the belief that spurred on equality of access to education throughout the twentieth century, eventually leading to comprehensive education: a belief that ordinary working-class people could use their minds as well as their hands and that they deserved the opportunity to do just this. MacDiarmid has at times been condemned for his supposed attacks on working-class culture, often equated with 'popular culture', and his contrary insistence on elitism. This is, however, a misunderstanding of his position. He certainly attacked *commercialised* popular culture such as Harry Lauder's stage impersonations of the traditional Scotsman, but the true folk culture that inspired Burns was another matter. And in relation to Burns, it was not Burns himself or his poetry that MacDiarmid frequently attacked, but the way this poetry was adopted and adapted to fit less demanding ideas and entertainment tastes; to act, as with Lauder, as a kind of self-congratulatory idea of Scottishness. Where MacDiarmid might be vulnerable to a charge of elitism is in his belief that not all of his fellow human beings were either motivated to use, or capable of using, their mental capacities to the full; but even in this belief he never limited the possibility of such full use of capacities to a certain class of society, and he always searched after this seemingly impossible dream of creating a human capacity beyond what we have now, as we see in his final long poem *In Memoriam James Joyce*.

To return to more mundane matters, and the *Cencrastus* speaker looking out from another window in Thrums, this whole sequence, with its intermingling of the day-to-day frustrations of the small town newspaper reporter, and his dream-like aspiration towards the achievement he believes lies within him, speaks not only of the pressures of MacDiarmid's own living situation at his time of writing, but also raises questions that are still relevant today in our increasingly commercialised, quick-read and time-short culture. In the 'Thrums' sequence, this dilemma is given form in two short lyrical stanzas, italicised in the text to mark their introspective status, followed by an ironic confrontation with the boss who comes in to find his reporter day-dreaming instead of working:

> *I wha aince in Heaven's height*
> *Gethered to me a' the licht*
> *Can nae mair reply to fire,*
> *'Neth deid leafs buriet in the mire.*
>
> *Sib to dewdrop, rainbow, ocean,*
> *No' for me their hues and motion,*
> *This foul clay has filed me till*
> *It's no to ken I'm water still.* (CP 234)

And then the boss enters:

> 'What was I dae'n sittin' in the dark?'
> 'Huntin' like Moses for the vital spark,
> – A human mole

> Wi' a hole for a soul?'
> 'I sud think o' my wife and faimly'
> I listen to him tamely. (*CP* 234, 235)

The advice given may be sensible for a career within the bounds of small-time journalism:

> 'Cut oot this poetry stuff, my lad. Get on
> Wi' advts. and puffs, and eident con
> The proofs; it's in you gin you care
> To dae't [...]
> Apply yersel' to what's worth while
> And I'll reward ye: that's my style.' (*CP* 235)

It is not relevant, however, for a writer whose aim (for himself and others) is the expansion of human consciousness: '*I'm no' the kind o' poet/That opens sales o' work.*' (*CP* 236).

For MacDiarmid's reluctant journalist in this *Cencrastus* sequence, his present occupation is the equivalent of the inward-looking community depicted by Barrie in his Thrums tales, satisfied with its self-limited horizons, its imaginative speculation directed only towards the well-established routine of everyday life. On the other hand, MacDiarmid's sequence title 'Frae Anither Window in Thrums' can be seen as double-edged. His speaker is trapped in a small-time world, as are Barrie's characters, yet the difference is that he knows he is trapped, economically and physically, in that he has to attend his work-place in order to obtain the money he needs to provide for his family. Despite his present frustrations, however, his window looks out not to another Thrums but to a world inhabited by his speculative imagination and an ambition to realise the potential he feels within him. And despite his frustration and his cursing of the 'system that can gie/A coof like this control o' me' (*CP* 235), the humorous, self-ironical 'Hokum' poem that ends the 'Thrums' sequence suggests that the journalist (and his poet author) will survive:

> I wish I was Harry Lauder
> Will Fyffe or J. J. Bell,

> – Or Lauchlan Maclean Watt
> For the maitter o' that!
> – Dae I Hell!
>
> Oh, it's hokum, hokum, hokum,
> And this is as near't as I'll get.
> The nearest I've got yet,
> Losh, but it's unco like *it*,
> – That sine-qua-non,
>   A soupçon
> O' precious hokum-pokum! (*CP* 254)

MacDiarmid's 'Frae Anither Window in Thrums' has on occasions been linked to the painting of the same name by William McCance. Andrew Nash, for example, in his chapter on the Kailyard in the *Edinburgh History of Scottish Literature*, brings poem and painting together as art works taking issue with any claim that Barrie's Thrums might stand for the life of Scotland, stating that MacDiarmid's poem makes 'an allusion to the painting by William McCance'.[18] Robert Crawford, who gives a feminised reading of Barrie in *Scotland's Books*, also brings poem and painting together, describing the painting as showing 'a man and woman energetically copulating, as if to reassert "normal" sexual and gender relations in the face of Barrie's subversions'. Crawford also claims that 'McCance's picture takes its title from a work by the masculinist Hugh MacDiarmid, who anxiously excoriated Barrie'.[19] Nash wins the battle of the influences, if any, here, for MacDiarmid's *To Circumjack Cencrastus* which includes the sequence 'Anither Window in Thrums' was not published until 1930, while the painting's date is 1928. Crawford's reference to the 'masculinist' MacDiarmid who 'excoriated' Barrie does not fit with the content and tone of the Thrums scenario presented in *Cencrastus*, and is false also to the nature of the comments made elsewhere by MacDiarmid about Barrie. Although he launched many an attack against 'Kailyard' writers, this derogatory epithet was, in MacDiarmid's use of it, attached principally to sentimental imitators of Burns in poetry. Contrary to public perception, there are surprisingly few negative comments about Barrie in his writings, and an equally surprising number of either neutral or endorsing references, although the latter are directed more towards his support of writers and related activities than towards the specificities of Barrie's own writing, especially those which brought him popular success and fortune. In the late book *The Company I've Kept* (1966), MacDiarmid lists the many literary 'friends' he has made over the years, and makes a particular point of saying that 'Sir J. M. Barrie is one of the few Scottish authors who lived in my time I did not know personally, although he was one of the signatories to a remarkable tribute to me in the 'thirties'.[20] And in a reference to Philip Mairet's book on Patrick Geddes, he quotes a passage that names Barrie as the Chancellor of Edinburgh University who attempted to persuade the university to honour Patrick Geddes with an LL. D., an attempt frustrated by members of the Establishment hostile to Geddes.[21] MacDiarmid would certainly be an unlikely 'Thrums' enthusiast, so far as the content of the stories is concerned. Yet he appears to have recognised Barrie's skill with spoken language, especially in his theatre writing. In an article on the Edinburgh Festival in 1948, for example, he quotes approvingly a report that 'a newspaper scribe had proposed that they should unearth Sir David Lindsay, *Scotland's only considerable dramatist before Sir James Barrie*' (my emphasis); and in the same quotation he includes a reference to Scottish drama 'being kept in abeyance by the Kirk from Lindsay to Barrie'.[22]

The 'critical conundrum' of Barrie's reputation is receiving more specialised attention at the present time, with increasing recognition of the importance of his post-Thrums writing, especially his drama, and a recognition also of the difference between Barrie's Thrums and its later Kailyard imitators. The modernist MacDiarmid, on the other hand, is still to a significant extent struggling to have his innovative poetry – in Scots and in English – recognised for its own literary and intellectual international worth, as opposed to being judged in the context of his more intemperate political writings. The Auld Lichts of Scotland's Thrums still have a lang reach.

Notes

1   C. M. Grieve, *Contemporary Scottish Studies* (London: Leonard Parsons, 1926), pp. 24, 25.

2   C. M. Grieve, 'Whither Scotland?', *Scottish Educational Journal*, 17 July 1931, reprinted in *Hugh MacDiarmid, The Raucle Tongue: Hitherto Uncollected Prose*, 3 vols, ed. Angus Calder, Glen Murray and Alan Riach (Manchester: Carcanet, 1997), Vol. II, p. 270.

3   R. D. S. Jack, 'J. M. Barrie', in *The Edinburgh History of Scottish Literature, Volume Two: Enlightenment, Britain and Empire (1707–1918)*, ed. Susan Manning (Edinburgh: Edinburgh University Press, 2007), p. 331.

4   C. M. Grieve, 'Sir James Barrie and Ourselves', reprinted in *The Raucle Tongue*, vol. 1 (1996), p. 220.

5   Ibid.

6   Hugh MacDiarmid, *Lucky Poet: A Self-Study in Literature and Political Ideas* (London: Jonathan Cape, 1943), p. 41.

7   Robert Crawford, *Scotland's Books: The Penguin History of Scottish Literature* (London: Penguin Books, 2007), p. 506.

8   Jack, 'J. M. Barrie', p. 331.

9   Edwin Muir, *The Estate of Poetry* (London: Hogarth Press, 1962), p. 80.

10 Hugh MacDiarmid, *Complete Poems 1920–1976*, vol. 1 (London: Martin, Brian & O'Keefe, 1978), p. 74. Page numbers for subsequent quotations will be abbreviated in the text as *CP*.

11 For a discussion of Orage's book in relation to *A Drunk Man*, see Margery Palmer McCulloch and Kirsten Matthews, 'Transcending the Thistle in *A Drunk Man* and *Cencrastus*', in *The Edinburgh Companion to Hugh MacDiarmid*, ed. Scott Lyall and Margery Palmer McCulloch (Edinburgh: Edinburgh University Press, 2011), pp. 54–58.

12 Alan Bold, ed. *The Letters of Hugh MacDiarmid* (Athens: Georgia: University of Georgia Press), 1984, p. 90.

13 See Alan Bold, *MacDiarmid: Christopher Murray Grieve, A Critical Biography* (London: John Murray, 1988), p. 223.

14 *Times Literary Supplement* (22 September 1927), pp. 650–51.

15 Bold, *Letters of Hugh MacDiarmid*, p. 91.

16 Edwin Muir, review of *To Circumjack Cencrastus*, *Criterion* 10:40 (April 1931), reprinted in *Modernism and Nationalism: Literature and Society in Scotland 1918–1939*, ed. Margery Palmer McCulloch (Glasgow: Association for Scottish Literary Studies, 2004), p. 81.

17 MacDiarmid, *Lucky Poet*, p. 17.

18 Andrew Nash, 'The Kailyard: Problem or Allusion', *Edinburgh History of Scottish Literature, Volume 2*, p. 320.

19 Crawford, *Scotland's Books*, p. 509.

20 Hugh MacDiarmid, *The Company I've Kept* (London: Hutchinson, 1966), p. 16.

21 MacDiarmid, *The Company I've Kept*, pp. 137–38.

22 Hugh MacDiarmid, 'After the Edinburgh Festival', *The National Weekly*, 25 September 1948, reprinted in *The Raucle Tongue* vol. 3 (1998), pp. 162–63.

7. Barrie, Sentimentality, and Modernity

ANDREW NASH

'With Mr Barrie, the fear of sentiment becomes an obsession.'[1]

'The unspeakable sentimentality. Doyle's problem. A fact. At the root of everything, every last thing.'[2]

Sentimentality is a theme that pervades much of Barrie's writing. Although he is often accused of being a sentimental writer, whose object in his fiction and plays was primarily to manipulate an emotional response from his audience, his preoccupation with sentimentality as a theme in itself is of far greater consequence for understanding the distinctiveness of his work and its place within literary history. This essay points towards new ways of understanding the importance of Barrie's fiction, both in terms of the shift from Victorian to modern fictional modes, and in terms of the tradition of modern Scottish literature.

To begin with what might seem an unlikely connection. It is not widely known that Barrie and D. H. Lawrence shared a mutual admiration for each other's work. Cynthia Asquith, who became Barrie's secretary towards the end of his life, recalls that Lawrence had 'long greatly liked' Barrie's *Margaret Ogilvy* (1896), and when Barrie read Lawrence's *Sons and Lovers* (1913) he wrote to the author praising the book.[3] Lawrence's friendship with Gilbert Canaan, with whom Barrie's wife had an affair, prevented a lasting association, but on reading *Kangaroo* in 1923 Barrie was still writing to Cynthia of Lawrence: 'There are power and poetry in him as in few.'[4] A simplistic response to the writers' mutual affection for their strongly (auto)biographical works would be to suggest that they shared a morbid obsession with their mothers. But Lawrence also had a fascination for Barrie's *Tommy* novels. In 1910 he wrote to his childhood sweetheart Jessie Chambers: '*Do* read Barrie's *Sentimental Tommy* and *Tommy and Grizel* [...] They'll help you understand how it is with me. I'm in exactly the same predicament.'[5] This was four years after Lawrence had told Jessie that he couldn't marry her because he didn't love her 'as a husband should love his wife.'[6] Lawrence scholars have passed over the connection all too hastily. In an article from 1969, H. A. Mason, who thought *Sentimental Tommy* 'facile' and not worth Lawrence taking out of the library, concluded that he 'was telling his sweetheart, not that he was Sentimental Tommy, but Peter Pan' – he didn't want to grow up.[7] Such a clichéd and ill-informed view of Barrie's work gets us nowhere. More helpful is the reference made to *Tommy and Grizel* in *The Lost Girl*, Lawrence's novel of 1920. Early on in the story, two of the male characters enter into a debate about Barrie's work:

> 'May I see what you're reading?' And he turned over the book. '*Tommy and Grizel*! Oh yes! What do you think of it?'
>
> 'Well,' said James, 'I am only at the beginning.'
>
> 'I think it's interesting, myself,' said Albert, 'as a study of a man who can't get away from himself. You meet a lot of people like that. What I wonder is why they find it such a drawback.'
>
> 'Find what a drawback?', asked James.
>
> 'Not being able to get away from themselves. That self-consciousness. It hampers them, and interferes with their power of action. Now I wonder why self-consciousness should hinder a man in his action? Why does it cause misgiving? – I think I'm self-conscious, but I don't think I have so many misgivings. I don't see that they're necessary.'
>
> 'Certainly I think Tommy is a weak character. I believe he is a despicable character,' said James.
>
> 'No I don't know so much about that,' said Albert, 'I shouldn't say weak exactly. He's only weak in one direction. No, what I wonder is why he feels guilty [...] That's the unnecessary part. The guilty feeling—'[8]

As this exchange makes clear, what appealed to Lawrence about Barrie's fiction was its preoccupation with the psychology and ethics of feeling and sentimentality, and, by extension, of self-consciousness. When he told Jessie Chambers that he was in exactly the same predicament as Tommy, Lawrence was identifying not with the impulse to remain forever young but with the links Barrie makes between sentimentality and artistic creativity, and specifically with the creative artist's compulsion to invent emotion.

Inventing emotion is a definition of sentimentality. The modern pejorative meaning of the word developed in the nineteenth century, partly as a reaction against the discourse of eighteenth-century sentimental literature. As Michael Bell argues, 'from being one of the most honorific terms in Enlightenment vocabulary', sentimentality had, by the twentieth century, been reduced to a term of near abuse, referring to 'self-indulgent and actively pernicious modes of feeling'.[9] Whereas in the eighteenth century the sentimental impulse was seen as the embodiment of benevolent sympathy, from the Victorian period onwards it was seen as leading to egoism and social irresponsibility. As a consequence, sentimentality became an important – though still under-documented – theme in the novel as it developed from the mid nineteenth-century into the modernist period.[10] It underpins the work of George Meredith, a writer whom Barrie much admired and about whom he published a critical essay, and it also underpins a novel like Ford Madox Ford's *The Good Soldier* (1915), a text that has several points in common with *Tommy and Grizel*. Ford's narrator, John Dowell, repeatedly refers to the eponymous Edward Ashburnham as a sentimentalist, a charge he then levels at himself towards the end of the novel. To writers like Ford, a sentimentalist is someone who places faith in forms of feeling that don't really exist, and thus provides a delusory answer to the existential crisis of modernism.

In tracking the modernist turn against sentimentality, Lawrence's non-fictional writings are especially important. In the course of a critical essay on John Galsworthy he offers a useful definition of the term:

> Sentimentality is the working off on yourself of feelings you haven't really got. We all *want* to have certain feelings: feelings of love, or sex passion, or kindliness, or anything else that goes at all deep. So the mass just fake these feelings inside themselves. Faked feelings! The world is all gummy with them. They are better than real feelings, because you can spit them out when you brush your teeth; and then tomorrow you can make them afresh.[11]

That couldn't be a better description of Barrie's sentimental anti-hero, Tommy Sandys. Tommy is only too eager to fake emotions. On one occasion in his boyhood he exchanges clothes with another boy who is in mourning but who wants to join in with the street games, and agrees to do the mourning for him. He sits in the corner of the yard, hunkering by himself and wiping his mournful eyes with the boy's hanky.[12] On another occasion he composes a letter for an illiterate woman who wishes to inform her mother about the death of a friend. Tommy revels in the opportunity to express powerful sentiments which do not belong to him, and not only do his words induce tears in the eyes of the reader of the letter, they also reduce Tommy to tears. Barrie's attitude towards sentimentality is ambivalent because, as R. D. S. Jack has argued, this capacity to take on another person's emotions is presented in his work as the epitome of the 'artistic personality'.[13] But these scenes are an important illustration of how Barrie's attitude towards sentimentality contrasts with that of eighteenth-century writers. Michael Bell has argued that in novels such as Henry Mackenzie's *The Man of Feeling* (1771), the sympathetic identification with another person's suffering fulfils Adam Smith's idea of sympathy as 'the capacity to reconstruct, imaginatively, the inner state of another person.'[14] To Barrie and Lawrence, however, the capacity for sympathy carries the danger of spilling over into a love of emotion for its own sake. In Mackenzie's text, the man of feeling is presented as a victim of a hostile world which operates against the code of benevolent sympathy he embodies. In Barrie, by contrast, the man of sentiment is the victimiser who – unwittingly or otherwise – manipulates vulnerable realists like Grizel; just as in *The Good Soldier* Edward's libertinism, which the narrator sees as deriving from his sentimentalism, drives one woman to suicide and another to madness. As Barrie wrote in one of his working notebooks: 'a sentimentalist always asks too much of people.'[15]

Before considering the *Tommy* novels in detail, it is necessary to look back to one of Barrie's early books – *A Window in Thrums* (1889). Critics who consider Barrie a sentimental writer can legitimately point to the rhetorical structure of this text, which seeks to arouse an emotional response in the reader. But even in this early work we can see Barrie developing an interest in sentimentality as a *theme* for his writing. The narrative structure and style is in part an exploration of the impulse towards sentimentality – to invent emotion. At the end of the story, the son Jamie, who has escaped Thrums for London, returns home too late to witness the death of his mother, father, and sister. Written at a time when Barrie was living in London and thus separated from his own family, the text appears autobiographical. But Barrie's parents were still alive when he published the book. What the text does is to imagine an unhappy experience in Barrie's life and what the emotions of that experience would be like. And six years later this imagined narrative became real when Barrie received a telegram in London informing him that his sister had died. Before he had arrived home in Kirriemuir his mother was also dead. The ending of *A Window in Thrums*, then, doesn't so much make patterns with facts (to evoke Muriel Spark's *The Prime of Miss Jean Brodie*), as make patterns with imagined facts that later became true. As Miss Brodie herself realised, 'Truth is stranger than fiction.'[16]

There is, however, another layer to the sentimental structure of *A Window in Thrums*. The narrator of the story, who is remarkably self-conscious throughout, frequently consoles himself by imagining a happy ending for the story:

> Away up in the glen, my lonely schoolhouse lying deep, as one might say, in a sea of snow, I had many hours in the long years by for thinking of my friends in Thrums and mapping out the future of Leeby and Jamie. I saw Hendry and Jess taken to the churchyard, and Leeby left alone in the house. I saw Jamie fulfil his promise to his mother, and take Leeby, that stainless young woman, far away to London, where they had a home together. Ah, but these were only the idle dreams of a dominie. The Lord willed it otherwise. (*WT* 181)

The lure of sentimentality is thus present both inside and outside of the narrative. And this essential self-awareness of Barrie's writing is what most autobiographical approaches to his fiction have failed to take into account.[17]

The *Tommy* novels are themselves often classed as autobiographical, though they are so only in the sense that *Sons and Lovers* and Joyce's *Portrait of the Artist as a Young Man* (1916) are autobiographical. Like these works, Barrie's novels raise the issue of what it means to transform life into art. It's instructive to compare the boy Tommy with Peter Pan. Both are presented as tyrannical in their fantasising nature. The brilliant episode when Tommy organises all his friends in an imaginary Jacobite uprising anticipates the way Peter stage-manages the battles in the Never Land. In *Peter Pan* we know that the battle between the pirates and Peter and the Lost Boys is a

ANDREW NASH

game, subject to the whims of Peter's creative imagination. So it is with Tommy's uprising. Barrie's presentation of the scene, with the characters constantly slipping in and out of their roles, with their real thoughts presented in brackets, makes the artifice visible on the page, forcing the reader to concentrate on the process of imaginative play. It also establishes the egoism of the creative artist. Tommy is in charge of the story, and he sometimes has to direct his slow-witted friends on how to play their parts. Significantly, however, when an adult (Mr McLean) enters the game and starts to take over the narrative, Tommy retreats into the background: 'sulky he remained throughout the scene, because he knew he was not the chief figure in it.' (*ST* 346). Like Peter, he is only happy when he is the author of the story.

In childhood, Tommy's egoism is implicitly excused by the narrative tone. In adulthood, however, his sentimental qualities take on some of Peter's dangerous manipulative power. In *Tommy and Grizel* Tommy's art is presented as a form of deception. His best-selling book, which becomes known simply as 'Sandys on women', leads everyone to assume that he has an intimate knowledge of women, has been jilted, or perhaps widowed. When he is thrust into literary society, Tommy is happy to go along with these misapprehensions, misleading one woman into thinking he is a widower and another into thinking he is proposing to her. Later, he falsifies his relationship with Grizel when he writes a book about unrequited love, leading Grizel – whose love Tommy is unable to return – to exclaim: 'No one was ever loved more truly than you. You know nothing about unrequited love. Then why do you pretend to know? [...] It is nothing but sentiment' (*TG* 304). Tommy's sentimentality, however, is what makes him a brilliant writer. His sentimental moments always leave him 'in splendid fettle for writing' (*TG* 39). But the novel suggests that artistic profundity comes at a cost. Grizel tells him that 'If writing makes you live in such an unreal world it must do you harm.' (*TG* 101). It does, but it harms her as well. Grizel is presented as entirely honest. Her name suggests the patient Griselda of literary myth – in *Sentimental Tommy* she calls her doll Griselda and is herself called Lady Griselda in the Jacobite games. She is contrived to be the complete opposite of Tommy so that the destructive potential of his sentimentality can be intensified. 'His individuality consisted in having none, while she could only be herself' (*ST* 187).

The novel makes clear that Tommy's failure to love Grizel is not in itself the problem. As Eve Kosofsky Sedgwick argues, the problem is that, having inadvertently led her to believe that he desires her, Tommy pretends to do so.[18] I have argued elsewhere that the novel can fruitfully be explored alongside the sexological debates that were taking place at the end of the nineteenth century.[19] Barrie was closely attuned to contemporary debates over gender and sexuality as his journalism – particularly the essays he wrote for the *Edinburgh Evening Dispatch* – make clear.[20] There is little doubt that Lawrence would have detected this aspect of Tommy's character when he explained to his former lover that he was in exactly the same predicament. Tommy's problem is that, because of his sentimentality, the only women he can fall in love with are those of his own imagination. We see this at the start of *Tommy and Grizel* when he is working as an amanuensis for the popular novelist Mr Pym. Left alone to polish Pym's grammar, he ends up rewriting the love passages, falling in love with the characters he creates:

> That was Tommy with a pen in his hand and a handkerchief hard by; but it was another Tommy who, when the finest bursts were over, sat back in his chair and mused. The lady was consistent now, and he would think about her, and think and think, until concentration, which is a pair of blazing eyes, seemed to draw her out of the pages to his side, and then he and she sported in a way forbidden in the tale. While he sat there with eyes riveted, he had her to dinner at a restaurant, and took her up the river, and called her 'little woman'; and when she held up her mouth he said tantalizingly that she must wait until he had finished his cigar. This queer delight enjoyed, back he popped her into the story. (*TG* 16–17)

Tommy here fulfils Lawrence's definition of the sentimentalist. The moment the author has finished his invented emotion he consigns the woman back to fiction and spits his faked feelings out like toothpaste.

Responding like this to an invented person is all very well, but when Tommy responds to Grizel in the same way it is destructive. When he pretends to love her, his attempts at emotion are seen as a calculated playing of a part. He reads Grizel's love for him as if it is a work of art he has created:

> The artist who had done this thing was entranced, as if he had written an immortal page. [...] He so loved the thing he had created that in his exultation he mistook it for her. He believed all he was saying. He looked at her long and adoringly, not, as he thought, because he adored her, but because it was thus that look should answer look; he pressed her wet eyes reverently because thus it was written in his delicious part [...]. He did not love, but he was the perfect lover; he was the artist trying in a mad moment to be as well as to do. (*TG* 157–59)

The sentimental artist has an egotistical desire to replace reality with his own artistic creation. At one point Tommy says openly to Grizel: 'what a delicious book you are, and how I wish I had written you!' (*TG* 185). Throughout the novel Tommy does attempt to write Grizel's life through his sentimental fantasies. At the end of the story, when Grizel goes missing, having followed Tommy to Switzerland, various imaginary scenes run through his mind, including one where he discovers Grizel dead and another where he is reconciled to her in Thrums. With each fantasy Tommy indulges in an imaginary emotional response, to the extent that he shares his faked feelings of grief with the occupants of a hotel reading room. When he actually returns to Thrums and discovers that Grizel has gone mad, having been driven insane by his false treatment of her, the harsh reality cuts through his sentimental fictions.

It is these sorts of episodes that make the narrative form of Barrie's novel so distinctive. *Tommy and Grizel* is about a sentimental, creative artist, but it is also a creative act in itself, and the self-consciousness of the narrator, who regularly uses the first-person pronoun, keeps us aware that this is an *imaginative, creative* record of Tommy's life (just as it is, in a way, an imaginative, creative record of Barrie's life). The narrator pointedly refuses to discuss Tommy's writing and his identity as a celebrity author and draws attention to his own efforts to persuade the reader to adopt a particular position towards the two protagonists. He confesses his own love for Grizel and openly admits to omitting details that would make the reader admire Tommy more. Right at the end he makes a direct appeal to his readers:

But here, five and twenty years later, is the biography, with the title changed. You may wonder that I had the heart to write it. I do it, I have sometimes pretended to myself, that we may all laugh at the stripling of a rogue, but that was never my reason. Have I been too cunning, or have you seen through me all the time? Have you discovered that I was really pitying the boy who was so fond of boyhood that he could not with years become a man, telling nothing about him that was not true, but doing it with unnecessary scorn in the hope that I might goad you into crying: 'Come, come, you are too hard on him!'

Perhaps the manner in which he went to his death deprives him of these words. Had the castle gone on fire that day while he was at tea, and he perished in the flames in a splendid attempt to save the life of his enemy (a very probable thing), then you might have felt a little liking for him. Yet he would have been precisely the same person. I don't blame you, but you are a Tommy. (*TG* 428)

The tone and effect here is remarkably similar to the closing pages of *The Good Soldier*, published fifteen years later, where John Dowell also reflects on his own response as a 'sentimentalist' to the characters in the story he has been telling, and admits that he cannot conceal his 'love' for Edward Ashburnham, however much he tries in his narrative to condemn the good soldier's actions.[21] In Barrie's text, the narrative awareness of the multiple ways in which a story might be shaped, and how different ways of telling the story will induce a different emotional response from a reader, is a reflection of the theme of sentimentality itself and therefore of the content of the novel. Like *A Window in Thrums*, then, the form of *Tommy and Grizel* reflects its content.

In his next work of fiction, *The Little White Bird* (1902), Barrie furthered this technique of fusing theme and content to create a metafictional text where the idea of inventing emotion and fantasies is folded into the narrative form of the work itself. The narrator, a retired soldier, tells stories to a little boy, David, in order to recreate him as a fictional character so that he can claim parental possession of him. (One of these stories is the fantasy of Peter Pan, whose early textual adventures are recounted in six self-contained chapters). At the end of the text, we learn that the story we have been reading is a book that the narrator has been writing in an effort to out-create David's mother, who is about to give birth to a second child. The series of 'creation conflicts' that R. D. S. Jack detects in *Peter Pan* have their origins in this text.[22] The explicit analogy between artistic creation and maternal creation allows Barrie to portray a narrator who is constantly tempted to replace reality with an artistic world of his own making. The characters in his fantasies are literally created by words or writing: he claims to have brought about David's birth by dropping a letter which reconciled his parents to one another; he announces the birth of David's sister in a newspaper while her mother is in Patagonia; he creates his own fantasy child, Timothy, during a conversation and then, with 'hasty *words*' (*LWB* 48, my italics), destroys him when the fantasy becomes complicated. Notebook entries show that Barrie considered making the narrator a theatre prompter, a playwright, or a reader of plays, whose theatrical mind leads him to 'assume characters'.[23]

The narrative style of *The Little White Bird* thus operates as a fabrication of the text's own reality, just as the text is itself a fabrication of Barrie's own reality and his relationship with the Llewelyn Davies family.[24] As in *A Window in Thrums*, the work makes patterns with imagined facts. Peter Pan is a character in *The Little White Bird*, but the germ of his fantasising, role-playing mind can be traced to the narrator of the story, just as it can be traced to sentimental Tommy. Space prevents detailed consideration of *Peter Pan* here, but it is clear that the theme of sentimentality allows for continuity to be drawn between Barrie's early prose works and his drama.

Barrie and Scottish Literature

In what remains of this essay, I want briefly to explore how the ideas developed above can help us place Barrie's work more effectively within the traditions of Scottish literature. Rather than looking backwards, to see how the treatment of sentimentality and the creative imagination compares with eighteenth-century writers or with the work of earlier Victorian novelists such as George MacDonald, I want to look forward to consider the presence of his work in modern Scottish literature. I have suggested how his novels can be read profitably alongside those of English modernist authors like Lawrence and Ford, but it is possible to see his fictional concerns as foundational to those cultivated by some of the most important Scottish prose writers of the twentieth century. Such an endeavour might seem surprising and rather unlikely. As Margery Palmer McCulloch's essay in this volume shows, the criticism of Hugh MacDiarmid contributed to Barrie's work being identified for much of the twentieth century as a tradition against which modern writers positioned themselves, both aesthetically and ideologically. Yet the thematic concerns of Barrie's writing – and specifically the issues of sentimentality and artistic creativity – have remained central to the concerns of modern Scottish writers. Novelists such as James Kelman, Alasdair Gray, Muriel Spark and John Burnside – each, on the surface of things, markedly different from Barrie in style and thematic interest – can be seen as responding to the themes and issues raised in this chapter.

A link with Kelman might seem fanciful, but it is striking how often Patrick Doyle, the central character in *A Disaffection* (1989), refers to himself as sentimental: 'It was enough to make ye burst out greeting. The unspeakable sentimentality. Doyle's problem. A fact. At the root of everything, every last thing.'[25] Like Tommy, Doyle's 'inclination towards the sentimental' is a trap of his own making; it is at the root of everything because it offers a retreat from reality and a self-deluding faith in forms of meaning that don't really exist: 'How fucking un-of-this-world-ness! Time to cut out all forms of sentimental drivel.'[26] Like Tommy, Doyle is haunted by his own fantasies, which he considers 'border on a very, a very dubious perception of the world'; at one point he explicitly references 'Peter Pan territory, Never Never Land, sentimental maudlinity.'[27] The 'unspeakable sentimentality' is the basis of his existential crisis, just as it is for Tommy, and Kelman hints that the problem is part of the Scottish psyche when Doyle coins the word 'sentimacbloodymental.'[28]

In formal terms, of course, Barrie's work has little affinity with that of Kelman. Alasdair Gray is a different matter. Gray's deployment of fantastic, satiric and farcical modes has much in common with Barrie. An epigraph to *The Fall of Kelvin Walker* (1985) uses a famous line from *What Every Woman Knows* (1908) – 'there are few more impressive sights in the world than a Scotsman on the make' – and Gray's novel, reworked from an earlier drama, might also owe something to an earlier Barrie play, *Walker, London* (1892). Both works are farces and involve a duplicitous central male character;

and Gray might well be following Barrie in playing on the nineteenth-century colloquialism 'Walker', meaning 'an exclamation expressing incredulity' (*OED*), in his presentation of a central character who, like Barrie's Jasper Phipps, is 'consciously and conscientiously remaking himself'.[29]

Barrie's fictional concerns are also present in the plot and themes of Gray's *Lanark* (1981). In a short but perceptive comparison, Cairns Craig has argued that when Duncan Thaw 'flees the real world' of Glasgow and 're-emerges as Lanark in the alternative world of Unthank, he repeats the flight of Barrie's Peter Pan to the Never Land of the imagination'.[30] And Thaw can also be seen as a descendent of Tommy Sandys. An artist trapped by his environment and his own sentimental fantasies, Thaw, like Tommy, is 'as much estranged from imagination as from reality'.[31] Where Tommy's fantasies end up driving Grizel mad, Thaw's failure to reconcile the imagination with reality leads him – apparently – to kill Marjory Laidlaw.

A writer with even closer links to the themes and concerns of Barrie's fiction is Muriel Spark. The layering of fictions, the blending of realism and fantasy, and the suspicion of the imagination (linked, of course, to her exploration of the influence of Calvinism on the Scottish psyche), all resonate with Barrie's work. Spark's explicit rejection of a sentimental aesthetic in favour of the 'art of ridicule' does not make her Barrie's opposite; indeed, her comment that 'I have never from my earliest memories known any other life or way of seeing things but that of an artist, a changer of actuality into something else', could easily have come from the author of the *Tommy* novels.[32] Spark's works are full of those Barriesque characters who use fiction to interpret – and in some cases to create – reality. The Tommy who writes letters for the members of his community, and so invents their lives and emotions, is like Dougal Douglas, the central character in *The Ballad of Peckham Rye* (1960), who conceives fictions for the men and women of his community and who ghost-writes the memoirs of an elderly actress, inventing for her a Peckham childhood that doesn't exist. The narrator of *The Little White Bird*, who like his creator rewrites the lives of the people around him, is not dissimilar to Fleur Talbot, the narrator of *Loitering with Intent* (1981), who fictionalises the memoirs of the members of the Autobiographical Association. It is intriguing in this context that Barrie himself invented a 'Society for Providing Material for Volumes of Reminiscences' in a satirical article of 1890.[33]

There are at least two direct references to Barrie in Spark's work. In *The Bachelors* (1960), it is recalled that the favourite childhood book of Patrick Seton, the spiritualist medium, was *Mary Rose* (1920). Patrick is described as 'a dreamy child', and when he is taken to the theatre to see the work acted he 'is sharply shocked by the sight of the real actresses and actors with painted faces performing outwardly on the open platform this tender romance about the girl who was stolen by the fairies on a Hebridean island'.[34] It is clear why Patrick, a fake psychic, should be affected by a play about a ghost returning from another world and a girl who once, unbeknownst to herself, disappeared for twenty days on a Hebridean island. The shock Patrick experienced when seeing the actors in Barrie's play putting on their roles is surely meant to indicate the shattering of the 'poetic innocence' that formed his 'dream of childhood', a dream that still remains in the mind of the adult man 'as that from which everything else [in his life] deviates'.[35] In the same passage we learn that on his 'first enchanted visit to the Western Isles' Patrick encounters the first of the 'unfortunate occurrences' which he believes have plagued him since childhood: 'having sat up reciting to an American lady far into the night and the next morning being accused of having taken money from her purse'.[36] The Western Isles thus become a scene of materialism, not enchantment, for this 'dreamer of dreams'.[37]

Both *The Bachelors* and *Mary Rose* explore the dialectic between the spiritual and the material. As Peter Hollindale perceptively summarises, *Mary Rose* is concerned with 'the tragic interplay between time and time-lessness, reality and fantasy-as-reality'.[38] So too, in Spark's characteristically ironic way, is *The Bachelors*, its dialectic dramatised in several ways but most obviously in the two central characters who pursue true and false vocations. As Bryan Cheyette argues, *The Bachelors* is a novel that 'is split asunder between body and soul': Patrick 'attempts to act as a medium between distinct spheres' but, in contrast to the epileptic Ronald Bridges, who 'build[s] bridges between people and different domains', Patrick 'splits them apart'.[39]

The second direct reference to Barrie in Spark's work comes in *The Hothouse by the East River* (1973). In this novel the central characters are already dead: they ghost 1970s New York having refused to accept their own mortality. The intertextual links with *Peter Pan* are explicit. Not only do we have a character whose shadow falls the wrong way, but during the course of the novel there is a production of Barrie's play where, in a parodic inversion, the actors are all geriatrics. Significantly, the play is produced by the son the central characters never had; not so much the boy who never grew up, as Spark critics inevitably suggest, but the boy who never was: the lost boy – the Timothy of *The Little White Bird*. There are echoes here, too, of the fantasy section of *Dear Brutus* (1917), where the characters enter an enchanted wood and experience what might have been had they taken different turnings in their lives. One of the characters, the alcoholic Dearth, meets the daughter he never had, before awakening at the climax of the play to the reality that he is childless.

Too many Spark critics, unfamiliar with Barrie, reach false conclusions about the intertextuality at work in *Hothouse*. Norman Page argues that the novel 'has no truck with Barrie's sentimental conclusion in *Peter Pan* that 'to die will be an awfully big adventure'.[40] But that famous phrase is not the conclusion of *Peter Pan*; it is the final line of Act 3. The published play of 1928 concludes with a clear rejection of Peter's decision to deny linear time and to cheat death. One of Barrie's closing prose observations at the end of Act 5 is: 'If he could get the hang of the thing his cry might become "To live would be an awfully big adventure!"' (*PP* 153). Spark's novel (regardless of authorial intention) is not a dismissal of Barrie's play but a re-articulation of its central message that the 'substance' of life, rather than the sentimentalised 'shadow' of fantasy, is always superior.[41] There is, furthermore, a structural comparison to be made with Barrie's work here, because Spark's metafictional strategy in *Hothouse* reminds us that the characters in her novel are unreal in a double sense: they are the fictions of Muriel Spark but they are also fictions inside the 'reality' of the novel, having created an existence for themselves that never was. That's strikingly similar to the way that the narrator of *The Little White Bird* likes to create false lives and identities for himself and for others within his own narrative.

One final example again makes visible the presence of Barrie in the development of twentieth-century writing, and here in terms both of modernism and of Scottish literature. Barrie's memoir of his mother, *Margaret Ogilvy* (1896), is his most maligned and misunderstood work. It has been seen by most critics as a deplorable lapse in taste; a cynical gesture by the author to cash in on his mother's death by writing a sentimental, commercialised account of her life. But the book is as much about its author as it is about Margaret Ogilvy, and it fits directly into a tradition of experimental forms of life-writing that proliferated at the end of the nineteenth century. Seizing on a term invented by Stephen Reynolds in 1906, Max Saunders has explored in magisterial depth this tradition of 'autobiografiction' – a hybrid form which he identifies as the origins of modernism.[42] Barrie's self-conscious construction of a fictionalised life in *Margaret Ogilvy* – 'the creation of a personal history more bearable than the truth'[43] as Lisa Chaney has it – lays bare the power of fiction, or fictionalised autobiography, to construct and sentimentalise the past. The text is everywhere concerned with deception. It begins on the day when Barrie was born, and the first chapter is thus composed not from memory but from stories subsequently told to the author. Barrie draws an immediate distinction between the writing self and the constructed self:

> On the day I was born we bought six hair-bottomed chairs, and in our little house it was an event […]. I so often heard the tale afterwards, and shared as boy and man in so many similar triumphs, that the coming of the chairs seems to be something I remember, as if I had jumped out of bed on that first day, and run ben to see how they looked. (*MO* 1)

The self that imagines here – that *seems* to remember – is a self constructed through memories; but they are memories of stories not facts. Thus Barrie can spend much of this book *imagining* events that took place before he was born, leading to observations such as this: 'I have seen many weary on-dings of snow, but the one I seem to recollect best occurred nearly twenty years before I was born.' (*MO* 24–5) As Chaney observes, 'in the end we no longer quite know where either the real Barrie or his mother might lie.'[44]

As a text that foregrounds the act of re-writing the past from memories of stories, the multi-layered imaginary structure of *Margaret Ogilvy* links Barrie to the genre of autobiografiction and also to a dominant trend in recent Scottish writing. *Margaret Ogilvy* can profitably be seen as a point of origin for 'autobiographical' texts such as John Burnside's *A Lie about my Father* (2006) and Janice Galloway's *This is Not About Me* (2008) and *All Made Up* (2011), whose titles alone parade the fictionality of their form of life-writing. In a preface to his book Burnside demands that it be treated as fiction but the ISBN cataloguing classes it as autobiography. Resonant of *Margaret Ogilvy*, which Barrie might easily have titled *A Lie about my Mother*, Burnside presents the story of his father's lies as a lie in itself – a life story that discloses its own fictionality. Take, for example, his account of the origins of his father (a foundling):

> I try from time to time to imagine the morning when he was found, wrapped in nothing but a blanket according to the story Aunt Margaret had heard […] Nobody I have ever known was there to witness his abandonment, so I can imagine it as I like: as a scene from a fairy tale, perhaps, the unknown baby left at the door of some unsuspecting innocents […] I could imagine it wet and windy, the blanket sodden, the child crying plaintively, weak with hunger and terrified. […]
>
> I could stick to this kind of grainy, wet Thursday morning realism, and I would probably be fairly close to the truth; but what I choose to imagine is a summer's morning.[45]

The choice of imagining is exactly what Barrie makes in *Margaret Ogilvy*, where, like Burnside, he sifts through the different ways in which he might visualise events from an imagined life. At the end of the text Barrie looks forward 'to a time when age must dim my mind and the past comes sweeping back like the shades of night over the bare road of the present'. What he chooses to anticipate seeing in the future, however, is not 'my youth […] but hers' (*MO* 163). The imagined future memory is of a time before he was born.

Memory, when transformed into art, works both backwards and forwards. However great the contrast in attitude and style, the technique of life-writing that Barrie and Burnside adopt stands comparison. Just as Barrie ends by imagining the future, *A Lie About My Father* closes with the author imagining how he will pass the story of his father on to his son:

> The memory I have of my father, caught between the night and his little prefab, is a story in itself, or at least, the beginnings of one. It is a father's tale, a myth, and I have to work out how to pass it on, in its best form, to the child with whom I am now walking, on the morning of the saints.[46]

All the author needs is 'one story, to start things off. The last thing I would want to do is make a lie of it.' As with *Margaret Ogilvy*, Burnside's memoir closes with a recognition that stories carry a truth of their own.

The links I have made with four modern Scottish writers merely scratch the surface of the many ways in which Barrie's work can be related to common themes in Scottish literature. Under the influence of MacDiarmid, we have been encouraged to view Barrie as the summation of a debilitating tradition, rather than as an important figure in the emergence of distinctively modern forms of writing. Detailed study of the formal qualities of his prose works and of the themes of sentimentality and the artistic imagination, however, can reveal the vital significance of his work in both the emergence of literary modernism and the development of distinctively Scottish literary traditions in the twentieth and twenty-first centuries.

Notes

1   Stephen Gwynn, 'The Autumn's Books', *Fortnightly Review*, 74 (1900), p. 1037.
2   James Kelman, *A Disaffection*, 1989 (London: Picador, 1990), p. 186.
3   *D. H. Lawrence: A Composite Biography*, ed. Edward Nehls, 3 vols (Madison: University of Wisconsin Press, 1957–59), p. 445.
4   *Letters of J. M. Barrie*, ed. Viola Meynell (New York: Scribner's, 1947), p. 200.
5   *The Letters of D. H. Lawrence*, Volume 1: 1910–1913, ed. James T. Boulton (Cambridge: Cambridge University Press, 1979), p. 175.
6   *D. H. Lawrence: A Composite Biography*, p. 59.
7   H. A. Mason, 'Lawrence in Love', *Cambridge Quarterly*, 4:2 (Spring, 1969), pp. 181–200, p. 198.
8   D. H. Lawrence, *The Lost Girl*, 1920, ed. John Worthen (Cambridge: Cambridge University Press, 1981), pp. 70–71.
9   Michael Bell, *Sentimentalism, Ethics and the Culture of Feeling* (Basingstoke: Palgrave, 2000), p. 2.
10 For a recent brief discussion of the modernist reaction against sentimentality see Jonathan Greenberg, *Modernism, Satire and the Novel* (Cambridge: Cambridge University Press, 2011), pp. 11–16.
11 D. H. Lawrence, 'John Galsworthy', 1928, repr. in *D. H. Lawrence: Selected Critical Writings* ed. Michael Herbert (Oxford: Oxford University Press, 1998), p. 216.
12 Barrie later identified this as an episode from his own childhood. See *The Greenwood Hat, being a Memoir of James Anon 1885–1887* (London: Peter Davies, 1930), pp. 1–2.
13 R. D. S. Jack, *Myths and the Mythmaker: a literary account of J. M. Barrie's formative years* (Amsterdam and New York: Rodopi, 2010), p. 32.
14 Bell, p. 44.
15 Beinecke Library, Yale University, Barrie Vault Shelves, A2/16.
16 Muriel Spark, *The Prime of Miss Jean Brodie*, 1961 (London: Penguin, 1965), p. 124.

17 The worst example being Harry M. Geduld, *Sir James Barrie* (New York: Twayne, 1971).
18 Eve Kosofsky Sedgwick, *Epistemology of the Closet*, 1990 (Harmondsworth: Penguin, 1991), p. 198.
19 Andrew Nash, 'Trying to be a Man: J. M. Barrie and Sentimental Masculinity', *Forum for Modern Language Studies*, 35:2 (June, 1999), pp. 113–25.
20 See Andrew Nash, 'J. M. Barrie and the Third Sex', in *Joyous Sweit Imaginacioun: Essays in Honour of R. D. S. Jack* (Amsterdam & New York: Rodopi, 2007), pp. 229–41.
21 Ford Madox Ford, *The Good Soldier*, 1915, ed. Martin Stannard (New York: W. W. Norton), p. 161.
22 R. D. S. Jack, *The Road to the Never Land: a Reassessment of J. M. Barrie's Dramatic Art* (Aberdeen: Aberdeen University Press, 1991), pp. 181–212.
23 Beinecke, A2/15.
24 On this relationship see Andrew Birkin, *J. M. Barrie and the Lost Boys* (London: Constable, 1979).
25 Kelman, p. 186. There are around twenty references to sentimentality in Doyle's narrative.
26 Kelman, p. 58.
27 Kelman, pp. 61, 83.
28 Kelman, p. 299.
29 Alasdair Gray, *The Fall of Kelvin Walker* (Edinburgh: Canongate, 1985), p. 106. For a brief discussion of the link with *What Every Woman Knows*, see Stephen Bernstein, *Alasdair Gray* (Lewisburg: Bucknell University Press, 1999), p. 92.
30 Cairns Craig, *The Modern Scottish Novel: Narrative and the National Imagination* (Edinburgh: EUP, 1999), p. 230.
31 Alasdair Gray, *Lanark*, 1981 (London: Picador, 1985), p. 159.
32 Muriel Spark, 'The Desegregation of Art', repr. in *Critical Essays on Muriel Spark*, ed. Joseph Hynes (New York: Hall, 1992), pp. 37, 33.
33 'Pro Bono Publico', *Fortnightly Review*, 48 (1890), pp. 398–407.
34 Muriel Spark, *The Bachelors* (London: Macmillan, 1960), p. 171.
35 Ibid.
36 Spark, *The Bachelors*, pp. 171–72.
37 Spark, *The Bachelors*, p. 171.
38 Peter Hollindale, 'Introduction', in J. M. Barrie, *Peter Pan and Other Plays* (Oxford: Oxford World's Classics, 1995), p. xxii.
39 Bryan Cheyette, *Muriel Spark* (London: Northcote House, 2000), p. 49.
40 Norman Page, *Muriel Spark* (Basingstoke: Macmillan, 1990), p. 88.
41 The terms 'shadow' and 'substance' are used by the narrator of *The Little White Bird* to contrast artistic creativity with maternal creativity. (*LWB* 201, 206).
42 Max Saunders, *Self Impression: Life-Writing, Autobiografiction, and the Forms of Modern Literature* (Oxford: OUP, 2010).
43 Lisa Chaney, *Hide and Seek with Angels* (London: Hutchinson, 2005), p. 139.
44 Ibid.
45 John Burnside, *A Lie About My Father* (London: Jonathan Cape, 2006), pp. 20–21.
46 Burnside, p. 324.

PART III: PETER PAN'S CONNECTIONS

8. Betwixt-and-Between: *Peter Pan in Kensington Gardens* and the Decadent Moment

PAUL FOX

'I think they have no portion in us after
We pass the gate.'
Ernest Dowson, 'Vitae Summa Brevis' (1896)

Maps are of fundamental importance in the several Peter Pan texts of J. M. Barrie. The opening sentence of *Peter Pan in Kensington Gardens* (1906) makes an immediate demand of the reader, that 'you must see for yourselves that it will be difficult to follow our adventures unless you are familiar with the Kensington Gardens' (*PPKG* 3). The children at play within the Gardens name landmarks according to their fellows' experiences upon those sites. The boundaries of the Gardens might be clearly marked, both internally and externally, by gates and stones, paths and persons, but the markers within the gates alter the readers' understanding of the physical space: what are boundary stones in the Gardens between the London parishes of Paddington and Westminster St. Mary's are simultaneously the gravestones of Phoebe Phelps and Walter Stephen Matthews, buried by Peter who discovered the babies' bodies after they had fallen from their perambulators. The Gardens are, then, a personalised space, understood via the experiences of those children who play, and occasionally die, within its boundaries. In *Peter and Wendy* (1911), with the latter instantiation of the children's garden playground as Neverland, Barrie remarks upon the near impossible task of 'trying to draw a map of a child's mind, which is not only confused, but keeps going round all the time. There are zigzag lines on it [...] and these are probably roads in the island; for the Neverland is always more or less an island' (*PW* 73).[1] Proceeding to describe the various imaginative interests and experiences within the minds of children that are realised on the island, Barrie then states that the cumulative weight of these reveals Neverland's cartography to be a palimpsest, 'map[s] showing through, and it is all rather confusing, especially as nothing will stand still' (*PW* 74). This confusion is made all the more apparent when Barrie informs the reader that even birds 'carrying maps and consulting them' (*PW* 102) cannot find their way to Neverland, for Peter gives directions to the island based solely upon what whimsically springs into his mind, altering each moment. But, then again, 'of course the Neverlands vary a good deal' (*PW* 74). What, then, can Barrie's maps signify to the reader? Are they simply a multiplicity of directions and markers whereby we can locate the various adventures had by Peter and other children? Do they plot the fulfilment of children's transitory desires or their actual experiences? Are they a shifting or a shifty plan of a mental or a physical space, or some combination of each? And why does Barrie claim to attach such great importance to his readers' understanding of the maps of his stories?

Hard on the heels of Barrie's injunction that readers must comprehend the map of Kensington Gardens, they are informed that 'no one has ever been in the whole of the Gardens, because it is so soon time to turn back' and that they are a 'tremendous big place' (*PPKG* 3). Mothers and nannies require that children sleep between midday and one, and, if only that were not the case, then perhaps, Barrie suggests, we might be able to appreciate the whole. Sadly, it is time itself, interpreted and imposed by adults, that impedes our few opportunities for adventuring. The map of the Gardens becomes necessary precisely because we do not have time to explore them for ourselves. 'The Gardens are bounded on one side by a never-ending line of omnibuses' (*PPKG* 3) that whisk children away to their homes and naptimes, a border that operates according to schedule and parental demand, where, by holding up a single, authoritative finger, an adult causes an omnibus to appear, always and immediately. Children may try to escape this adult world and to stay in the Gardens, such children as Marmaduke Perry who refuses to leave the little wooden house off the Gardens' Broad Walk, or Maimie Mannering (an earlier characterisation of Wendy) who spends the night in the Gardens and meets Peter Pan, but Lock-Out time always comes, the moment when children are barred from entering, their play forbidden until another day. Only Peter, disjunct from the world of adults, is able to reside in the Gardens and it is that adult world from which he himself is, literally, barred. But being in exile from the adult world allows Peter to remain upon an island in the Gardens, the space itself separated from the exterior noise and bustle of London life. Kensington Gardens exist as an atemporal enclave within the world of adult time, and, thus, Peter Pan is, as the first sentence of *Peter and Wendy* informs us, the one child who never grows up. He is 'ever so old, but really always the same age' (*PPKG* 12) depending upon whether one views him from the temporal standpoint of the adult world or that which exists within the Gardens. The later instantiation of Kensington Gardens as the *Neverland* would operate further to mark the fundamental significance of time within the maps and mapping of Barrie's worlds.

In the Gardens, Peter is told by the wise, old bird, Solomon Caw, that he now resides in an unusual existential state: he is a Betwixt-and-Between, neither bird nor human, a 'poor little half-and-half' (*PPKG* 16–17). Barrie presents a curious natal mythos in *Peter Pan in Kensington Gardens*: human mothers send their requests for children (boys or girls, dark or fair) to Solomon Caw by writing a letter, folding it up into a boat, and sailing it across the Serpentine to the birds' island. On receipt, Solomon decides whether or not the request is viable. The babies mothers might eventually receive are originally birds born on the island and they become human once delivered. After a period in this new state, children forget what it was to fly, to speak the language of birds, and what it is to be without the mothers to whom they have been delivered. Peter neither exists in the state of an unborn baby, nor yet is he fully born into the human world: he is 'betwixt-and-between' the two in a liminal moment all of his own, an interstitial period between the pre-temporal and time itself. He occasionally and only partially recalls his human mother, but doesn't fully remember what it was to be a bird. He does not grow up because he does not exist in the adult world of dynamic, linear temporality. Equally, he is free from that world's constraints, of being locked out of, or forced to leave, Kensington Gardens; he is at liberty to play when and as he wishes, and will, by the time he appears in Neverland, be capable of adopting and switching various identities and roles as his whims demand rather than abiding by the identities imposed upon other children by adults. If in Neverland he desires a mother to tell him stories, this is simply because his personality is acted out according to those narratives of himself that he creates, and it is in this type of creative role-playing that Peter's essence is revealed, one which is fluid and always changing, based upon an aesthetic of play unconstrained by fixed identity and the adult world's expectations of what it means to grow up. Barrie's own fear of an externally imposed identity, one fixed in writing for all time, is evident when he stated: 'May God blast anyone who writes a biography of me'.[2] In the adventures had by Peter in Kensington Gardens, we see the impositions of, and expectation about, identity already constraining children's playfulness at an early age, and this is the world from which Peter is free.

This temporal characterisation of Peter Pan at play in Kensington Gardens and Neverland is one derived from an aesthetic that had been at the foreground of British literature and perceived by the general public as the dominant literary movement for much of the preceding fifteen years: that of Decadence. *Peter Pan in Kensington Gardens* was published in 1906, two years after the play *Peter Pan, or The Boy Who Would Not Grow Up* was first produced. In 1902, Barrie had published *The Little White Bird*, five chapters of which were extracted with only the most minor of alterations to constitute the *Kensington Gardens* text. A number of critics have seen the themes of Peter Pan's stories evident in an even earlier Barrie work, *Tommy and Grizel*, published in 1900. That all these literary endeavours would be influenced by the themes and aesthetic of Decadence should then be unsurprising in that they were conceived by Barrie during, or very soon after, the latter years of the *fin de siècle*. The aesthetic of Decadence was fundamentally concerned with the effects, and affective nature, of time, and was primarily derived by the *littérateurs* of the 1890s from the impressionistic philosophy of Walter Pater, specifically that articulated in the 'Conclusion' to his *Studies in the History of the Renaissance* (1873), what Oscar Wilde would refer to as his 'golden book'. Pater had there described existence, both physical and mental, in perpetual and fluid motion, and the ontological and epistemological necessity of 'fixing' the moment within the flux of a dynamic temporality. The nature of our lives was one in which

> those impressions of the individual mind to which, for each one of us, experience dwindles down, are in perpetual flight […] all that is actual in it being a single moment, gone while we try to apprehend it, of which it may ever be more truly said that it has ceased to be than that it is. To such a tremulous wisp constantly re-forming itself on the stream, to a single sharp impression, with a sense in it, a relic more or less fleeting, of such moments gone by, what is real in our

life fines itself down. It is with this movement, with the passage and dissolution of impressions, images, sensations, that analysis leaves off – that continual vanishing away, that strange, perpetual, weaving and unweaving of ourselves.[3]

Pater suggested that it was only by aesthetically fixing the moment, artificially rejecting time's movement and existing outside its destructive dynamism, that any impression of life might be ascertained, that even our very sense of identity must be artistically created, for within a world of constant change, only the aesthetic could bring any sense of existential quietude. Our fixed identities would be artfully arranged, not imposed externally by mothers and nannies, nor by the external standards of the world at large. The critical suggestion that Decadent aesthetes were 'secretly wishing for an island or similar aesthetic envelope'[4] is answered by the liminal spaces of Kensington Gardens and Peter's existence within the temporal 'betwixt-and-between' or the Paterian 'fixed moment'. Therein the artist could create himself, performing and justifying a variety of roles and adopting a succession of identities, in a manner that Wilde would later qualify as 'the truth of masks' in his essay of the same name.

Decadent literature is rife with an angst-ridden attitude to time's passing. In Wilde's sole novel, *The Picture of Dorian Gray* (1891), the eponymous anti-hero is introduced to the Decadent aesthetic by his new friend, Lord Henry Wotton, who tells Dorian:

What the gods give they quickly take away. You have only a few years in which to live really, perfectly, and fully. When your youth goes, your beauty will go with it, and then you will suddenly discover that there are no triumphs left for you […] Every month as it wanes brings you nearer to something dreadful. Time is jealous of you, and wars against your lilies and your roses […] You will suffer horribly.[5]

Dorian hears Lord Henry's views in a garden artfully separated, like Peter's Kensington Gardens, from the hubbub of London, and is granted a new aesthetic perspective that will affect the course of his life to a dramatic extent. He will, via the artful rendering of his portrait, 'fix' the moment of his youth in the midst of the turbulence of life's passing, existing beyond the deleterious effects of time's skirmishes against his 'lilies and roses'. In the spotlight on the stage of London society, Dorian goes untouched by the passing years, much as, in the directions given by Barrie in the printed version of his dramatic rendition of *Peter Pan* (1928), the Boy Who Would Not Grow Up is specifically remarked as going untouched by other characters as they move about the stage throughout the play. Each youth is set apart from the effective influence of time upon their lives but also from the imposition of others' desires or expectations. Once Dorian has made Lord Henry's advice part of his own personality and character, he remains uninfluenced by others for the majority of the remainder of the novel. Peter, once he understands the words concerning his identity as voiced by Solomon, accepts them and moves on, making his games and character on the birds' island one that is governed solely by his own desires, and his own immediate sense of self-performance. Pater's philosophy had 'set a high premium on the present impression, the life of immediate sensation'[6] and Peter will follow his momentary whims in expressing himself within his world. Dorian ends an aesthetic failure only because he treats his experiences, the roles he plays, as trappings for what he believes to be his essential, unchanging character, donning masks and setting them aside, but always seeing them as disguises behind which his own real self is hiding; Peter completely inhabits the roles he plays, actually becoming the characters he enacts. In *Peter and Wendy* he can swap sides in fights as he does at the Battle of Slightly Gulch, announcing mid-fray that he is a member of the Piccaninny tribe, thereby causing great confusion to the other combatants who, nevertheless, follow his aesthetic lead; after the death of Hook, Peter comes dangerously close to becoming the erstwhile Pirate Captain, sitting in a dark cabin wearing his old nemesis' clothes, his finger held aloft, hooked threateningly. Whatever Peter performs, he does so thinking 'that whatever he was doing was a thing of vast importance' (*PPKG* 18). A life at play is a very serious affair, after all.

The performative is fundamental to the Decadent aesthetic and is, perhaps, most succinctly expressed in Wilde's oft-quoted imperative that one should make oneself a work of art, and that, in doing so, no other purpose exists beyond the artistic statement itself. Peter artfully renders himself throughout Barrie's texts, inhabiting the roles he plays, becoming the characters in actuality rather than simply adopting various guises. But

Peter's performative aspects extend beyond his own self. His aesthetic personalities affect and effect the identities of those around him, as occurs during the Battle of Slightly Gulch. In Kensington Gardens, Peter goes much further, effecting nature and the acts of birth and bloom. His 'heart was so glad that he felt he must sing all day long, just as the birds sing for joy, but, being partly human, he needed an instrument, so he made a pipe of reeds' and with it he plays the 'sough of the wind and the ripple of the water' and catches in his tunes 'handfuls of the shine of the moon' (*PPKG* 18). Most startlingly, he plays the birth of birds and the beginning of summer when he desires the season to begin, causing mothers to look for newly-laid eggs, and a chestnut tree to flower early. Peter's pan-pipes play the world into being, the most consummate of aesthetic acts, in a wonderful rendition of Walter Pater's claim that '*all art constantly aspires towards the condition of music*. For while in all other kinds of art it is possible to distinguish the matter from the form, and the understanding can always make this distinc-tion, yet it is the constant effort of art to obliterate it.'[7] Peter fulfils this aesthetic obliteration, the form of his music composing the matter of life, performing the world based on his immediate whims and desires, and to a tune of his own making. Lord Henry had told Dorian that if an individual 'were to live out his life fully and completely, were to give form to every feeling, expression to every thought, reality to every dream – I believe the world would gain such a fresh impulse of joy that we would [...] return to the Hellenic ideal'.[8] Peter, playing his pan-pipes, named after a Greek god, riding a goat, the animal associated with the deity, will be the realisation of this Hellenic ideal. He is full of the gaiety and merriment Lord Henry believes would arrive with the advent of a New Hedonism, that joy capable of remaking the world through the feelings, thoughts, dreams, and vital impulsiveness of a latter-day Epicurean. Pater's 'Conclusion' to his Renaissance studies had been attacked by critics for promoting just such a neo-Hellenic philosophy and was judged by many to be amoral, irresponsible, and inher-ently dangerous. Pater's response would be to publish his single novel, *Marius the Epicurean* (1885), in which he explored and explained just what the Hellenic ideal might afford the modern world. Lord Henry's words are a restatement of Pater's ideal, just as Peter will be the embodiment of this new Pagan attitude, forged in joy, performatively expressed in music, capable of creating a self and new worlds from moment to moment. If the perceived failure of Decadence is, as one critic suggests, a 'failure to bring together the real and the ideal' then Peter remedies that failure.[9]

There is, perhaps, no more startling a rendition of the performative aesthetic in Decadent literature than that which appears towards the conclusion of John Davidson's poem 'Thirty Bob a Week' (1894). The poem is an attack upon the miserly, modern treatment of the working man attempting to survive on a material pittance, and written in the colloquial idiom of a late nineteenth-century London clerk. The narrative description of the clerk's banal, quotidian struggles in life is suddenly interrupted by the following verses:

> And it's this way that I make it out to be:
> No fathers, mothers, countries, climates – none;
> Not Adam was responsible for me,
> Nor society, nor systems, nary one:
> A little sleeping seed, I woke – I did, indeed –
> A million years before the blooming sun.
>
> I woke because I thought the time had come;
> Beyond my will there was no other cause;
> And everywhere I found myself at home,
> Because I chose to be the thing I was;
> And in whatever shape of mollusc or of ape
> I always went according to the laws.
>
> I was the love that chose my mother out;
> I joined two lives and from the union burst;
> My weakness and my strength without a doubt
> Are mine alone for ever from the first:
> It's just the very same with a difference in the name
> As 'Thy will be done.' You say it if you durst![10]

Davidson overturns so many commonly held assumptions in these few lines that a reader at their conclusion is left confronted by and within an entirely different world: time, evolutionary law, parentage, genealogy, the creative role of God in composing the universe, responsibility, the biological will, choice and freedom, are all represented from the perspective of the Decadent aesthetic. Richard Le Gallienne, another critic and poet of the *fin de siècle*, had written that Davidson's art was a 'vindication of the free play of human vitality [...] expressive of the best energies and ideals of the 1890 Renaissance'[11] and certainly the views stated in these few verses combined with the manner in which Davidson expresses them are a perfect summation of the Decadent aesthetic. The speaker is not caused by anything other than himself; was conscious before the galaxy was formed; awoke to consciousness through his own singular will; can become, and expresses himself as, whatever form of life he wills himself to be; rejects all external causes and impositions upon his selfhood and embraces evolutionary necessity as coming about through his own volition; chose his parents rather than being a product of their procreative act; joyfully maintains that his life is solely his own responsibility; and concludes that he is a self-willed expression of life itself, the biological will expressed in his being coming about through the expediency of his own performative sense of self-identification. Davidson maps the history of the universe, rolling it up into the momentary and momentous consciousness of the aesthetic individual, making time itself a creation of the artist's performative will.

Origins are of vital important importance to Barrie and to Peter Pan, the author describing at the end of the dramatic version of Peter's story that there is a 'riddle of his being' that lies undiscovered (*PP* 153). *Peter Pan in Kensington Gardens* affords the reader greater detail about Peter's origins than does *Peter and Wendy*; how he came to arrive in the Gardens; whence he came and considers returning; the manner in which children arrive into the human world of parents, adult expectations and rules; and the liminal, existential situation in which Peter finds himself, the betwixt-and-between of identity in the interstitial space of the Gardens but also that of the temporal moment after existence has begun but before birth occurs. It is this time outside time, preceding it, or encapsulated unbreached within it, that allows Peter to give birth to himself repeatedly in continually different forms and to will existence according to the tunes he plays on his pan-pipes. The artful rendition of the Paterian moment within which Peter resides, repeatedly recreating his identity alongside the world around him, living *as if* each moment is an eternity unto itself, is the mark of the Decadent aesthetic. Like Davidson's expression of self-creation, an endeavour in which the world

comes into being simultaneously alongside and through each newly embraced
artistic perspective, Peter joyfully plays the universe into being over and
over again with each new narrative he adopts, every new song he pipes, and
through all the games in which he happily engages. Peter Pan does not evolve
and so he does not age, but he is constantly renewed according to his
own whimsical will, and so remains forever young. He has no need of a
mother unless it appears to him that he requires new stories within which
to conceive himself once more; he has no history other than those several
he believes himself to have had at any particular moment. Like Davidson's
clerk, Peter chooses continually to be the thing he is from moment to moment.

Even death itself is no more than the passing away of a former identity,
for, as Peter playfully says in *Peter and Wendy* when it appears that he will
be drowned by the rising Lagoon in Neverland: 'To die will be an awfully
big adventure' (*PP* 125). To avoid making the mistake of Dorian Gray, the
Decadent aesthete must allow each new volition its expression, must accept
the passing away that the movement of time affords, whilst simultaneously
'fixing' each passing moment as if it is the reality that has always been
eternally necessary, a product of the entirety of the universe's causative,
linear history. Expressed then, as Davidson had shown, as an act of the
aesthetic will, passing away becomes as negotiable as it is necessary in
avoiding the sterility and stasis devoid of life's vitality and joy, the failed
position in which Dorian finds himself in Wilde's novel. The poet Ernest
Dowson encapsulates the temporal conceit of Decadence in his short poem
'Vitae Summa Brevis Spem Nos Vetat Incohare Longam' (1896), and, like
Peter's conclusion as he faces his apparent demise in the waters of the
Lagoon, 'death is not all that conclusive'[12] in Dowson's poem:

> They are not long, the weeping and the laughter,
> Love and desire and hate;
> I think they have no portion in us after
> We pass the gate.
>
> They are not long, the days of wine and roses:
> Out of a misty dream
> Our path emerges for a while, then closes
> Within a dream.[13]

Dowson's title is taken from Horace's Odes I: 4 and has been translated variously, two possibilities being 'our brief sum of life forbids us to embark upon a protracted hope' and 'the brief sum of life forbids us the hope of enduring long'. Both translations emphasise the brevity of our sojourn, our 'days of wine and roses' that emerge from, and return to, the 'dream' of Dowson's poem. Like Barrie's map of Kensington Gardens, this space separated off from the past and present, the before and after of dynamic temporality, is bounded by at least one gate and the experiences we endure disappear once that threshold is crossed. The everyday affairs of the adult world that impose themselves upon us, as they do the children who yearn to escape into the Kensington Gardens, are dissolved once we pass through this gate. It may be death, it may be simply a marker for the passing away of impositional cares, the emotions associated with a life as brief as a moment, and, consequently, appears to afford us little pleasure and no hope whatsoever. But Dowson also suggests that the moment of life is more real than the past and future of linear temporality, that it is those latter two aspects of time that are dreams. The 'days of wine and roses' may be short and bring to mind Lord Henry's words concerning time warring upon Dorian's 'lilies and roses', but they are as necessary as the past and future are illusory figments. Insulated from linear time within the pocket of the aesthetic moment, that moment can and should be the vital expression of possibilities for living. Like the vagrant paths that lead to the Round Pond where all the games are played at the centre of Kensington Gardens, paths that have the capacity to 'Make Themselves', Dowson's path leads to the happy quietude of the moment between the mists of past and future, and it is only from the position of the linear movement of time into the mists surrounding life that any sense of poignancy or despondency is possible. Within the moment lies the fulness of life, and that life is complete in and of itself, 'days of wine and roses' to be experienced to the utmost. It is only when Peter remembers his past and his mother, or considers his future and his possible departure from the Gardens, that any sense of grief or anxiety imposes itself upon his world.

To escape these illusory hopes and fears, one must live in the moment unaware of any possible, let alone necessary, alteration of circumstances; to escape regret, guilt, longing, desires that cannot be enacted, one must forget the past. By the moment of Peter's arrival in Neverland, even a mother is replaceable, but it is his uncanny ability to forget things, places, events, and names, that allows him to live merrily by multiplyling his momentary instantiations of self-created identity.[14] At the conclusion to *Peter and Wendy*, Peter is capable of forgetting time itself, arriving haphazardly at the moment for spring-cleaning only when he feels the urge. In Kensington Gardens, the fairy Queen Mab requests the time from her Lord Chamberlain, and he is able to tell her by blowing upon a dandelion. This means of telling the time, its flightiness, random and accidental nature, the manner in which time is spread, shared, and seeded thoroughout the map of the Gardens in a multiplicity of singular moments, is a final summation of the Decadent formulation of aesthetic time in Barrie's artfully constructed worlds, and the basis to the liminal character of the consummate artist, Peter Pan.

Notes

1   For a fuller explanation of Neverland's map, see Paul Fox, 'Other Maps Showing Through: The Liminal Identities of Neverland', *Children's Literature Association Quarterly* 32.3 (2007), pp. 252–68.

2   From the Notebooks of J. M. Barrie. Quoted in *J. M. Barrie, The Annotated Peter Pan: The Centennial Edition*, ed. Maria Tatar (New York: W. W. Norton & Co., 2011), p. xxviii.

3   Walter Pater, *Studies in the History of the Renaissance*, ed. Adam Phillips (Oxford: Oxford University Press, 1990), pp. 151–52.

4   Jan. B. Gordon. '"Decadent Spaces": Notes for a Phenomenology of the Fin de Siècle', in *Decadence and the 1890s*, ed. Ian Fletcher (London: Edward Arnold, 1979), p. 46.

5   Oscar Wilde, *The Picture of Dorian Gray*, in *Collins Complete Works of Oscar Wilde: Centenary Edition* (Glasgow: Harper Collins, 1999), pp. 17–159 (p. 31).

6   Jerome Hamilton Buckley, *The Triumph of Time: A Study of the Victorian Concepts of Time, History, Progress, and Decadence* (Cambridge: The Belknap Press of Harvard University Press, 1966), p. 132.

7   Pater, p. 86.

8   Wilde, p. 28.

9   R. K. R. Thornton, *The Decadent Dilemma* (London: Edward Arnold, 1983), p. 200.

10   John Davidson, 'Thirty Bob a Week', in *The Yellow Book*, 2 (London: Bodley Head Press, July 1894), pp. 99–102 (pp. 101–02).

11   Richard Le Gallienne, *The Romantic Nineties* (1926; London: Putnam & Company, 1951), p. 121.

12   Linda Dowling, *Language and Decadence in the Victorian Fin de Siècle* (Princeton: Princeton University Press, 1986), p. 205.

13   Ernest Dowson, 'Vitae Summa Brevis Spem Nos Vetat Incohare Longam', in *Verses*, (Oxford and New York: Woodstock Books, 1994), p. v.

14   For the significance of forgetting to the aesthetic life lived fully, see Friedrich Nietzsche, 'On the Uses and Disadvantages of History for Life', in *Untimely Meditations*, (Cambridge: Cambridge University Press, 1997), pp. 57–125. John Davidson was, incidentally, the motive force behind the introduction of Nietzsche's ideas to the British public.

9. *Peter Pan*'s Make-Believe:
Place, Uncertainty, and Wonder

RALPH JESSOP

One by one as you swung monkey-wise from branch to branch in the wood of make-believe you reached the tree of knowledge (*PP* 75–76).

We had a sufficiently mysterious cave, that had not been a cave until we named it.[1]

She is never quite sure, you know; indeed the only one who is sure about anything on the island is Peter (PP 128).

You just think lovely wonderful thoughts and they lift you up in the air (*PP* 103).

J. M. Barrie's *Peter Pan* is one of the most famous works to emerge from literary and theoretical antecedents involving playful make-believe transformations and subversions of oppressive ideas of how things must be. The topics of place, uncertainty, and wonder interrelate through elements of Barrie's childhood and education. Through considering these topics the play fittingly becomes a participant in broader literary and intellectual oppositions to some dreaded aspects of modernity, especially with regard to an identification of uncertainty with stasis/death. *Peter Pan* constitutes a response to Victorian pessimism born of modernity's disenchantment of the world, the new scientific prediction of the total destruction of the universe, and the critical condition informing such nihilism – the absolute uncertainty of eighteenth-century scepticism. This uncertainty's pessimism is nihilistic through its apparent tendency to avail visions of an absolute stasis and thereby universal annihilation; the destruction of humanity, possibility, wonderment, and place itself. *Peter Pan*'s opposition to such grave pessimism is thus an artistic attempt to redeem humanity, childhood, and our connectedness with the world and others from the overbearing terror of complete dissolution and universal death, through the relished enactment of childish irreverence – 'To die will be an awfully big adventure' (*PP* 125).

Place, uncertainty, and wonder are additionally related to one another through the play's pervasion by, and the transformative power of, make-believe. The play performs a transformation of theoretical discourse into an art form of playful opposition to what some of this discourse dreadfully implies. In re-scripting elements in Barrie's literary, philosophical, and scientific education, *Peter Pan* constitutes a thoroughgoing exercise of make-believe. Making-believe a place of fun and magic, involves wonder as a state of absorption in what is being made, in the game. It also involves wonder as uncertainty; some things that are real, bound by physical laws, or unquestionable, become doubtful as making-believe is at once also a wondering whether these certainties may not exist, may not come to pass, or may be somehow different. Make-believe puts in doubt even the most resilient truth or prevalent power. As make-believe transforms otherwise ordinary objects or spaces into wonderfully special things or hallowed places, the generation of an imaginary place or identity proportions, defies, eschews, or contradicts realities or hegemonic pronouncements. However, if make-believe involves wonder as uncertainty (a radical doubting), almost paradoxically it can liberate us from the pessimism of total uncertainty's inertia. The principal result of extreme uncertainty/scepticism postulated by one of the most inescapable presences of Barrie's university education, David Hume, is a complete inability to act.[2] Contrary to this envisioned stasis or absolute inertia implying death, making-believe is an exercise of our capacity for agency, a gesture of defiance against an overshadowing uncertainty concerning the reality or reasonableness of this capacity.

So markedly characteristic of childhood play, make-believe involves some attempt to make the world anew, often overturning or playing with reality, conventions, and the most binding rules. Pivotally, the vital light-sparkle that is Tinker Bell is restored from death through everyone playfully enacting a public commitment to belief in fairies, an assertion of our capacity in making-believe to think an alternative through imagining or entertaining (and being entertained by) what cannot be, yet which may be suggested. The anarchically sceptical aspect of the activity of making-believe is therefore inherently, if transitorily, liberating and optimistic. Consecrating the value of the child's capacity to make-believe, *Peter Pan* affirms the wondrously creative potential to make something out of virtually nothing, the pleasure of apparently purposeless vitality, the potency of communal unity, and the efficacy of human agency. Believing in fairies, or an eternal, flying boy, involves contradiction of the mundane laws of physical nature and mortality. The play's playful contradiction of unbreakable laws recalls and encourages the pleasures of wonderment, transgression, of overcoming impossibilities, of fantasising places and identities of play through make-believe's wanton power to transform fragments of sand into citadels, to build castles out of air, or to re-situate the Darling house from its 'rather depressed street in Bloomsbury' to 'anywhere you like' (*PP* 87). This is a pretending that involves the idea that the child's – humanity's – condition can be imagined as significantly other than they appear destined or doomed to become. Inasmuch as this making-believe endorses the notion, that what so inescapably *is* or must happen, *may* not be, it partakes in a basic, deceptively innocuous assumption of scepticism: what *unshakeably* must be believed may not be as we think it is. But, as a sceptical process of philosophical argumentation with the potential to subvert even the most well-established facts or beliefs may be commenced in opposing propositions, literary characters have frequently been presented or significantly named in ways that initiate a crucial ambiguity or dynamic relation of opposite tendencies or characteristics. Such a combining of opposites thus generates a vivifying dialogical iteration that in some cases so intensifies conflicts that it eventually self-destructs – one need only recall Emily Brontë's Heathcliff, R. L. Stevenson's Jekyll and Hyde, and Oscar Wilde's Dorian Gray.

Peter Pan's name is similarly enigmatic, ambiguous, finally irresolvable, multi-layered in its allusive significance – a combination of Pan (the multiply significant Greek God of the woods or Nature) with 'the rock' (Christianity's Saint Peter), of the Greek prefix '*pan*' (meaning 'all') with a particular little boy (most obviously, Peter Llewelyn Davies), an identification of universality with particularity, an ultimately unfathomable fused dichotomy incapable of conception, a being whose ability to understand Wendy's recognition of his constraints, and yet whose inability to understand this '*has something to do with the riddle of his being*' (*PP* 153). In his embodiment of contradiction, of uncertainty, Peter Pan's being is the stuff of make-believe, a subjective power to generate subjects and objects out of mere props, or participants, or almost nothing.

This much-used literary device of yoking together opposites to form fictional characters, such as Peter, suggests a consonance with a long and ancient history of enduring notions concerning humanity as a combination of the rational and the animal, good and evil, flesh and spirit, reason and the passions. According to the Bible's opening words in Genesis, the place of our habitation itself, commencing through a distinction between heaven and earth followed by a fundamental distinction of gender, has played an enormous role through so narrating humanity's mythic origins within and as an integral part of a duality of substance or properties. The Christian notion of the *Deus Homo* (God-man), combining the human with the divine, is distinctly constructed for the purposes of human salvation. But, the combination of opposites in the construction of literary characters has another, foreboding resonance during the nineteenth century through the similarity it bears to the most extreme scepticism of the Enlightenment philosopher, Hume. In the Edinburgh of Barrie's university education, this had been occasionally understood, at least since the 1830s, in terms of a self or 'intellectual nature [...] divided against itself', a notion encapsulated in the now more famous term 'divided self' that would later gain prominence in the work of William James (contemporaneous with *Peter Pan*) and R. D. Laing.[3]

The bleak character of the prodigious uncertainty of this scepticism, its disenchantment of and apocalyptic threats concerning humanity's place, coupled with some responses to its unsustainable pessimism, are peculiarly pertinent to a cultural environment of Barrie's youth and education. The places in which this occurred – Dumfries, Edinburgh, and more generally, the Scottish Lowlands – mainly become relevant to these topics and to *Peter Pan* through writers and philosophers closely connected with this part of the world. Among the most internationally influential literary, philosophical, and scientific figures in Scotland, a substantial number of writers and thinkers – including Hume, Thomas Carlyle, and the theoretical physicist, James Clerk Maxwell – lived and worked in the South of Scotland, the place of Barrie's education and formative experiences.

Barrie's consciousness of literary-informed games of making-believe places and identities of adventure is specifically situated in the southern

Scottish town of Dumfries. According to Piers Dudgeon, Barrie's boyhood games with his friend, Stuart Gordon, in a garden on the banks of the river Nith, would later become transformed into the piratical adventures in Peter Pan. Barrie mentions this place on the banks of the Nith in his 1913 introduction to R. M. Ballantyne's novel, *The Coral Island* (1858): 'We had a sufficiently mysterious cave, that had not been a cave until we named it, and here we grimly ate cocoa-nuts, stoned from trees which not even Jack nor Ralph nor Peterkin would have recognised as likely to bear them.'[4] Dudgeon notes that this was a time of intense friendship in Barrie's life and importantly it marks the beginning of his fictional writing in the 'Log-Book' of the boys' adventures, 'the prototype for *The Boy Castaways*'. But, as Dudgeon claims, these childhood adventures were inspired by *The Coral Island*, Barrie's 'favourite book'.[5] This fusing in childhood, of his experience of make-believe with the literary imaginary and the commencement of his writing career, imbues the place now known as Moat Brae House[6] with a special status; a place of memorial celebrating the seemingly ordinary but profoundly important childhood activity of making-believe as elevated by the combined factors of Barrie's childhood literary-inspired make-believe experiences, the historic cultural prominence of *Peter Pan*, and informed by a number of other elements, including some of Barrie's literary and philosophical antecedents, some of which he first encountered in the South of Scotland, not least of all through his education at Edinburgh.[7]

Barrie attended the University of Edinburgh from 1878 where he was taught by a number of eminent scholars including: Peter Guthrie Tait, the Professor of Natural Philosophy and co-author with Glasgow University's William Thomson (Lord Kelvin) of the *Elements of Natural Philosophy*, a text Barrie later described as being 'better known in my year as the *Student's First Glimpse of Hades*' (*EE* 49); Alexander Campbell Fraser, the Professor of Logic and Metaphysics and successor of the outstandingly erudite Sir William Hamilton; Henry Calderwood, the Professor of Moral Philosophy and a major critic of Hamilton; and, David Masson, the Professor of Rhetoric and English Literature, an admirer of Hamilton's work, close personal friend of Carlyle, and greatly respected as a teacher by Barrie: 'I seem to remember everything Masson said, and the way he said it' (*EE* 20). The University of Edinburgh therefore exposed Barrie to a range of now largely ignored yet once prominent figures, inheritors of the illustrious past of the Scottish

Enlightenment and early post-Enlightenment periods. Until recently, this intellectual background to Barrie's work has received virtually no critical attention.

Commenting broadly on Barrie's work, Andrew Nash rightly claims that:

> Barrie has often been accused of being an insufficiently Scottish writer, yet the investigations into the relationship between illusion and reality that recur throughout his work place him at the centre of a visible tradition in Scottish fiction, traceable from James Hogg to Alasdair Gray, that has been produced by a culture engaged with the question of the apprehension of reality.[8]

Supplementing Nash's observation, at the heart of Scottish philosophical traditions, at least from the time of Hume, are major epistemological/ metaphysical concerns with perception, the extent to which the physical world may be known directly if at all, and the severity of Humean scepticism/uncertainty as intimately involved in such speculations. While a student at Edinburgh, Barrie was substantially inducted into such philosophical obsessions by scholars including Calderwood, Masson, and Fraser.

In Barrie's reminiscences of his student days, *An Edinburgh Eleven*, there are some intriguingly personal recollections of his university professors. These sketches are riddled with Barrie's humour of understatement, wry innuendo, or an irony that at times indicates an undisclosed biographical narrative or veiled mockery, at which Barrie playfully hints:

> Professor Calderwood has such an exceptional interest in his students that he asks every one of them to his house. This is but one of the many things that makes him generally popular; he also invites his ladies' class to meet them. The lady whom you take down to supper […] asks what you think of the metaphysics of ethics. Calderwood sees the ladies into the cabs himself. It is the only thing I ever heard against him. (*EE* 45)

Perhaps Calderwood is being gently mocked for preventing whatever might have followed from such a potentially risqué question to do with the sceptical nature of 'the metaphysics of ethics', hinting at missed opportunities for some flirtatious subversions of the female students' moral conduct. Nevertheless, if Barrie treats his university reminiscences with a light humour, glimpses are given that additionally suggest a more studious side to his formative years, as, for example, when he quotes some of his own marginalia in his copy of Campbell Fraser's *Selections from Berkeley*:

> I see that I was once more of a metaphysician than I have been giving myself credit for. The book is scribbled over with poses in my hand-writing about dualism and primary realities. Some of the comments are in shorthand, which I must at one time have been able to read, but all are equally unintelligible now. Here is one of my puzzlers:— 'Does B [the philosopher George Berkeley] here mean impercipient and unperceived subject or conscious and percipient subject?' (*EE* 67)

By the time of writing *An Edinburgh Eleven* Barrie was a famous and rich author and playwright. He could well afford to make light of the great seriousness of his University days and arguably *Peter Pan* had already in a sense being doing just that.

*

Peter Pan's success has much to do with how the play provides a wonderful on-stage recreation and restoration of the intensity and enjoyment of make-believe and its magical world of a liberated imagination, fantasy, and fun. In opposition to the '*cadaverous and blackavised*' Hook, Peter declares: 'I'm youth, I'm joy, I'm a little bird that has broken out of the egg' (*PP* 145). This unavoidably brings home the optimism of believing that we are capable of rebutting the fearful oppressor, but also of escaping or re-enchanting this prosaic, materially orientated world of terrifying horrors. But such re-enchanting possibilities and tensions with a workaday world that represses the inherent liberty of imagination are also evident in one of the play's greatest and earliest English antecedents, Shakespeare's *A Midsummer Night's Dream*, a play upon which Barrie drew for his later *Dear Brutus* (1917).

Through acting that expressly relies on the device of two opposing worlds of oppressively regulated reality and space-and-time bending magic and play, and that crosses barriers between stage and audience, both plays hint at enacted oppositions – by the chaotic, poetic, hyperphysical, anarchic, and playfully indeterminate – against the ordered, prosaic, physical, controlled, and rigidly determined. In Shakespeare's play, Athenian youths venture into the wood as a place of escape, confusion, madness, saturnalian licence, magic, supernatural agency. This is a place that defies, disrupts, humanises, and is radically alternative to Theseus's world of brutal conquest and the order of stark choices – 'I woo'd thee with my sword' (1.1:16; and see 1.1:46–78).[9] Theseus's literal-minded, cool rationality confines and dismissively describes the poet's imagination – the transformative power of make-believe – as excessively emotional, insane, merely subjective in its derivation of things and places *ex nihilo*, a power that, according to Theseus, foolishly 'gives to airy nothing/ A local habitation and a name' (5.1: 16–17). Both plays portray spirits of mischief that violate the laws of custom and of nature. Bottom is transformed into an Ass; Puck encircles the world in a minute; the Queen of the Fairies becomes enamoured of Bottom as a donkey; and, the self-unawareness of Bottom and the rude mechanicals' play-acting, through exposing pretence, warmly encourages the audience to value the complex relations of play and make-believe as Puck re-enters at the end, inviting the audience to affirm their friendship with the players by clapping (5.1: 423). In *Peter Pan*, Nana, the children's nursemaid, is humorously a human transformed by the actor into a rather special dog of make-believe fun, though indicative of the Darlings' impecunious condition; Peter enables the Darling children to fly with abundant scope for ridiculous antics, but in teaching them how to fly Peter's recourse to wonder reaffirms its importance and hints at the equivocal nature of language as terms hover between the literal and metaphorical meanings – go-betweens uniting make-believe with reality that momentarily disclose a symbolic significance of the play's enactment of flying: 'You just think lovely wonderful thoughts and they lift you up in the air' (*PP* 103); As the play begins to draw to a close, the audience is called upon by Peter to affirm their belief in fairies to save Tinker Bell, also by clapping. Such enactments of playing, of staging a world chaotically liberated from natural and man-made rules, invite the audience to relax their constraining detachment and censure of the performance, reclaim their capacity for absorption in playful make-believe, and participate in the activity of making-believe through feeling the pleasure and potency of linguistic shifts in meaning. The sprinkling of this complex fairy-dust promises at least some temporary restoration of a sense of childlike, beneficent intimate relation with the world, with our fellow creatures and people, our ideals, and dreams – the audience and the players thereby become warmly humane, combined in a quasi-holy communion that a maleficent workaday world relentlessly attempts to destroy.

Through the magic of its lighting, props, recreations of make-believe games and conjuring escape to the utopian Never Land, *Peter Pan* is an *activity* involving the absorption of wonder and the mental play of wondering or questioning whether the world and human existence must be entirely as they appear (or are by adult authority) determined to be. The play thus involves rejections or questionings of what the adult world prescribes – as in Peter's specific rejection of adulthood. It does this through its sustained presentation and celebration of childhood make-believe, informed not only by *Coral Island* but also by its major eighteenth-century precursor, Daniel Defoe's *Robinson Crusoe* (1719). That is to say, some of *Peter Pan's* literary precursors are importantly fantasies of self-sufficiency and adventurous capability that foster belief in the reader's capacity for agency and a certain independence from the constraints of the adult world. The play's entertainment is also reliant upon wonder as something that absorbs or engages the audience in the visually magical spectacle of flying children and electrical lighting effects – the Never Land's 'wonders […] might hurt your eyes' (*PP* 105); through the 'blue haze […] we see numberless nests all lit up' (*PP* 152).

But the modernity of such techniques of the spectacular also permeates how Barrie uses wonder to insinuate doubt or uncertainty concerning the adult worldview. It does this through generating, as greatly more desirable, the children's alternative vantage point of a utopian place of play. The places and identities of this playfulness are brought to life by wonderful scenery, stage effects, by Tinker Bell's minimal existence as light and sound combined with enactments of her recognition, by Peter's asserted embodiment of eternal youth. Such suggestions of an airy nothingness and the dramaturgic playing with visual effects, place, time, uncertainty, and wonder, so animates the world of the stage that its making-believe escape from the mundane through dreams of adventure, the magic of flight, the offer of eternal youth, and the cramming of space and time into the on-stage representation of the Never Land (as described in Act 2) stands in opposition to the pessimism of adulthood's oppressive consciousness of space and time-regulated reality and its horrors of the inevitability of cruelty, dullness, conformity, economic hardship, decline, and death.[10]

*

Notwithstanding *Peter Pan*'s indebtedness to English literature, theatre, culture, the timing and context of the play's early and later successes, and insights provided by literary criticism through examining aspects of Barrie's life, some more recent studies indicate ways forward for Barrie scholarship that tend to emphasise the relation of his work to broader philosophical and cultural ideas. This is particularly true of the seminal intervention by R. D. S. Jack in *The Road to the Never Land*. For example, Jack brings to the fore some highly intriguing connections between Barrie's art and the work of Nietzsche.[11] Cairns Craig's *Intending Scotland* (2009) has more recently supplemented such notions by ambitiously suggesting ways of reading *Peter Pan* through a largely neglected Scottish literary and intellectual history, a great deal of which pertains to certain writers and thinkers closely associated with the places of Barrie's education in the South of Scotland.[12] To assist understanding of the play's cultural significance as a work of modernist drama that translates, plays with, and attempts to subvert certain oppressive aspects of modernity, *Peter Pan* needs to be brought into relation with some of the ideas of people important to Barrie's formative years.

Rightly, given the strong likelihood that Masson influenced or was a key person in Barrie's development as a writer, Craig's reading of *Peter Pan* is partly informed by Masson's *Recent British Philosophy*, the third edition of which was published in 1877, one year before Barrie commenced his studies at Edinburgh. *Recent British Philosophy* discusses several topics and includes a response to a work cited by Barrie in *An Edinburgh Eleven* – the *Elements of Natural Philosophy* by Thomson and Tait.[13] Masson claims that the new scientific theory of the second law of thermodynamics (elucidated in Thomson and Tait's *Elements*), entailed that the entire universe would ultimately run down, that 'all the starry systems shall also run [...] together at last in an indistinguishable equilibrium of ruin.'[14] Finding this whole notion immensely disturbing, in its implications for science, metaphysics, and theories and beliefs concerning the human condition, Masson claims that:

> [No] man into whose mind this idea of the exhaustibility of the Sun's Heat, and consequently of the force energizing our system, had once entered, could ever think a thought about anything whatsoever that should not, in shape and colour, be influenced by that idea![15]

The ultimate truth of all existence had emerged as a certain prediction of complete extinction. As a scientific matter of fact, all hope of a better future state had been effectually abolished. Masson must have made some effort to impress this upon his students, including Barrie.

Thomson's theory of thermodynamics articulated an overarching law of physics, namely, the famous principle known as the *conservation of energy*. As Craig points out, contrary to what one might at first assume by the phrase 'conservation of energy', what this great law of Physical Science effectually entails is 'the ultimate dissipation of energy'[16] – in other words, the very scenario described by Masson as the 'equilibrium of ruin'; the scenario that this highly inspiring and dynamic Professor would have impressed upon the young Barrie as dismally nihilistic in its prediction of an ineluctable dissipation of all vitality. This helps to explain what Barrie means when he recalls that Thomson and Tait's *Elements* was 'better known in my year as the *Student's First Glimpse of Hades*' (*EE* 49). With typically understated humour, Barrie is here alluding to nothing short of the absolute death of our universe, a glimpse of the most momentous loss imaginable, a realisation of just how hollow and dispiriting the world had become for later Victorians beginning to sense the drenching away of all that they once thought of as so permanent and adapted to serving their progressive ends. The irrefutable fact was that the universe was *necessarily* in decline; to learn of that, from Masson if not from certain other sources, must have been akin to losing all one's innocent beliefs in present worth and future well-being and rewards. However, it is perhaps fortunate that such oppressive ideas of how things *must* be, can provoke playful responses that ridicule or subvert the overweening authority they assert – it seems likely that if Thomson and Tait's *Elements* were known amongst Barrie's fellow students as their '*First Glimpse of Hades*' this may have been voicing some gallows humour.

Craig argues that Peter Pan may be modelled on an altogether more serious response to the dreadful prognosis of universal death, namely, James Clerk Maxwell's scientific thought experiment, known as the demon in the ether – this too is arguably playful. Maxwell has recently been honoured by a number of books and by a statue in Edinburgh. According to some, and expressly asserted in the title of Basil Mahon's recent book about him, he was *The Man Who Changed Everything*.[17] Maxwell spent much of his highly productive time working at his estate at Parton near to the town of New

Galloway, some twenty miles or so from Dumfries. His demon in the ether is effectually an attempt to refute or subvert the deterministic force of the second law of thermodynamics. Heat, *of necessity*, according to the second law, must flow from hotter substances to cooler ones. But, by means of Clerk Maxwell's demon in the ether this is *not* a necessary law but is instead a probability. Maxwell's demon is postulated to demonstrate that the second law of thermodynamics could be reversed by something unknown and unobservable – the demon in the ether could operate a shutter between any two substances, such that particles in the cooler substance may be made to flow into the hotter. Though not capable of empirical proof, Maxwell's demon brilliantly illustrates that there is nothing *formally necessary* about the normal transition of heat and what that means is that there was nothing absolutely necessary about Kelvin's thermodynamics and its prognosis of an entirely determined ultimate equilibrium or final rest and death of the universe.

Craig's ambitious reading of *Peter Pan* as a literary and dramatic re-enactment of Clerk Maxwell's theory of the demon in the ether is alluring, since Peter does seem to function in some similar ways to Maxwell's demon. For example, as Craig explains:

> Like the Demon, Peter is the guardian of the shutter that keeps two spheres – the sphere of Edwardian London and the sphere of the Neverland – separate, but unlike the Demon, Peter can move between them. At Peter's invitation, however, certain particles – certain children – are allowed to cross from one sphere into the other, thus renewing the energy of the Neverland at the expense of the domestic sphere from which they escape. [...] This continual transfer of new energy safeguards Peter's experience of the Neverland from the entropy which haunts his adversary, Captain Hook.[18]

For Craig, Captain Hook is haunted, much as Masson might have claimed everyone would be who had understood Thomson's theory of thermodynamics, by time ticking towards the end of time when the clock will stop and all will be consumed, all the stars will go out, and everything will cease.

The similarities between Maxwell's demon and Peter are certainly suggestive, not least of all because part of Craig's achievement involves bringing to attention some of the ways in which *Peter Pan* may be better understood in relation to Victorian and early Edwardian pessimism. That is to say, Craig is effectually initiating a potentially much more extensive discussion concerning the ways in which the pessimism that typifies an important dimension of the modern human condition may be seen as being acutely pertinent not only to the play's origins but also to its popularity. But there are other elements involved in the construction of Peter's character germane to the grim predictions of an 'equilibrium of ruin' which relate to that earlier but still deeply troubling strand in Scottish intellectual history of Hume's extreme or absolute scepticism.

If some of his professors at Edinburgh introduced Barrie to ideas concerning, for example, Berkeley's idealism, Hume's scepticism, the grim consequences of the second law of thermodynamics, and perhaps also Clerk Maxwell's playful antidote of the demon in the ether, he would also have known, at least through Masson, of the cultural significance of the work of one of the University's most famous former Rectors, a model of literary achievement and of opposition to certain aspects of the Enlightenment legacy, the literary and intellectual guru greatly admired and celebrated by Masson and by a number of his eminent colleagues at Edinburgh – Carlyle.[19] Barrie recalls a time during his attendance at Professor Masson's memorable Literature class at Edinburgh University, in 1881: 'When the news of Carlyle's death reached the room, Masson could not go on with his lecture. […] Here were two men who understood each other' (*EE* 19).

Born in 1795 at Ecclefechan, close to the border with England and the town of Dumfries, Carlyle produced his most foundational work while situated some fifteen miles from Dumfries during his Craigenputtoch period (1828–34), including the famous essay, 'Signs of the Times' (1829), and his novelistic treatment of the human condition, *Sartor Resartus* (1834). Barrie recalls frequently seeing Carlyle while living at Dumfries:

> When I was at school in Dumfries I often saw Carlyle in cloak, sombrero and staff, mooning along our country roads, a tortured mind painfully alone even to the eyes of a boy. He was visiting his brother-in-law, Dr Aiken, retired, and I always took off my cap to him. I daresay I paid this homage fifty times, but never was there any response. Once I seized a babe, who was my niece, and ran with her in my arms to a spot which I saw he was approaching; my object

that in future years she would be able to say that she had once touched
the great Carlyle. I did bring them within touching distance, but
there my courage failed me, and the two passed each other to meet
no more. (*GH* 38)

As Dudgeon points out, Barrie's mother idolised Carlyle and, according
to Barrie, this was well known. As Barrie reports his mother's words, she
even seems to have regarded Jane Welsh Carlyle (so often and understandably regarded by many as particularly long-suffering and aggrieved) as 'a
glorious woman' because, Jane would have known that: 'The whole world
is ringing with his fame, and he is my man!'[20] Perhaps not surprisingly,
given Carlyle's fame and his mother's adoration of him, Barrie comments
in *The Greenwood Hat*: 'In our Scottish home the name that bulked largest
next to Burns was Carlyle … indeed he was the only writer I even tried to
imitate' (*GH* 37).

Barrie's youthful studentship at Edinburgh (1878–82) was unavoidably
conditioned to some extent by Masson's great admiration for Carlyle as one
of the century's most prominent and influential critics of the Enlightenment
legacies of Lockean materialism or mechanistic metaphysics, and of at least
one major outgrowth of the Lockean tradition, Benthamite utilitarianism.[21]
As a moral theory, but also as an approach of much wider practical application in, for example, education, utilitarianism seemed to be unstoppably
and disastrously in the ascendant. This is evident in a number of stories by
one of the century's most prominent novelists, Charles Dickens, a close
friend of Carlyle and highly regarded by Masson.[22] Dickens's work in many
instances constitutes a fascinating literary elaboration and translation of
Carlyle's thought. This can be clearly detected in his harshest satire on the
utilitarianism of the modern educational system, *Hard Times* (1854), which
as Michael Goldberg claims, 'bears the unmistakable imprint of Carlyle's
influence'.[23] This also resonates in Barrie's rather similar stance against
educating children with a poor diet of mere facts. *Peter Pan*'s pervasive
enactments of make-believe playfulness and fearless adventure, effectually
continues an older, Carlyle-inspired, critique of the utilitarian legacy of the
Enlightenment, a legacy relentlessly satirised in the memorably insistent
demand in *Hard Times* for education that exclusively concentrates on: 'Fact,
fact, fact!'[24]

In *An Edinburgh Eleven* Barrie comments on Professor Tait's pedagogical approach which involved the notion held by Tait that, according to Barrie, 'the less his students know of his subject [physics] when they join his class, the less, probably, they will have to unlearn'. Tait's view about ignorance being a valuable starting point for learning, according to Barrie, had become outmoded in an age when children are fed 'on geographical biscuits in educational nurseries with astronomical ceilings and historical wall-papers' (*EE* 60). Interestingly, a similar notion appears in *Peter Pan*: it is the child who has been fed 'geographical biscuits' and who thus cannot wonder, as Barrie points out, who has the greatest difficulty learning how to fly. Thus, when John at first fails to fly, Barrie comments: '*He tries; no, he has not got it, poor stay-at-home, though he knows the names of all the counties in England and Peter does not know one*' (*PP* 103). Barrie later comments in Act 4, scene 1 that facts are: '*the only things that puzzle*' Peter (*PP* 129). Barrie's seemingly light comment on Tait's pedagogical approach is an easily missed sideswipe at the utilitarian or instrumental/goal-obsessed nature of the teaching of young children during the early twentieth century. However, if Barrie's views on education were shared by some of his Edinburgh professors, such as Tait, and by novelists such as Dickens, his work is certainly indebted to Carlyle as incontestably one of the most influential writers from the South of Scotland.

Through decades of the nineteenth century Carlyle's work saturated the thought, literature, and culture of the many divergent ways in which Victorian writers and artists attempted to resist, or to some extent, to mitigate the legacies of the preceding century's modernising transformations. In *Sartor Resartus* Carlyle provides one of the most profoundly influential models of fictional character formation in his self-consciously fictive representative of human existence, the highly general duality that is Diogenes (God-born Teufelsdröckh (Devil's dung). Through several texts including 'Signs of the Times' and *Sartor Resartus* Carlyle articulated ideas of foundational importance to nineteenth-century literature and culture's numerous struggles with modernity's deeply embedded materialistic and mechanical assumptions concerning both nature and the human condition.[25] Part of this tendency to oppose the mechanical metaphor's viral propensity to spread itself upon virtually everything, involved emphasising a number of human characteristics including human free will or agency, the social and fundamentally dualistic character of human existence, the complex weave of human social relations, the organic changefulness of the natural world and of human existence as an unfolding process, the great immensity and plenitude of nature, the vastness of human ignorance, the relativity of our knowledge and even of the most abstract of the sciences, the symbolic and ultimately inexplicable character of everything from the Universe itself to the humblest building of a hut, the deadening inanity of modernity and paralysing effects of Enlightenment scepticism and mechanism, and hence the great importance of regaining the experience of wonderment to restore a sense of meaning and vitality to an otherwise stale, flat, and doomed human existence.[26] In *Sartor Resartus* Carlyle notably drew attention to the importance of wonder, as one of his great watchwords of opposition to the mechanistic/materialist conception of the human condition, as for example when he writes of 'wonder everywhere lying close on us'.[27] Carlyle figures his extraordinarily preposterous yet profound Diogenes Teufelsdröckh, 'As a wonder-loving and wonder-seeking man', who potently describes a symbol's embodiment of the real and the imaginary by claiming that in a symbol 'Fantasy with her mystic wonderland plays into the small prose domain of Sense'.[28] Early in the text, the topic of wonder is introduced in sharp contrast to 'That progress of Science, which is to destroy Wonder', and Teufelsdröckh declares that 'The man who cannot wonder [...] is but a pair of Spectacles behind which there is no Eye'.[29]

Carlyle's work upholds the huge importance of wonder for humanity amidst the deadening crisis of modernity's hollowness and impending stasis, and in doing so he provides a leading light for Barrie's turn to wonder in *Peter Pan*'s making-believe. However, uncertainty also profoundly haunts Carlyle's work as a spectre of the modern condition inherited from the Enlightenment, in particular from how Hume's absolute scepticism was understood by the father of Scottish Common-Sense philosophy, Thomas Reid, and by his greatest proponent in the nineteenth century, the greatly admired friend of Carlyle and much respected teacher of Clerk Maxwell, Sir William Hamilton (Professor of Logic and Metaphysics at Edinburgh). In Hamilton's interpretation of Hume, it is as though Hume's philosophical system comprises a set of mutually undermining positions between which one can make no difference – and hence, one is led towards a condition of complete indifference or a resulting stasis; an inertia akin to the effect described by Masson of 'an indistinguishable equilibrium of ruin' and to an extent linked by Masson with what he regards as Hume's nihilism.[30] In other words, the theory of thermodynamics that spelled out doom for all existence as the necessary outcome of the natural laws of the universe had been already articulated in general, highly theoretical terms, at least some decades previously by Hamilton's definition of Hume's scepticism. Importantly, this notion of Hume's scepticism resulting in a complete stasis of absolute uncertainty, is something that Hamilton's successor in Logic and Metaphysics at Edinburgh, Campbell Fraser, touches on in his *Selections from Berkeley*, the text to which, as noted above, Barrie refers as he reflects on his studies of Fraser's edition, 'I was once more of a metaphysician than I have been giving myself credit for'. Fraser defines the paralysis of Hume's scepticism as typifying the modern condition: 'Hume's paralysis of human intelligence was the chief crisis in the epoch of philosophy that was inaugurated by Locke, and in which we are living.'[31]

The basic problem with the condition of equilibrium enounced by Masson inheres in the stasis and hence complete cessation of everything – the 'ruin' effected by the *process* of equilibration or running down to the moment of equilibrium, the final moment of cessation. But this is also the great threat of uncertainty, of the metaphysical theory of an absolute scepticism or total indeterminacy, but now translated into the cosmos as a whole as the ultimate fact that our place is ineluctably heading towards complete ruination, a destruction, through the final equilibrium of energy, of place itself. But, in opposition to this fearfully oppressive big idea or theory of how things – how the universe that is our condition – *must* be, Maxwell's demon and Peter Pan both seem to be almost paradoxically embodiments of uncertainty that, as it were, fly in the face of such a relentlessly deterministic outcome for humanity, the world, and the whole universe. That is to say, by introducing embodiments of complete uncertainty (in particular, of irresolvable contradiction) both Maxwell and Barrie offer hope through liberating us from the necessity that determines, or the absolute uncertainty that entails, stasis.

By introducing a playful, vital embodiment of uncertainty, the demon or sprite that the Enlightenment's anti-superstition project had sought to eradicate as unobservable figments of mere fancy, Barrie brings to life an object of wonder, something that revives that self-absorbed state of make-believe in which places and identities are generated or displaced as if from nothing.[32] By embodying uncertainty in the persona of Peter, Barrie activates the audience's participation in wonderment and in the play. With the play's emphasis on the importance of belief and wonderment, *Peter Pan*'s crucial device of wonderment, belief, and of course magic, is the very ambiguity or uncertainty that Peter himself embodies as an eternal boy. Hence, all the often playful but at times disturbing strangeness of Peter: his linguistic dislocation or ignorance of the meaning of terms such as 'kiss' (*PP* 101); his sexual ambiguity or ambivalence; his total immersion in pretence and how this operates to render uncertain whether he is telling the truth or just pretending; his evocation of sadness or pity in the audience that can so quickly switch to feelings of distrust or dislike; his puzzling forgetfulness betokening his being only in the present – in all of these things Peter consistently so embodies ambiguity or uncertainty that he is at once a fascinating *dynamic force of indeterminate conduct* (a truly free spirit) and is thereby the play's gateway for the Darling children and for the audience to a freedom from dull reality, from the threat of Hades contained in that life-changing theory of thermodynamics that must have so struck Barrie and his generation. According to Granville Barker:

> Much of the charm of all [Barrie's] work might be explained by the fact that he never loses and never lets his audience lose the exciting hovering of the mind between make-believe and reality which so endears the Theatre to a child. I am not sure that this half-dread of reality is not a source of weakness to some of the other plays, but it is an obvious strength to Peter Pan.[33]

It would seem that, pivotal to that experience of hovering between opposites is the way in which Peter exemplifies or embraces a cluster of opposites that generate the irresolvable uncertainty that typifies responses both to Peter himself and to the play as a whole. Yet, importantly, so to embody the paradox of uncertainty for us in the real world, Peter himself is, as Barrie notes: '*the only one who is sure about anything on the island*' (*PP* 128).

*

Peter Pan participates in a philosophical literature of resistance to the Enlightenment's legacies of pessimism concerning humanity's future and modernity's disenchanting or voiding of the world's vibrant meaningfulness.

A significant part of this literature was produced by writers closely associated with the places of Barrie's education in the Scottish Lowlands. Inasmuch as *Peter Pan* transforms theoretical discourses that Barrie encountered while a student at Edinburgh, the play partakes in elements at the heart of Scottish intellectual life during the eighteenth and nineteenth centuries. But it does this through a pervasive playfulness, a continual stream of humour that burbles throughout the action, characters, verbal exchanges, and Barrie's stage directions and comments on the action and props. The play also opposes foreboding elements of disenchantment and pessimism through absorbing, and in effect inverting, profound uncertainty to return the audience to the emancipating fun of believing in the impossible – extreme scepticism and credulity are closely related.

Absorbed in playrooms of make-believe, we enjoy a participation in its transformative power as we come to care passionately about the imagined existence of Tinker Bell, signified by light, sound, and the actors' responses to her as a presence. As childhood games of make-believe also often involve imaginary enhancements of spatial entities, dignified by naming, but engagingly mysterious and wonderful, the play involves making onstage places wonderfully real – the Never Land, the Mermaids' Lagoon, the Home Under the Ground. As Barrie comments on the staging of Never Land: 'In the daytime you think the Never Land is only make-believe, and so it is to the likes of you, but this is the Never Land come true' (*PP* 105). Reified for the audience, *Peter Pan* manifests imaginary places that otherwise are too easily denigrated as merely solipsistic. But, though the crafting of sufficiently wonderful spectacle may help the play to become compellingly enthralling for a paying public, Peter Pan's undaunted capability affirms childhood games of make-believe as wonderful mental activities of place- and identity-making. He is a hero of boyish competence; the lost boys cheer at Peter's command to build a house around Wendy because '*no difficulty baffles Peter*' (*PP* 114).

By involving the audience in fantasies of competence, in audacious contraventions of natural laws, and in the joy of the transformative and absorbing power of making-believe, Barrie is recovering an important childhood capacity to generate out of airy nothing wonderfully absorbing places and identities. This capacity of make-believe resembles the adult's potential sense of autonomy to reject or doubt and critique people, concepts, or predictions that otherwise would make us quail into dangerous compliance. Emerging from the Edenic world of playful make-believe into the adult world of moral knowledge, may be a seriously compromised process if connection with this capacity is lost. Thus, redeeming something of make-believe's transformative and emancipatory power (through our participation in the play) involves the subversive act of recovering an important dimension of our humanity that intricately inheres in our ability to wonder, to be absorbed in the mystery of our existence, to imagine an alternative while being subjugated by assertions that there are no alternatives, to believe in what seems impossible, to doubt and question what appears to be or is authoritatively deemed beyond question – making-believe considered in this way is tantamount to a refusal to be silenced.

The play's thorough permeation by the activities of making-believe involves uncertainty as a key element within the modern adult condition of pessimism and the dreaded loss of place, certitude, wonder, autonomy, loved ones, and the self. Mr Darling's undoubtedly humorous slippery-slope remarks about the consequences of not being able to get his tie on articulate the precarious uncertainty of the family's existence if governed by the rigidly deterministic logic of an inhumane economic system: 'if I don't go to the office again you and I starve, and our children will be thrown into the streets' (*PP* 91). But uncertainty and such fears are treated playfully and are at the heart of the play's renewal of wonder through Peter Pan's combined agency and embodiment of that agency-negating state of self-division or contradiction, the absolute scepticism that Barrie's Professor of Logic and Metaphysics, Campbell Fraser, described as the modern condition of 'Hume's paralysis of human intelligence'. However, as uncertainty in one mood is threatening, depleting all vitality and hope through the stasis it appears to imply, in another, playful, humorous mood, uncertainty evokes fascination, wonder, and through the drama's generation of something wonderful/mysterious and dynamic/vital, the optimism of being able to do virtually anything that one wills to do.

Wonder, uncertainty, and place beautifully and complexly function in the play, beckoning us towards further explorations of their fluid relations to oppose the terrifying bleakness of the modern world's philosophical and scientific eschatology. Fundamental to humanity's profound need for participation in meaningful work and for social enjoyments of play that are fully absorbing and freed from all too often prevalent distractions of despair, anxieties, and oppressive controls and uncertainties that counterproductively threaten to eradicate autonomy, Barrie's playful make-believe fosters an awareness of being vitally yet perhaps too precariously dependent on imagination, courage, and a strongly held belief in our capacities to act. *Peter Pan's* making-believe translation of literary and theoretical discourses and of experience invites the audience to recover or escape to a precious world of childlike wonder and make-believe fun. In this, humanity's redemption potentially inheres. Though this may be regarded as gratifyingly optimistic, unless the conditions of unfettered making-believe are adequately protected and its activity is sufficiently valued, the play risks being so haunted by the seriousness of what it attempts to oppose or escape from that, as an antidote to the darkness visible of the deeply conflicted condition of modernity, it may also be haunted by its impotence.

Notes

1   J. M. Barrie, 'Preface', in R. M. Ballantyne, *The Coral Island*, 1858 (London: James Nisbet, 1913), p. vii.
2   David Hume, *Enquiries Concerning Human Understanding and Concerning the Principles of Morals*, ed. L. A. Selby-Bigge, third edition (Oxford: Oxford University Press, 1979), p. 160. For two examples of how Hume was referred to by Barrie's Professors at Edinburgh University, see Alexander Campbell Fraser, 'Introduction', in *Selections from Berkeley with an Introduction and Notes for the Use of Students in the Universities*, revised edition (Oxford: Clarendon Press, 1891), pp.ix, xxxix–xlvi); and David Masson, *Recent British Philosophy: A Review with Criticisms*, third edition (London: Macmillan, 1877), pp. 31–32.
3   Sir William Hamilton, 'Philosophy of Perception', 1830, in *Discussions, Works of Sir William Hamilton*, intr. Savina Tropea, 7 vols (Bristol: Thoemmes Press, 2001), I, pp. 39–99 (p. 94). Self-division was earlier described by one of Hamilton's favorite authors, Pascal, in terms of a division between reason and the passions: having both reason and passions, man 'cannot be free from war [...]. Thus he is always torn by inner divisions and contradictions' (Blaise Pascal, *Pensées*, trans. A. J. Krailsheimer, revised edition (London: Penguin, 1995), pp. 207–8. William James, *The Varieties of Religious Experience: A Study in Human Nature*, 1902, ed. Martin E. Marty (Harmondsworth & New York: Penguin, 1982), chapter 8; R. D. Laing, *The Divided Self: An Existential Study in Sanity and Madness*, 1960 (London: Tavistock, 1969).
4   Barrie, 'Preface', p. vii.
5   Piers Dudgeon, *Captivated: J. M. Barrie, the du Mauriers and the Dark Side of Neverland* (London: Chatto & Windus, 2008), pp. 61–62.
6   The connection with Moat Brae House is made explicit in Roger Lancelyn Green, *Fifty Years of Peter Pan* (London: Peter Davies, 1954), pp. 6–8.
7   The Peter Pan Moat Brae Trust, under the patronage of Joanna Lumley, is thus rightly attempting to restore this derelict property in order to establish a centre for children's literature. There can be few places in the world more deserving of such efforts.

8   Andrew Nash, 'Introduction', in *FMJL*, pp. xviii–xix.

9   William Shakespeare, *A Midsummer Night's Dream,* ed. Harold F. Brooks, The Arden Shakespeare (London and New York: Routledge, 1979), 1.1: 16; and see 1.1: 46–78). Further references are in the text.

10 For example, there are several hints concerning economic worries, such as Barrie's stage direction comments, including: 'Mrs Darling's wedding gown […] was such a grand affair that it still keeps them pinched' (*PP* 87–8); 'The Darlings could not afford to have a nurse' – hence Nana (*PP* 88).

11 R. D. S. Jack, *The Road to the Never Land: A Reassessment of J M Barrie's Dramatic Art* (1991, repr. Glasgow: Humming Earth, 2010), pp. 85–91.

12 Cairns Craig, *Intending Scotland: Explorations in Scottish Culture since the Enlightenment* (Edinburgh: Edinburgh University Press, 2009).

13 Sir William Thomson and Peter Guthrie Tait, *Elements of Natural Philosophy,* 1872, second edition (Cambridge: Cambridge University Press, 1879).

14 Masson, p. 146. Quoted by Craig, p. 102.

15 Masson, p. 144. Quoted by Craig, p. 103.

16 Craig, p. 103.

17 Basil Mahon, *The Man Who Changed Everything: The Life of James Clerk Maxwell* (Chichester: Wiley, 2003).

18 Craig, pp. 127–8.

19 Masson was the main organiser of Carlyle's eightieth birthday tribute which included a long list of signatories, several of whom were Masson's colleagues at Edinburgh and teachers of Barrie, including Calderwood and Campbell Fraser. See Ralph Jessop, *Carlyle and Scottish Thought* (Basingstoke: Macmillan, 1997), pp. 15–16.

20 Letter from J. M. Barrie to Mrs Oliver, 21 December 1931, quoted by Dudgeon, pp. 64–65.

21 Masson, pp. 67–69.

22 Jack, p. 119.

23 Michael Goldberg, *Carlyle and Dickens* (Athens: University of Georgia Press, 1972), p. 79. Ralph Jessop, 'Counter-Cultural Scepticisms of the Long Enlightenment: Hume, Reid, Hamilton, Carlyle, Dickens and Beyond?', *Journal of Scottish Philosophy*, 4 (2011), pp. 75–94 (pp. 92–94).

24 Charles Dickens, *Hard Times,* ed. Paul Schlicke (Oxford University Press, 2006), p. 11.

25 See Ralph Jessop, 'Coinage of the Term Environment: A Word Without Authority and Carlyle's Displacement of the Mechanical Metaphor', *Literature Compass* 9/11 (2012), pp. 708–20.

26 For example, see Thomas Carlyle, *Sartor Resartus,* ed. Rodger L. Tarr and Mark Engel, Strouse Edition (Berkeley: University of California Press, 2000), pp. 162–3.

27 Carlyle, p. 192.

28 Carlyle, p. 153; p. 162.

29 Carlyle, pp. 52–53.

30 Masson, p. 148.

31 Fraser, p. xxxvi.

32 For an example of the play's displacement of identities, see Peter's mimicking of and exchanges with Hook in Act 3.

33 Granville Barker, 'J. M. Barrie as a Dramatist', *The Bookman* (Oct. 1910), pp. 13–20 (p. 14).

10. Barrie and Bloomsbury

ROSEMARY ASHTON

Ask people which London location they associate with J. M. Barrie and especially *Peter Pan*, and most will reply not 'Bloomsbury' but 'Kensington'. Peter Pan himself tells Wendy in the opening scene of the play as published in 1928 that he ran away as a baby to Kensington Gardens. Sir George Frampton's famous statue of Peter Pan was installed in Kensington Gardens in 1912; Barrie lived in the area when he wrote the play; and it was in the Gardens that he befriended the family of boys, the Llewelyn Davies children, to whom the printed text was dedicated. Of the five boys, John (known as Jack), Peter, and Michael contributed their names to characters in the drama. Barrie used the collaborative games he played with the boys in his 'terrible masterpiece', as the third son, Peter Davies, later described the celebrated play.[1]

The original appearance in Barrie's writings of the eternal boy Peter Pan comes in the loose, anecdotal fictional work, *The Little White Bird*, published in 1902. In 'this disconcerting book', as Leonee Ormond describes it,[2] Peter's story is interpolated into a whimsical narrative written in the first person by a narrator who, like Barrie, owns a St Bernard dog called Porthos; he meets a little boy and his mother in Kensington Gardens. Peter Pan makes his appearance in chapter fourteen, illustrating the narrator's claim that all children are born birds first. As a one-week-old baby Peter flies out of his bedroom window, 'right over the houses to the Gardens', where he meets fairies and, on the island in the Serpentine, a wise old bird, Solomon Caw, who tells Peter that he is neither bird nor human, but 'a Betwixt-and-Between' (*LWB* 104). Though Peter is thus immediately associated with Kensington Gardens, the exact location of the home from which he flies is not given; indeed he appears not to live in the immediate area, for 'standing on the ledge he could see trees *far away*, which were doubtless the Kensington Gardens' (*LWB* 100, [my italics]).

After the success of *Peter Pan*, first performed in 1904–05 (but not published as a text until 1928), Barrie tinkered with the story further, publishing a narrative version as *Peter and Wendy* in 1911. The action of the play is reproduced, and a back story added, in which Mr and Mrs Darling hire Nana the Newfoundland dog as their nanny because, though middle-class, they are 'poor', but wish to keep up with the neighbours by having a nanny for their children. They meet Nana in Kensington Gardens, where she impresses by being more solicitous about children than the 'careless nursemaids' (*PW* 71) who frequent the Gardens with their small charges. In 1906 Kensington Gardens had featured in the title of a text brought out by Barrie's publishers, Hodder and Stoughton, a reprinting of the Peter Pan section from *The Little White Bird* as a separate book, *Peter Pan in Kensington Gardens*, accompanied by fifty illustrations by Arthur Rackham.

Finally, when Barrie printed the text of the play in 1928, he wrote in his dedication to the Llewelyn Davies boys, 'We first brought Peter down, didn't we, with a blunt-headed arrow in Kensington Gardens?' (*PP* 75). Small wonder, then, that both Peter Pan and the Darlings are widely thought to live near Kensington Gardens, from where Peter and the Darling children fly off to have their adventures in the Never Land.

The fact – little commented on by editors and critics of Barrie – is that though he met the boys who inspired his play in Kensington Gardens in 1898 while walking his dog Porthos and became friends with the family, who lived nearby in Kensington Park Gardens,[3] and though he based the play's adventures on games they played together there, when he came to write it in November 1903, he placed the Darlings' house not in Kensington, but in Bloomsbury. The manuscript of the first draft, written between 23 November 1903 and March 1904, is headed simply 'ANON. A Play'. It has a drawing of the children's bedroom, and the scene is entitled 'The Night-Nursery of the Darling Family'. In his stage instructions Barrie specifies that the production must adhere closely to the details of his drawing. The room is 'to look as snug & small as possible', and should have all the accoutrements of 'a cosy nursery in a middle[-]class family'. 'The house is in a London street in Bloomsbury, and the houses opposite may be vaguely seen thro' the windows.' No more is said about the location, as the instructions move on to describe how the black and white Newfoundland dog Nana, to be played 'by a *boy*', bustles about the nursery preparing a bath for the youngest Darling, Michael in the final version, but here called Alexander.[4]

The playscript, which should have been submitted to the Lord Chamberlain for approval before the play opened, is not among the Lord Chamberlain's Plays in the British Library,[5] but a typescript survives, adorned by cues on lighting and staging, and clearly intended for use in the first production of the play at the Duke of York's Theatre from 27 December 1904 to 1 April 1905 (a run of 150 performances).[6] Like the manuscript, it specifies that the Darlings' house is in Bloomsbury. One might wonder why Barrie should name the particular setting for the production, given that a Bloomsbury house is not much different from other London houses built in the late eighteenth or early nineteenth century, and that unless someone mentions the location in a speech, or some visual clue is given, there is no way an audience could know of it.

While there is, therefore, no obvious theatrical reason for the play to open in a house in Bloomsbury, there is an emotional one which has been largely overlooked by students of the play's complicated textual history. The text of the play underwent changes in production between 1904 and its publication in 1928, many of which have been discussed by Green, Peter Hollindale, Jacqueline Rose, and Jack.[7] But these discussions do not affect the account of Bloomsbury in the present essay, as none of them mentions the Bloomsbury setting or connections.[8] When Barrie printed *Peter Pan* in 1928, he expanded on the Bloomsbury theme, giving the reasons in his stage directions for the opening scene:

> The night nursery of the Darling family, which is the scene of our opening Act, is at the top of a rather depressed street in Bloomsbury. We have a right to place it where we will, and the reason Bloomsbury is chosen is that Mr Roget once lived there. So did we in days when his *Thesaurus* was our only companion in London; and we whom he has helped to wend our way through life have always wanted to pay him a little compliment. The Darlings therefore lived in Bloomsbury.
>
> It is a corner house whose top window, the important one, looks upon a leafy square from which Peter used to fly up to it, to the delight of three children and no doubt the irritation of passers-by. The street is still there, though the steaming sausage shop has gone; and apparently the same cards perch now as then over the doors, inviting

homeless ones to come and stay with the hospitable inhabitants. Since the days of the Darlings, however, a lick of paint has been applied; and our corner house in particular, which has swallowed its neighbour, blooms with awful freshness as if the colours had been discharged upon it through a hose. Its card now says 'No children', meaning maybe that the goings-on of Wendy and her brothers have given the house a bad name. As for ourselves, we have not been in it since we went back to reclaim our old *Thesaurus*. (*PP* 87)

Though the very next paragraph tells us that we 'may dump' the Darling house 'down anywhere you like, and if you think it was your house you are very probably right', the relish for particularity with which Barrie makes the house a Bloomsbury house suggests that its location was significant for him. Early in the opening scene of the published play, Mrs Darling enters the nursery, and once more Barrie mentions Bloomsbury in the directions, though the audience could hardly intuit it. Mrs Darling, he says, 'is the loveliest lady in Bloomsbury' (*PP* 89). The 1903–4 manuscript and 1904 typescript merely say, 'At that moment enter Mrs Darling R[ight]. She is a young beautiful woman in evening dress.'[9]

And Bloomsbury certainly was significant for Barrie, as we find from the more expansive account of his own experience of the area in his auto-biography, *The Greenwood Hat*, privately printed in fifty copies in 1930, and reissued in 1937 by one of the Llewelyn Davies boys, the publisher Peter Davies, after Barrie's death. The very title, with its subtitle 'Being a Memoir of James Anon 1885–1887', teases. 'ANON. A Play' was written in 1903–4 by the man who was by then a successful author of novels and especially plays (*Quality Street* and *The Admirable Crichton* had both been produced with success in 1902), but who had arrived in London from Scotland in March 1885 at the age of twenty-five, hoping that Frederick Greenwood, editor of the *St James's Gazette*, would print more of his articles, enough to allow him to live in London as a writer. Over the next few years Greenwood took plenty of his articles, many of them stories and anecdotes set in Barrie's homeland, either his birthplace of Kirriemuir, Angus (the 'Thrums' of his early journalism and fiction), or Dumfries, where Barrie had been to school. The *St James's* contributions were published over the name 'Anon'.

The Greenwood Hat, which, as R. D. S. Jack notes in a recent book on Barrie's youth, is seldom referred to by critics,[10] is informative on the subject of Bloomsbury. The writing is at once revealingly direct and playfully vague. Bloomsbury joins Kirriemuir and Kensington Gardens as a place associated with an important time in his life. If Kirriemuir is significant as the location of his childhood, and Kensington as the place where he lost his heart to Sylvia Llewelyn Davies and her boys, then Bloomsbury is significant as the all-important first destination on his arrival in the metropolis, and the place where his writing career took off.

In the 1928 directions to *Peter Pan* he locates the Darlings, perhaps surprisingly, in a 'rather depressed street' in Bloomsbury. One might expect a middle-class family house in or near one of Bloomsbury's famous garden squares – Russell, or Bedford, or Gordon Square, say – with their solid brick houses built by James Burton or Thomas Cubitt, two of the new breed of speculative builders who enlarged and enhanced parts of London, including Bloomsbury, between 1790 and 1840. Much of Bloomsbury was built for, and inhabited by, professional men and their families – lawyers, who could easily get to their place of work in the nearby Inns of Court, doctors who practised in one of the many hospitals in the area, upwardly mobile merchants who had their businesses in the City of London (people like the Sedleys and Osbornes, whom Thackeray knowingly places in Russell Square in *Vanity Fair*), or academics employed by University College London, opened, under its original name of the University of London, in Gower Street in 1828.[11]

Barrie's friend E. V. Lucas described the Bloomsbury of most people's imaginations when he wrote in 1906 of the area as 'a stronghold of middle-class respectability and learning':

> […] the British Museum is its heart: its lungs are Bedford Square and Russell Square, Gordon Square and Woburn Square: and its aorta is Gower Street, which goes on for ever. Lawyers and law students live here, to be near the Inns of Court; bookish men live here, to be near the Museum.'[12]

It was to 46 Gordon Square that the four Stephen siblings, Vanessa (later Bell), Thoby, Adrian, and Virginia (later Woolf) moved from their late father Leslie Stephen's gloomy house (in Kensington) in late 1904, just as rehearsals were starting for the first production of *Peter Pan*. They and their literary and artistic friends were soon to become famous as the Bloomsbury Group, and the Bloomsbury they inhabited was the one described by Lucas, the intellectual heart of London, with the British Museum as its geographical and symbolic centre.

But Bloomsbury covered an area which went beyond these squares built on the well-managed estate of the Duke of Bedford. Eastern Bloomsbury, stretching through meaner streets to Gray's Inn Road, was less affluent. Charles Booth's famous 'poverty maps' of 1889, published as *Life and Labour of the People of London* from 1892 to 1897, while classifying most of Bloomsbury, leading west to Tottenham Court Road, the boundary with Fitzrovia, as 'yellow' or 'red' housing (meaning that inhabited by wealthy people of the upper-middle and middle classes), identified a few small pockets to the south and east as purple ('mixed'), light blue (poor), dark blue (very poor), and even black (the resort of 'loafers and semi-criminals').[13] The street where the Darlings live seems to be located in the less salubrious eastern region of Bloomsbury. Mr Darling is a modestly paid clerk in the City, and his house is in a street in which there is a 'steaming sausage shop' (unthinkable in the Duke of Bedford's Bloomsbury to the west) and cards in windows offering rooms to let.[14]

The stage directions at the beginning of the 1928 text of *Peter Pan* explain that the Darlings, though middle-class, are hard up. Mr Darling works for little money, and his wife is a clever homemaker who has used 'all the scrapings of her purse' to make the coverlets on the beds out of her own wedding gown, and whose evening dress, in which she appears on her first entrance into the nursery, is 'a delicious confection made by herself out of nothing and other people's mistakes' (*PP* 87, 89). Though it might seem that Barrie's presentation of his characters' circumstances and his placing them in the poorer part of Bloomsbury deviates widely from the situation of their originals, in fact the Llewelyn Davieses, though impeccably middle-class, living in a comfortable house in Kensington and employing servants, were by no means wealthy. Arthur Llewelyn Davies was a young barrister when he married Sylvia Du Maurier in 1892; Sylvia, according to her son Peter, did have a struggle to manage the household on her husband's salary, and did indeed make her own, and her children's, clothes.[15]

Barrie might have placed the Darlings in Kensington, but he chose Bloomsbury. There was a twofold reason, as he tells us in the stage directions in the published text: Peter Mark Roget of *Thesaurus* fame had lived there, and so had Barrie himself on arriving in London in 1885 to make a living and a name, when at first Roget's *Thesaurus* 'was our only companion'. The *Thesaurus* was significant enough to Barrie for him to make two references to it in the 1928 *Peter Pan* (though not in the 1903–04 manuscript or 1904 typescript). In Act One, Scene One, when Wendy cries out that her father is 'chaining Nana up', the author interpolates: 'This unfortunately is what he is doing, though we cannot see him. Let us hope that he then retires to his study, looks up the word "temper" in his *Thesaurus*, and under the influence of those benign pages becomes a better man.' (*PP* 96). Once again, this must be for the benefit of the reader rather than the spectator of the play. One further reference to Roget's work comes towards the end of the published text. In Act Four, Scene One, when Hook is planning to give poison to the sleeping Peter, and Tinker Bell intervenes to save Peter by taking it herself, we are told – perversely and mischievously in the circumstances – that Hook 'is not wholly evil: he has a *Thesaurus* in his cabin, and is no mean performer on the flute' (*PP* 136).

As Barrie says, Roget lived in Bloomsbury. He spent most of his adult life in the area, graduating from rooms in Great Russell Street in 1800 to a house in Bernard Street leading east to Brunswick Square, and finally, as he became more affluent, to Upper Bedford Place leading north from Russell Square. Before he turned at the age of nearly seventy to compiling his celebrated *Thesaurus*, which was published in 1852, Roget was a practising doctor and Fellow of the Royal Society.[16] Whether Barrie knew about the many years Roget had spent in Bernard Street in particular is not clear; perhaps he did, and so valued the fact that his own first addresses on coming to London in 1885, fifteen years after Roget's death, were very close by.

The Greenwood Hat fills in the details merely hinted at in the opening scene of the *Peter Pan* text. This idiosyncratic autobiography takes the form of a reprinting of some of Barrie's short pieces by 'Anon', which Greenwood had printed in the *St James's Gazette* in the 1880s, accompanied by reminiscences written in 1930 of the circumstances in which he originally composed them. The hat of the title, he tells us in one such explanatory passage, was bought shortly after his arrival in the capital; it was 'bought for the subjection of Greenwood', the young author believing that 'without a silk hat he could not advance upon a lordly editor' (*GH* 19).

Barrie's description of the arrival in London is striking. Having travelled by overnight train on 28 March 1885, he arrived at St Pancras station on Euston Road, the northern boundary of Bloomsbury, 'gauche and inarticulate, as thin as a pencil but not so long' – a rueful reference to his very small stature, about which Barrie was obsessively anxious. He gives a thumbnail sketch of his younger self, amused and patronising, but at the same time honestly revealing the hurt he still felt about his lack of height:

> Wears thick boots (with nails in them), which he will polish specially for social functions. Carries on his person a silver watch bought for him by his father from a pedlar on fourteenth birthday (that was a day). Carries it still, No. 57841. Has no complete dress-suit in his wooden box, but can look every inch as if attired in such when backed against a wall. Manners, full of nails like his boots. Ladies have decided that he is of no account, and he already knows this and has private anguish thereanent [...] Pecuniary asset, twelve pounds in a secret pocket which he sometimes presses, as if it were his heart. (*GH* 8–9)

Having been excited by spotting in St Pancras a placard of the *St James's Gazette* advertising a piece of his already accepted for publication by Greenwood, a moment which he recalls, forty-five years later, as 'the romance of my life', the young Barrie set about finding cheap lodgings. He knew London only from maps, and as he hoped to become a frequenter of the Reading Room at the British Museum, he stayed in the immediate area, at first finding temporary quarters in Guilford Street, then moving after a short while to 'little Grenville Street' round the corner. Both these streets are close to Roget's Bernard Street, the first parallel to it and leading eastwards to the Foundling Hospital, the second a narrow street running from north to south, joining Guilford Street with Bernard Street at the angle of the south-west corner of Brunswick Square. Barrie remembers spending 'many months' of poverty in Grenville Street, 'emerging to dine quite agreeably on four provocative halfpenny buns from a paper bag', before moving, when his financial circumstances improved, to a better room than the one at the back in which he started, which 'looked on to a blank wall' (*GH* 17–20).

According to one of his earliest biographers, Denis Mackail, Barrie vacated the dark little room at the back when his friend T. L. Gilmour came to share his lodgings in September 1886; the pair sent regular 'letters from London' to the *Scotsman* newspaper using the signature 'Grenville'.[17] It is reasonable to suppose that the Darlings' house is based on the house in Grenville Street, for we are told that the all-important top window at the front 'looks upon a leafy square', presumably Brunswick Square. In commenting in his autobiography on the pieces done for Greenwood between 1885 and 1887, Barrie remembers how 'Anon' facetiously 'described himself as having been so pestered by the Waits [messengers sent by the editor] that he buried them in Brunswick Square' (*GH* 153).

Whether Barrie knew it or not, some of the people closest to him, a number of whom were concerned in the creation and production of *Peter Pan* in 1904, had, like him, Bloomsbury connections. Most important to him emotionally was Sylvia Llewelyn Davies, beautiful mother of five beautiful boys, the original of Mrs Darling, 'the loveliest lady in Bloomsbury'. The third child of George Du Maurier, the *Punch* artist and author of the best-selling novel *Trilby* (1894), she had been born in Great Russell Street in 1866.

George Du Maurier himself had more than one Bloomsbury connection. Not only did he live for five years in Great Russell Street, taking three rooms on the second floor of No. 46, a house above a soap shop 'just opposite the British Museum', and renting 'a jolly studio' on the ground floor of the same house at the time of his marriage in January 1863,[18] but he had briefly studied chemistry at University College London in Gower Street between 1851 and 1853. He mentions his time as a reluctant chemistry student in the last of his three semi-autobiographical novels, *The Martian*, published in 1897, the year after his death, in which he also talks, through Robert Maurice, his *alter ego* in the novel, of living in Brunswick Square.[19] In his first novel, *Peter Ibbetson* (1892), a semi-fictional account of Du Maurier's early life in Paris and London, the narrator tells of his boyhood love of Dumas's *Three Musketeers* and his acquiring of a St Bernard dog, which he christens Porthos in honour of his favourite novel.[20] Barrie in his turn named his own first dog, also a St Bernard, Porthos after the dog in *Peter Ibbetson*.[21] (Nana in

Peter Pan is based not on Porthos, but on Luath, a black and white Newfoundland who succeeded Porthos as Barrie's companion in Kensington Gardens in 1903 and whose coat was copied for Nana's costume.[22])

George Du Maurier's youngest child, Sylvia's younger brother Gerald, was the first actor to play the important part of Captain Hook in *Peter Pan*, at first doubling it with the less significant part of Mr Darling.[23] He was hugely successful as a menacing Hook, catching Barrie's ambivalence towards his monster-with-a-*Thesaurus* by playing him as both frightening and comic.[24] By 1906 Gerald was playing only Hook, the last time he acted in the play; in 1924 and 1925 he produced *Peter Pan* with his daughter Angela playing Wendy.[25]

It was towards the Du Maurier side of the Llewelyn Davies family that Barrie felt drawn. Sylvia's great beauty was constantly remarked on – her niece Angela Du Maurier wrote of 'the ravishing Aunt Sylvia'[26] – as was the fact that her husband Arthur was as handsome as she was pretty. George Du Maurier rejoiced that his daughter's choice had fallen on a good-looking, if rather prim, young man, a '*joli garçon*', as he remarked, giving him hopes, which were to be spectacularly fulfilled in the five Llewelyn Davies boys, of pretty grandchildren.[27] Undoubtedly Sylvia's charm and the slight air of bohemianism which she brought with her as part of the Anglo-French artistic Du Maurier milieu, appealed to Barrie. The Du Maurier family's connections to Bloomsbury, if known to Barrie, would have added to the romance the place already held for him.

As *Peter Pan* enjoyed its successful first run, one Bloomsbury resident in the audience in January 1905 noted in her journal that the play, though sentimental, was 'imaginative & witty like all of his', and all in all 'a great treat'.[28] Virginia Stephen's circle was to become synonymous with 'Bloomsbury', cementing the area's reputation as the home of intellectual, literary, and artistic pursuits, a reputation which in truth it had already acquired during the nineteenth century, when Dickens, Thackeray, William Morris, Millais, Dante Gabriel Rossetti, Edward Burne-Jones, and Du Maurier were among its inhabitants. To that list we must add J. M. Barrie, the man who celebrated Bloomsbury by giving it a place in his most famous and enduring work, *Peter Pan*.

Notes

1   Quoted in Andrew Birkin, *J. M. Barrie and the Lost Boys* (London: Constable, 1979), p. 1.

2   Leonee Ormond, *J. M. Barrie* (Edinburgh: Scottish Academic Press, 1987), p. 103.

3   See Janet Dunbar, *J. M. Barrie: The Man Behind the Image* (London: Collins, 1970), p. 117.

4   'ANON. A Play', MS given by Barrie to the American actress Maude Adams; extracts quoted courtesy of the Lilly Library, Indiana University, Bloomington, Indiana. Four pages of MS notes leading towards *Peter Pan*, dated 14 October 1903 and now in the Beinecke Rare Book and Manuscript Library, Yale University, do not specify any location.

5   Roger Lancelyn Green, *Fifty Years of Peter Pan* (London: Peter Davies, 1954), gives a full account of the versions of *Peter Pan*, including the MS 'ANON. A Play'; his book benefits from his relations with two of the Llewelyn Davies 'boys', the youngest, Nico, and Peter Davies, the publisher of Green's book, both of whom gave him material. But his remarks about the playscript submitted to the Lord Chamberlain in December 1904 (pp. 83, 87) are mysterious, since, as R. D. S. Jack correctly points out in 'The Manuscript of *Peter Pan*', *Children's Literature*, XVIII (1990), pp. 101–13 (p. 102), there is no 1904 playscript in the Lord Chamberlain's Plays in the British Library.

6   Typescript of three-act version of *Peter Pan*, Beinecke, P45 1904–1905b.

7   See Green; Peter Hollindale (ed.), *J. M. Barrie: Peter Pan and other Plays* (Oxford: Oxford University Press, 1995) pp. xxvi–xxix; Jacqueline Rose, *The Case of Peter Pan, or The Impossibility of Children's Fiction* (London: Macmillan, 1984); Jack, 'The Manuscript of *Peter Pan*'.

8   Nor does Maria Tatar in *The Annotated Peter Pan* (New York and London: W. W. Norton & Co., 2011), which concentrates on the fictional version, *Peter and Wendy*.

9   'ANON. A Play', Scene 1, p. 3.

10 R. D. S. Jack, *Myths and the Mythmaker: A Literary Account of J. M. Barrie's Formative Years* (Amsterdam & New York: Rodopi, 2010), p. 16.

11 For a history of the building of Bloomsbury in the nineteenth century and in particular the establishment of educational institutions in the area, see the website of the UCL Leverhulme-funded Bloomsbury Project, **www.ucl.ac.uk/bloomsbury-project**. See also Hermione Hobhouse, *Thomas Cubitt: Master Builder* (London: Macmillan, 1971), Donald J. Olsen, *Town Planning in London: The Eighteenth and Nineteenth Centuries* (New Haven, Connecticut and London: Yale University Press, 1964, revised 1982), Richard Tames, *Bloomsbury Past: A Visual History* (London: Historical Publications, 1993), Roger Hudson, *Bloomsbury, Fitzrovia, & Soho* (London: Haggerston, 1996), and Rosemary Ashton, *Victorian Bloomsbury* (New Haven & London: Yale University Press, 2012).

12 E. V. Lucas, *A Wanderer in London* (1906, revised edn, London: Methuen, 1913), pp. 189–90.

13 The manuscripts of the Booth notebooks, which describe streets and their occupants in detail, are in the British Library of Political and Economic Science at the London School of Economics. The maps themselves are available online at the Charles Booth Online Archive, **booth.lse.ac.uk**.

14 For the strict lease restrictions imposed by the Bedford Estate, see Olsen, *Town Planning in London*, pp. 39–73.

15 For an account of the Llewelyn Davies family, which makes use of Peter Davies's 'Family Mausoleum', or *Morgue*, his annotated collection of family papers in 1945, see Birkin, *J. M. Barrie and the Lost Boys*, pp. 48–55, 83 and n.

16 For Roget's life, see D. L. Emblen, *Peter Mark Roget: The Word and the Man* (London: Longman, 1970), and Joshua Kendall, *The Man Who Made Lists: Love, Death, Madness, and the Creation of 'Roget's Thesaurus'* (New York and London: G. B. Putnam's Sons, 2008). Both discuss the writing of the *Thesaurus* in detail. R. D. S. Jack briefly discusses the shared fascination with language of Roget and Barrie in *The Road to the Never Land: A Reassessment of J. M. Barrie's Dramatic Art* (Aberdeen: Aberdeen University Press, 1991), pp. 223–25.

17 Denis Mackail, *Barrie: The Story of J. M. B.* (London: Peter Davies, 1941), pp. 119, 123.

18 George Du Maurier to Tom Armstrong, November and December 1862, and to his mother, April 1864, *The Young George Du Maurier: A Selection of his Letters 1860–67*, ed. Daphne Du Maurier (London: Peter Davies, 1951), pp. 182, 183, 234.

19 George Du Maurier, *The Martian* (1897), in *Novels of George Du Maurier, with introductions by John Masefield and Daphne Du Maurier* (London: Peter Davies, 1947), p. 533.

20 Du Maurier, *Peter Ibbetson* (1892), in ibid, pp. 77–78.

21 Dunbar, p. 99.

22 Birkin, pp. 98, 111.

23 Daphne Du Maurier, *Gerald: A Portrait* (London: Victor Gollancz, 1934), pp. 62, 94. Gerald was replaced in the part of Mr Darling in February 1905 by A. E. Matthews, see Green, p. 100.

24 See James Harding, *Gerald Du Maurier: The Last Actor-Manager* (London: Hodder & Stoughton, 1989), pp. 60–61.

25 Green, pp. 222, 229; Angela Du Maurier, *It's Only the Sister: An Autobiography* (London: Peter Davies, 1951), p. 77ff.

26 Angela Du Maurier, p. 6.

27 Daphne Du Maurier, pp. 52–53.

28 Virginia Stephen, Journal, 25 January 1905, Virginia Woolf, *A Passionate Apprentice: The Early Journals 1897–1909*, ed. Mitchell A. Leaska (London: Hogarth, 1990), pp. 227–28.

11. 'A love that is real': Children's Responses to Wendy

VALENTINA BOLD

Dear "Wendy",
    After having been to see Peter Pan and your wonderful acting I
feel as though I can never be happy unless I am watching it [...] You
[...] acted so well that you made people think that the love between
you and Peter Pan was real. I wish you would tell me whether it was.[1]

The quotation above, from a letter by fourteen-year-old Kenneth Morrison,
dated 31 December 1911, expresses the emotional impact of *Peter Pan* for its
first child audiences. Equally, it suggests the lasting impact the play had for
them. This chapter explores a set of twenty-three letters, written by twenty-
one correspondents, including Morrison, to Hilda Trevelyan, the first
'Wendy'. Written between 1906 and 1918, they are at once intimate, and
intensely personal, reflecting a characteristic which Nina Auerbach has
identified in the theatre of the previous century as a form of 'collaborative'
storytelling, between audience and theatre, creating a medium through
which 'audiences understood the world'.[2] There is certainly blurring of
personal and external experience, then, in the children's minds, probably
related to their developmental stage; for the youngest writers, in particular,
there is a sense that the actors' gaze is directed outwards, just as theirs is
directed towards the stage. For the older correspondents, particularly those
already in their teens, there is more of a direct admiration for the actress
and, in several cases, a desire to emulate her creation through their own
creativity. Arguably, they also respond to the 'liminal' connotations Paul
Fox has noted in Wendy: she 'role-plays the mother of the Lost Boys at
Peter's behest, remaining capable of comprehending Neverland in childish
delight, yet knowing her delight is childish'.[3] This might explain why the
children here identify with an adult actress depicting a child rather than,
for instance, the child actors who played other members of the Darling
family. The letters show, in short, how disbelief can be suspended in theatre
audiences – in several cases, beyond the duration of the act of theatregoing.

These children, it seems, have the ability to connect with actors in a way which is very direct and, in some cases, might even be transformational.[4]

Broad characteristics can be identified among the correspondents. Around two-thirds are girls, one-third boys; they are aged between six and eighteen (most at the younger end of that range) and so, it seems, within the final years of 'belief' in figures such as the Tooth Fairy or Santa Claus. The nature of their responses is very characteristic of their age. In *Developing Response to Fiction*, Robert Protherough observes that 'at the primary stage or early in the secondary school pupils may respond to novels in such terms as these: "It was the best book I've ever read, and I'm going to read it right through again"'; Protherough also observes that younger children generally envisage fiction 'in terms of a direct relationship between their own lives and the imagined life of the book', with a sense of 'total immersion'. In effect, it can be seen that the youngest correspondents are writing directly to Wendy; the older to Hilda Trevelyan, conspiratorially considering her part in creating the play. All Protherhough's observations are very visible in the letters considered here.[5]

The majority of the correspondents live in the English Home Counties, although one is from Edinburgh (with connections to the performers) and one County Clare (from a highly literary family). There are families from all over Britain, who have seen the play in its various locations: London (in the majority of cases), Liverpool, Oxford, Manchester and Edinburgh for instance. Most, like the Darlings, are middle to upper class, from elite (in one case aristocratic) backgrounds. *Peter Pan*, then, is seen within the context of being a suitable entrée to the cultured world of the theatre: a Christmas treat for the privileged which would become something close to a *rite de passage* – in Ashley Dukes' 1923 *The Youngest Drama*, seven-year-old twins are paraded around Kensington by their mother as exceptional among their age and class, for disliking *Peter Pan*.[6] I have found some biographical information about some of the children, at the time of their writing and subsequently. Some perhaps drew lasting inspiration from the play – at least one went to sea; others were as independently minded as their Wendy or aspired to the professional prowess of Trevelyan. I hope I have treated their letters with respect: I am conscious of having enjoyed a rare privilege in reading private mail which has allowed me to share, by proxy, the experience of the youngest, and earliest, audiences for *Peter Pan*.

Because there will be living people who may remember the writers as adults, I have not included exact addresses, except in a few specific cases where I hope this may allow the identification of family members or friends, without compromising confidentiality.[7]

The letters are, as might be expected, inherently childish in their composition and production. Many are on their parents' headed paper; they are full of spelling errors, and some are in capitals; they include long lines of hugs and kisses. Several have inclusions: a picture of the family dog, or a poem. Key scenes are mentioned repeatedly – Wendy darning stockings, Wendy flying – along with specific lines: 'I *do* believe in fairies'; the reference in the play to 'thimbles'. These children remember specific details, too, of the performance, including its costumes. Daphne Moss, for instance, in a short missive from South West London remarks:

> My dear Wendy
>   you acted the best i think you Flew very well. i think you looked very pretty in that little brown hat.
>   ~~Your~~ house was very prety
>   You are very pretty
>   Do you not think Tinker Bell was very rude to Peter Pan?
>   ~~Do~~ Did you like ~~P~~ Peter Pan? i can think ~~not~~ of nothing but you ~~as~~ and Peter Pan.
>   Your nana was very nice.
>   When i am in bed i alweys [*sic*] think you and Peter Pan are coming in after me.
>   Love from DAPHNE Moss[?]
>   XXXXXXX (ff. 121–22)

Arthur Coventry, wrote to 'Wendy' from Chippenham, aged nine, in a letter stamped Tuesday Feb 9 [?1911]. Coventry thought Trevelyan 'did the part very well indeed' and particularly liked her 'brown dress with the brown bonnet with the holly on it', as did several other children. This child went on to have real adventures at sea, as Captain Arthur Beauclerk Coventry (1900–1971). Born in Wiltshire, he was the youngest child of Henry Robert Beauclerk Coventry and Lady Mary Muriel Sophie Howard, daughter of the eighteenth Earl of Suffolk. He served in the Royal Navy and was decorated with the Distinguished Service Cross and an OBE.[8] He had given his attention to the stagecraft in the performance, as well as to Wendy, and notes that 'I have read the book of peter pan so many times over that I can say it all off by heart'. He had considered, too, the relative importance of the character of Wendy within the play, showing his conceptual melding of actress and character by his use of the second person in his analysis: 'I like you much better than Peter and I thought you flew so well. I wish I could fly. I did think tootles was horrid to try and shoot you, I have been talking about you ever since I came home. I thought you looked so sweet when you sat darning the stockings in the underground Home'. He hoped, too, 'you will be in the play next year'. (ff. 129–30)

All of these writers express an intensely felt love for Wendy, described in more than one as 'darling', 'mother' and friend. Writing from Brondesbury, for instance, the eight-year-old Mary Allison (her surname is illegible), including a charming picture of a bunch of flowers, after demanding 'Tell Piter [sic] I do believe in fairies *always*' – addresses 'Darling little Wendy' as 'a lovely little Mother to the lost boys'. She adds:

> I am nearly eight but I am not such a good little mother to my children in my beautiful Dolls house it is all covered with roses and creeper [sic] I wish you could fly and see me. I go to school every Day and to Dancing on Thursday. I wish Petter [sic] could fly into our nursery window. I went to see you on Monday afternoon and should love to come every day and please give my best love to Petter [sic] and all the lost boys specially to little Michael.
>
> Lots of love and kisses to you from annother [sic] little mother. (f. 150)

In this instance, evidently, the character is the focus of admiration. These children 'adore' Wendy. Several have seen Trevelyan perform more than once, in *Peter Pan* and other plays, particularly Barrie's. Writing from Edinburgh, Oona Macpherson addresses 'My dear Wendy' directly, and notes a canine link, along with her family's theatrical connections:

> We have a dog called Toy. He is exactly like 'Nana'. I enclose a photograph of him and Mummy and me. When you come here, will you

come and see him? Daddy was at Oxford with Mr Bourchier, and when he was here some time ago we had him and Mrs Bourchier to supper. They *are* nice. I have seen 'Peter Pan' five times, three times this year and twice the year before. We all love it. Yours affectionately.

The letter refers to the English actor/manager Arthur Bourchier (1868–1927) whose wife, Violet (1867–1942) was the sister of Irene Vanbrugh. Irene, who also worked with Bourchier, had her first major role in *Ibsen's Ghost* (1891) with others including Lady Mary in *The Admirable Crichton* (1902); she also performed, like Trevelyan, for Dion Boucicault. Despite this access to information about the actress, the child is obviously focussed on the characters, even equating a performed dog with her own canine companion.

The writers' shared love for Wendy is expressed in language typical of this period. The actress is 'simply sweet' and 'ripping', for instance, in a letter written on 30 December 1910. Many of its features (admiration for Wendy; recall of her dresses, a desire to know the actress personally, while a coyness about approaching her) are characteristic of the others:

Dear Miss Trevelyan

I do hope you will not be angry at me writing to you. I am twelve years old, and I admire you very much. I have seen you in Peter Pan, What every woman knows, & A Single Man. You are simply sweet in all of them. I am making a collection of postcards of all the plays I have been too [sic] [&?] I have 900. Your cards are on the first page, I would like to be able to have a card signed by you, so would you please autograph this card. We are going to Peter Pan this year but it will not be the same without the darling little Wendy we all know & admire so much. I am begging Mother to take me to see you again, because you fascinate me so. I say you did look ripping in that sweet dress. My chief ambition is to know you, but as I never shall I must be content to go and see you from the stalls. I am sending you an addressed envelope as you must be so busy, so if you have time one day to sign my postcard. Nobody knows I am writing to you, not even my mother. Now I must close as we are going to 'the Piper' at the St James's. With lots of love from your ever devoted Slave & admirer. Lita. Who adores you. (ff. 125–26)

Lita (there is no further information although, from a realisation that she shall never know her 'darling' Wendy, she is one of the older correspondents) is one of the most ardent and sophisticated theatre-goers, her collection of memorabilia witnessing her fascination with performers and performance and a knowing admiration for Trevelyan as Wendy.

Other writers make straightforward expressions of fandom for Wendy, rather than specifically Trevelyan. Joyce McLeod, from Eastcote House, Pinner, for example, writes simply in January 1912: 'Dear Wendy / Don't go away from Peter Pan. / Love from Joyce McLeod / PS. One of my Eastcote favourite Teddy Bears went to Peter Pan today' (ff. 134–35). Joyce was the daughter of Charles Campbell McLeod, who rented the house and grounds from R. H. Deane at this time.[9] 'Marjorie', writing on 22 February 1907 in capital letters, simply asks, 'DEAR WENDY / WILL YOU PLEASE WRITE YOUR NAME ON THIS POSTCARD FOR ME? WITH LOVE' (f. 117). Similarly, Ruth Russell, writing from Skipton, near Liverpool, in 1906, states simply: 'My dear Wendy, / I came went to see you & Peter on Saturday. I DO LOVE YOU MY NAME IS Ruth Russell do write to me please Love Ruth Russell / You dear little Mother / XXXX. (f. 115)

Six-year-old Hugh Bridson, writing in 1907, goes one step further in his aim to be close to his 'darling' Wendy, whom he has seen performing '**three** times'; 'you act *very, very nicely*': 'I like you *so* much I would like to *marry you*. I hope you are not going to marry anybody else, because **I** want to marry you'. His mother (Mrs J. C. Bridson) is amenable, apparently – 'she *would* like to have you for her daughter-in-law', and his ten and a half year old sister, Dickie, is also 'very, very fond of you'. Writing from Lathbury House, Oxford – he gives his address so that his respondent will 'know where to write to' – Hugh asks her address, and says his mother 'will ask you to come + see me some time'. He finishes by asking 'Please give my best love to Peter, & tell him I hope he is quite well. Pleas [*sic*] give my love to M^r and Mrs Darling'. This letter is signed with many hugs and kisses, with a promise of '9,000,000,000' more (f. 118). The family appears in the 1911 census, with Hugh's year of birth as 1901; it is possible they are part of the Ridgway Bridson family – Hugh was a family name for them – who are later linked to the family of Tony Blair.[10]

Trevelyan (1880–1959) does seem to have been the sort of performer worthy of such passionate responses. Some background information is useful in understanding the children's reactions. She had moved in similar circles to Barrie, although he did not know her before casting her as Wendy. Her name appears regularly in theatrical records as a jobbing actress, usually in musical and comic theatre, from the age of nineteen onwards. She first features on the playbills of 1898 in *Trelawny of the 'Wells'*, a comic operetta by A. W. Pinero, at the Court Theatre, which ran for 140 performances, fairly far down the bill as one of three actresses listed for 'Avoninia Bunn'. More prominent members of the cast – particularly relevant to *Peter Pan* – include Gerald Du Maurier as Ferdinand Gadd, and Dion C. Boucicault as Vice-Chancellor Sir William Gower and Director.[11] Trevelyan appears again several times, for instance in Eille Norwood's *The Talk of the Town* (a revised version of *The Noble Art*) which ran for forty-five performances at the Strand from August 1901, again in a minor role (Winifred Tiverton) (1/168). In the musical play *A Chinese Honeymoon* at the Strand, with libretto by George Dance, that same year in May, which ran for 1071 performances, she was one of the three actresses in the role of 'Fi Fi' (1/193). Later in the year, she had climbed the bill for *Two Little Vagabonds* by George R. Sims and Arthur Shirley, a melodrama at the Princess's (an adaptation of Pierre Decourcelle), which had twenty-one performances from October, as Dick, in a smaller cast of five starring Ernest Leicester and Alfred Ibberton (1/99). Other roles prior to Wendy included that of Henrietta in Cosmo Gordon Lennox's adaptation of *Coralie et Cie, The Little French Milliner* (2/41), and Girl in Fred Wright and Hubert S. Ryan's *The Wicked Uncle*, both at the Avenue in 1902 (2/52), Marie (alongside her future husband Sydney Blow as Billy) in Walter Sapte's *The Crammers or a Short Vacation* at the Strand in 1903 (3/137), and then, as mentioned, Amanda Afflick in Frederick Fenn and Richard Pryce's *'Op-O-Me-Thumb* in 1904 (4/51) at the Court and then St James (4/73). In the same year she was Daisy at the Strand in Hall and Lehmann's *Sergeant Bruce*, a musical farce (4/124), and the little Marchioness in an operetta by B. W. Findon, based on *The Old Curiosity Shop, The Marchioness*, at His Majesty's (4/142).

Although she had toured in Barrie's *The Little Minister* in 1899, Barrie had not seen Trevelyan act then. He scouted her when he was casting *Peter Pan*'s inaugural 1904 season at the Duke of York's theatre. According to Trevelyan's husband, the actor and writer Sydney Blow (1878–1961), Sir John Hare, who was then touring *Little Mary* and *'Op o' my thumb*, persuaded

Barrie to see this versatile young actress in the latter play. She was unaware of his presence until the end of the performance but, several days later, received an invitation to the Duke of York's to meet Dion Boucicault. Boucicault engaged her for the play – then unknown to her – with an enigmatic first call to 'Rehearsal – 10.30 for Flying'. Blow describes the rehearsal experience as both active, and somewhat baffling:

> That morning, after putting on a harness, she was instructed how to fly across the stage by a Mr. Kirby. Then she had to be insured against accidents. It certainly was a most odd play. She heard that there was to be a crocodile and wolves and mermaids in it and during her flying rehearsal the stage-manager loudly called out, 'Will all the pirates please go into the stalls.' So not only a crocodile, wolves and mermaids, there were to be pirates as well! A little later another command rang over the stage: 'Will all the Indians please go into the stalls.' It was all very bewildering.

The actors were sworn to secrecy about the effects, in an effort to maintain the surprise of 'a bit of whimsey and true Barrie' on the opening night.[12]

Despite this, arguably, rather detached introduction, after the opening night of December 27 1904, the play ran at the Duke of York's for 145 performances. Trevelyan played Wendy over 900 times; Barrie considered her 'incomparable' and his regard, and affection, for the actress is seen in a letter of 12 February 1911, written in condolence for the loss of her mother: 'I don't need to tell you to be brave, for you have been it too long to change. You are always a pleasant thought to me, I respect you so much.' She has been described as a 'joy' to see and 'the ideal Wendy', alongside Nina Boucicault as Peter Pan, Gerald Du Maurier as Mr Darling and Captain Hook, and Dorothea Baird as Mrs Darling. Her success, however, was initially a surprise to the writer and director, as Blow comments:[13]

> Neither Boucicault nor even Barrie knew then what Hilda was going to do to the part. I don't think Barrie realised what a good part 'Wendy' really was [...] I am sure he never saw the laugh she was going to get when she told Peter he was 'frightfully fascinating'. Bit

by bit Hilda built up the part of 'Wendy' as she rehearsed [...] The ones that saw those first years of 'Peter Pan' have never forgotten her 'Wendy' [...] I hear it so often. They all loved 'Wendy'.[14]

Blow's account of responses to the play is both witty, and revealing: 'After the Christmas seasons of "Peter" when the children had to go back to boarding-school, the furniture vans of Messrs. Heals, Maples and Harrods would drive up to many, many houses to collect beds that had been broken [...] because the late occupants had all tried to learn to fly like Michael and John'; equally, 'the Post Office was always kept pretty busy during the "Peter Pan" Christmas seasons. Girls had to write letters to "Peter" and boys to "Wendy"' [although the evidence in this chapter shows that girls could write to Wendy as well]. '"Hook" never got any letters, not even an envelope with a hiss enclosed in it.'[15] Although I have been unable to see any of Trevelyan's responses, incidentally – readers' information would be very welcome – manuscript references show she did reply.

Perhaps one of the most key, and yet elusive, questions to consider with these letters is to whom the children's letters are actually addressed. Although many of the child correspondents appreciate that Wendy 'acts' a part, they have little notion what this means. It is difficult to know, in most instances, whether they think they are writing to a real 'Wendy' or a made-up theatrical character or (as is sometimes clear) to the actress. In the majority of letters, there is no sense of distance; and most relate to 'Wendy' as if she is another child. For example, in one undated letter, 'Dear Wendy, / Thank you very much for the Post Card you sent me. When is your Birthday. I hope you had a happy Xmas, up a tree. I went to a party Yesterday and got two Whistles. I send you lots of thimbles. / With love from Findlay Rea' (f. 160). A mother writes, on an undated envelope addressed to 'Wendy': 'Our small daughter saw you this other day in Peter Pan & it was her wish to write to you after. She is under the impression that you are a little girl of her own age' (f. 146). This is followed by a letter, perhaps from the child in question, or possibly unrelated, from Shepherd's Bush, dated January 26. This little girl, whose name is difficult to read (perhaps Frcs – Frances? – or possibly Tris), like several others, had been to the play more than once, and had thought about the implications of the plot line, and Wendy's behaviour:

My darling Wendy,

We were at the theatre last night. And what a sweet little mummy you were to the Faries [*sic*]. We had a box near the stage and some times you came quite near us. I hope you will excuse my writing in pencil but mummy does not like us writing in ink when we are writing on our own because we spoil our frocks. What a lot of children Mrs Darling had when she adopted the Faries [*sic*] this is the second time we have been and we have been in the same box so I hope we shall come again

With love and kisses from your loving friend (f. 147–48)

As implied above, there is an implicit idea that the Darlings, and Peter, inhabit the theatre and, linked to this, a sense of the possibility of access to them between shows. More than one writer asks if they can visit them at the Theatre, or suggests they could come out to tea. For instance, in a letter addressed to 'Miss Wendy Darling, Duke of York's Theatre, St. Martin's Lane, London W', written in February 1915, Sheila Spurrier writes, 'My Dear Wendy / I came to Peter Pan the other day I am a little girl you don't know came in the thing you were in they were so pretty will you come to tea next Sunday about 3-3-0 our house is 11 Woodlands Road Barnes with love from Sheila Spurrier' (ff. 139–40). Her parents were probably Lancashire-born Arthur Spurrier (1866–1941), and Florence (b. Newcastle 1867). He became Director of Leyland Motors and London Central Omnibus Company and is listed at this address in the 1911 census. His obituary appeared in *The Times* on 15 November 1941.

Similarly, there is a brief undated message on a postcard, from Denise du Cros, of Canon's Park, Edgeware: 'Please Wendie [*sic*] could you come to tea with me, and please will you come as Wendy you can come tomorrow if you can' (f. 149). This little girl, born in Staines in 1901, came from a prominent family who, at the time of writing, were at the peak of their prosperity. She was the fourth child, and third daughter, of Sir Arthur Philip Du Cros (1871–1955), the first baronet of this title, and his first wife, Maude Gooding (whom he divorced in 1923). He was a successful businessman, who had developed the Dunlop Rubber Company, and a Conservative member of parliament (between 1908 and 1918 for Hastings; later Clapham). His personal wealth was such that during the First World War he financed three motor ambulance convoys, and he was a patron of the arts too. Denise's childhood home at Canons, originally owned by the first Duke of Chandos, and bought by Sir Arthur in the 1890s, was magnificent, with extensive grounds; Sir Arthur added notable terraces, designed by C. E. Mallows. Other properties included Craigweil House in Bognor Regis, where George V stayed during his convalescence in 1929. Du Cros, however, was dogged by controversy. In 1913, his home at St Leonard's, Hastings, was burnt down by suffragettes; in 1929 his company, Parent Trust and Finance, lost £3 million during linked criminal fraud proceedings. Canons Park was then sold to cover the debts and bought by North London Collegiate School. Sir Arthur was married three times, divorcing Denise's mother in a well-reported case. Despite the comfortable existence she must have enjoyed at the time of writing, then, this little girl's family went through, and would go through, difficult times. She married in 1923 but divorced in 1927, with a dispute over the paternity of her child.[16] It is tempting to think of her love of Wendy as a calm point amidst a sometimes tempestuous life.

Seeing *Peter Pan* was certainly a big occasion, starting with the journey to the theatre, and usually continuing to tea. The friendliness of address reflects the intimacy such a fulfilling encounter engendered, to 'my dear' Wendy. Rex Hayward, for instance, an eight year old writing from Cheadle, Cheshire (probably in 1906), expresses deep tenderness, showing how the enjoyment of *Peter Pan* in the theatre fits his comfortable life:

> My dear Wendy
> We did so like seeing you and Peter Pan on Tuesday afternoon, especially the Nursery scenes. We went out to luncheon and then we five children and M^r and Mrs Mosley motored to the Theatre. Then we had tea in Manchester and motored home afterwards. Will you come to tea on Sunday? Please do because I want to see you and show you my horses and my parrot. Do come because I am eight years old and we are going to a school called Street Court at Westgate. With best love to you all, I am your loving Rex W. Hayward. (ff. 113–14)

There is a familiarity in the invitation to tea and in the phrase 'you and Peter Pan' which is both touching and intriguing – is the reference to the character or the play; is the 'and' a synonym for 'in'?). The piece expresses, in addition, a loving picture of Edwardian life which would soon be shattered, too suddenly, by the First World War.

At least one child writes from boarding school. Aileen Edwards (her full name Aileen Dorothy de Lacheur Edwards) was born in 1897 and her family home was in Hampstead. She was a pupil at Roedean, in Brighton, between 1908 and 1914, and is mentioned in the *Roedean School Magazine* for competing in a gymnastic competition in 1910 and, in 1912 and 1913, for passing music examinations. She wrote from Junior House[17] there, in an undated letter presumably of around 1910 or 1911. She writes thanking Trevelyan for sending her autograph and expressing her love for the theatre and of theatricality:

> I have been to Peter Pan four times and am going this year again. I have been to What Every Woman knows once. I simply adore both of them. We have just been dancing the lancers to Peter Pan[']s music. It will be so sad with out [*sic*] you as Wendy I hope they wont [*sic*] have a terrible person instead I am eleven years old. Sorry I have made a smear. Much love (f. 152)

The evocative description she gives here, of dancing, and that personal attachment to Trevelyan in the role, perhaps reflects the appeal of Edwardian performance style. As Joseph Donohue has noted, despite the shift from the overtly emotional presentation favoured in Victorian theatre both shared, a 'gestural basis [...] a unitary concept of effective acting – namely, that it required, as Hamlet profoundly phrased it, "the motive and the cue for passion".[18] The reference to music, too, is revealing, as a powerful aspect of stagecraft. Russell Jackson is not alone is stating that, as well as 'mood and atmosphere', and 'characterization', music can have a powerful emotional effect in its dramatic contexts: 'music may also work at a subconscious level to make audiences more susceptible to extraordinary situations onstage' as part of the staging whole.[19]

Several children show a keen interest in the theatre. Myles Anthony Murphy, for instance, followed the progress of the play, writing to 'Dear Wendy, / I hope that you are well, that you like playing in Glasgow. I have been looking at photographs of yourself and like them very much. Please come back to London as soon as you can, because I would like to see you again. With best wishes and a big thimble / I remain, Dear Mother Wendy, Ever yours Affectionately (f. 155). Similarly, Eva Marie Thompson, of Lancaster Cottage, in the pretty Buckinghamshire village of Chesham Bois, feels a kindred spirit in Trevelyan, as a fellow actor. She wrote to Wendy first on 18 February 1910:

> My Dear dear Wendy
>   I am writing you a little letter to tell you that I think you acted the best you looked a little darling with that pretty cherry cap on.
>   I came to see you act on the fifth of January and I am sure you acted best that day.
>   I must tell you that I am a little actress after I acted as Vedainte a wiced [*sic*] Fairy in a play called Santa Claus. I had to have a great big bunchy white dress with a wand which had a red light in it that meant that I was dangerous.
>   Dear wendy I wonder if you have time to write me a little note I would so like one
>   I must close
>   I am Dear Wendy your loving
>   Eva Marie Thomson. (ff. 123–24)

Eva was probably the daughter of Henry Sewell Thompson, listed in Lancaster Cottage in the 1911 and 1915 *Kelly's* directories.[20] Trevelyan evidently responded, kindly, to her message; the child wrote again, a year later, on 8 January 1911; her intellectual development (and the spelling of her name) has progressed in the meantime. At this point, too – and unusually for the set of letters considered here – the child is well aware of the distinction between actress and role:

> My Dear Wendy (Miss Trevelyan),
>   I am sorry you are not Wendy this year. I am sure Peter will miss you.
>   I wrote to you last year & I was very pleased when you answered my letter. There is no picture of you in Home Notes you look very pretty you have got pretty red berries in your hair & on your dress

Do you like acting in a 'Single Man' with Nancy Price? I have seen a picture of her.

Are you going to act Wendy again? I hope you do.

I hope you will have time for a little reply.

I am

your little admirer

Eva Thompson

PS. Two Thimbles for you.

PPS. I acted at a Concert a little while ago as a beggar-maid.

I had to sing two solos. (f. 127)

While letters like Eva Thompson's show *Peter Pan* woven into the fabric of a happy, and stimulating, childhood, not all the correspondents, as already seen, were so fortunate; it seems Wendy's mothering characteristics could offer a perceived consolation in the face of loss. There is a heartbreaking example from County Clare, initially from Ennistyman House, which is scored out and replaced in pencil with Doolin House. On 18 August (year unknown), Suzette Majolier writes:

My dear Wendy

Thank you so much for writing your name in my birthday book and signin [sic] your postcard. Do you collect postcards. I do, if you like any sort spestually [sic] I would love to send you some. Have you a mummy. I have not. I have a nurse. I would like you for my mummy but daddy says you don't want me and he would not let me go and of course I don't want to leave him but I would like you to write letters like one.

I think it was very sweet of you being so sweet to me. Do you like being Wendy better than anything with lots of love and XXXXXXXXXXX' (ff. 161–62)

The writer was a member of the Majolier family who were related to the well-known artistic Macnamaras, profiled in Nicolette Devas's *Two Flamboyant Fathers*, who lived at both Ennistymon House, and Doolin House, County Clare.[21] Henry Valentine Macnamara was shot in the face and arms during the War of Independence in 1919 and, in 1922, the Óglaigh na hÉireann confiscated Ennistymon House as a barracks, and burnt down the Doolin house; Macnamara left for London and never returned. His son Francis (1886–1946) was a poet, whose daughter Caitlin married Dylan Thomas; guests at Doolin during the time Suzette would have known it included J. M. Synge, George Bernard Shaw and Augustus John. Francis later converted Ennistymon House into the Falls Hotel, selling it as a business in 1946.

Some children were inspired to creativity themselves, enclosing poetry with their letters. M. R., in a letter addressed to Miss Hilda Trevelyan at the Duke of York's Theatre, and postmarked 14 January 1912 (f. 136), encloses the following:

> TO Wendy
> How we all adore her in the fairy "Peter Pan"
> In the charming part of Wendy
> Lovely, sweet & dainty span,
> Dont we frantically admire her,
> As she plays it on & on.
> Tweeny also, she is charming,
> Rather different though to Wendy,
> Ever Beautifull [sic] in all things,
> Very Sweet & very tender,
> Every one seems just to love her;
> Lovely, Dearest, little Wendy,Years may go but we shall
> Alter our opinion of her never,
> No we shall love her forever on,
> & on, & on, for ever.
> M. R. (ff. 137–38)

Among those who send poems are some of the older correspondents. Gertrude Sullens, for instance, writing from 47 Par Avenue, Wood Green on 3 February 1918, offers an 'Acrostic on your name – of the actress, rather than the character, here – with best wishes for a Happy Birthday, and many thanks for some of the most delightful afternoons of my life' (f. 145). There is a woman of this name listed in the 1911 census as a resident of Middlesex living with her parents Emily (b. 1854) and James (b. 1854), along with Kenneth, presumably her brother (b. 1880). Gertrude was born in 1885. The poem is, reflecting the age of the correspondent, accomplished, and typed:

> Her tiny feet can make their way
> Into our hearts wth steps way
> Life's cares and fears so swift all fly away,
> Dull clouds of doubt "as to lift", [22]
> And on time's clock she turns the hands
> Till we are 'striking twelve' again
> Renews the hour glass 'lasting sands:-
> Expurging years of toil and pain
> Venus, forsooth! What thing so cold
> Encroaching years could thus dislodge
> Letting us, with fresh 'days of old',
> Youth's Pace enter, 'on the dodge'
> Ah! May Life's Balls of fair delight
> Ne'er fair to bring her her 'Invite'. (f. 144)

This, perhaps, reflects an affection born through seeing earlier versions of the play.

Other poetic enclosures include the following, from an anonymous admirer, addressed – indicating, as with the previous piece, that (evidently) older children most actively understood the difference between actress and character – 'To Miss Hilda Trevelyan':

> Good Western Winds
> Whose luck it is
> (Made rivale with the aire)
> To Give sweet Hilda's lip a kiss,
> And fan her wanton haire.
> Bring me but one I'll promise thee
> (Instead of Common showers,
> Thy wings shall be embalmed by me
> (And all beset with flowers)
> (adapted from RH).

The Greatest Night of the 4th Year
For Wendy Darling
From a Pittite who has spent ever so many delightful hours in her
'artfully fascinating' company with a row of footlights & many rows
of stalls in between.
Front Row Middle of the Pit (ff. 155–56)

While some of the letters, particularly those from the older correspondents, profess a regard for Wendy's professional competence, they all demonstrate an immense affection – implicitly preferring Wendy to Peter. The letter quoted at the start, from Kenneth Morrison (an older writer at fourteen), however, considers Wendy as part of the whole; he thought her a 'splendid mother' but liked Pauline Chase as Peter; it was their combination that made love seem 'real'. He asks for autographs from Trevelyan and Chase, pardoning himself for being 'ungentlemanly' or 'impertinent': 'if you knew how fascinated I was with your play, you would not blame me'; 'I shall *never never* forget Peter Pan and Wendy'. This boy, on the verge of growing up himself, is possibly, like Peter, reluctant to leave the pleasures of the play behind. The letter, written on New Year's Eve, concludes:

> I think it is the most sweet and beautiful play I have ever seen or ever hope to see. I think you make a splendid mother, and I think it must be 'fascinating' to act in it […] I have a boy friend considerably smaller than myself whom I love better than anyone in the world except my parents and perhaps the thought of Peter Pan and Wendy which I am sure I shall never forget.
>
> Please write and tell me whether your love for Peter Pan ('Miss Pauline Chase') is real, I should so love to know […] Please remind Miss Chase to write to me also.
>
> P.P.P.S Even if neither of you reply as I scarcely hope you to I shall *never never* forget Peter Pan and Wendy (ff. 132–33)

This correspondent, as can be seen, shows an unusual awareness both of Trevelyan's privilege in portraying a 'fascinating' part, and of the relationship between her character and Peter's, as acted by Chase.

Trevelyan/Wendy's child audiences offer a range of responses to the play, experiencing the play and its captivating actress in particular age-related ways. For the younger, they are at a special age when fiction and fact are not fully distinguished and, of course, during the heightened pleasure of their Christmastime, offer a rare insight into the precise responses of *Peter Pan*'s first audiences. They want to know the actress, to invite 'Wendy' to tea and to enjoy, again, the happy, emotive feelings brought out by this spectactular event, as Morrison described. The older respondents are more interested in the actress and the part, understanding the distinction between (beloved) artifice and art. All, however, in writing to the 'mother' and friend they perceive in Wendy, exhibit a love that is real, at least for the duration of their memories, and certainly for the duration of their childhoods.

Notes

1   'Miscellaneous Letters', NLS MS 9755, f. 131. All references to manuscript letters which follow are given in brackets after each letter, and refer to this volume. I am grateful to the National Library of Scotland for permission to quote from it and, in particular, to Sally Harrower for drawing my attention to these letters during the 2010 conference in Dumfries which was the starting point for this book. I wrote in brief about them in the NLS's magazine *Discover* (Winter 2011) in 'Letters from the Lost Boys and Girls', p. 29.

2   Nina Auerbach, 'Before the Curtain', in Kerry Powell, ed. *The Cambridge Companion to Victorian and Edwardian Theatre* (Cambridge: Cambridge University Press, 2004), p. 4.

3   Paul Fox, 'The Time of His Life: Peter Pan and the Decadent Nineties', in *J. M. Barrie's Peter Pan. In and Out of Time: A Children's Classic at 100*, ed. Donna R. White and C. Anita Tarr (Lanham, Maryland: The Scarecrow Press, 2006), p. 26.

4   Child actors like Nellie Bowman, for instance, appeared in *Peter Pan* between 1906–1910, as part of a four-child acting family; see Anne Varty, *Children and Theatre in Victorian Britain: 'All Work, No Play'* (Basingstoke: Palgrave Macmillan, 2008), p. 9.

5   Robert Protherough, *Developing Response to Fiction* (Milton Keynes: Open University Press, 1983), pp. 9, 21. I would like to thank my colleague Anne Ferguson, programme convenor of Primary Education, for drawing my attention to this text.

6   Ashley Dukes, *The Youngest Drama. Studies of Fifty Dramatists* (London, 1923), p. 10.

7   I have made every effort to contact the families of the original writers and would be grateful for further information; I can be contacted at: **valentina.bold@glasgow.ac.uk**

8   Arthur Coventry is listed in the 1911 census records, and there is further information on him and his career at **www.thepeerage.com**. See Charles Mosley (ed.), *Burke's Peerage, Baronetage and Knightage*, (Wilmington, Delaware: *Burke's Peerage*, 2003), vol. 1, p. 932.

9   I am grateful to the Ruislip, Northwood and Eastcote Local History Society, and in particular its chairman, Eileen Bowlt, secretary, Susan Toms, and to Karen Spink for their generous assistance in finding information on the McLeod family. Lesley Crowcroft, who

is involved in a current bid alongside Hillingdon Council to raise funding to restore the remaining Tudor Building at Eastcote House Gardens, was also immensely helpful; there are photographs of the house and garden at **www.eastcotehousegardens.weebly.com**

10 I would like to thank Stella Wentworth of Oxfordshire Libraries for confirming the presence of the Bridson family in the census records of 1901 and 1911 at Lathbury House, and drawing my attention to additional records relating to the family at Oxford Central Library. See too **www.boltonsmayors.org.uk/tree-bridson-t-r.pdf**

11 See J. P. Wearing (ed.), *The London Stage 1890–1899. A Calendar of Plays and Players*, 2 vols, (Metuchen, NJ: The Scarecrow Press, 1986), 98/6. All references to Trevelyan's performances which follow are to this work and appear in brackets within the text, in the format used therein giving year of production followed by item number.

12 Sydney Blow, *Through Stage Doors. Or Memories of Two in the Theatre* (Edinburgh; Chambers, 1958), p. 163.

13 *Letters of J. M. Barrie*, ed. Viola Meynell (London: Peter Davies, 1942), p. 57. See also H. M. Walbrook, *J. M. Barrie and the Theatre* (London: F. V. White, 1922), p. 101; A. E. Wilson, *Edwardian Theatre* (London: Arthur Barker, 1951), p. 149.

14 Blow, p. 163.

15 Blow, p. 163.

16 See the entry by G. K. S. Hamilton-Edwards, rev. Geoffrey Jones, on Sir Arthur Philip Du Cros in the *Oxford Dictionary of National Biography*, accessed online in May 2013; further information is taken from the Canons' Park Estate website **www.cpea.org.uk/ history.htm**. Du Cros's *Wheels of Fortune* (London: Chapman & Hall, 1938) profiles the history of the pneumatic tyre and those who pioneered it. I am grateful to Myra Stephens, of the Canons Park Estate Association, and Karen Morgan, the historian at North London Collegiate School, for their help in accessing information about the family and for providing me a useful copy of Grace Fuller's 'Canons & Du Cros in the spotlight' from *Optima* magazine of 28 May 2010, pp. 12–14 **www.optimamagazine.co.uk**

17 I am extremely grateful to Jackie Sullivan, the archivist at Roedean School, for this information about their former pupil.

18 Joseph Donohue, 'Actors and Acting', in Powell, ed. *The Cambridge Companion to Victorian and Edwardian Theatre*, p. 32.

19 Russell Jackson, 'Victorian and Edwardian Stagecraft', in Powell, ed. *The Cambridge Companion to Victorian and Edwardian Theatre* , p. 71.

20 I am grateful to Alison Bailey, of the Chesham Bois Council Local History Project, and to Cathy Wooveridge, clerk to the Parish Council, for finding information about Eva Thompson on my behalf, and for including an item in the Chesham Bois magazine, appealing to readers for further information. See also L. Elgar Pile, *A History of Chesham Bois* (1976), and *Chesham Bois – A Celebration of the Village and its History* (1999).

21 I am grateful to Peter Beirne of Clare County Library for providing information about the Majolier family. See also Nicolette Devas, *Two Flamboyant Fathers* (London: Collins, 1966).

22 I have been unable to locate the implied reference here, but it possibly alludes to the Browning lines, 'One who never turned his back but marched breast forward, / Never doubted clouds would break' in the 'Epilogue' to *Asolando* (1889). See *The Poetical Works of Robert Browning, Volume XV: Parleyings and Asolando*, ed. Stefan Hawlin and Michael Meredith (Oxford: Oxford University Press, 2009), p. 487.

12. Dumfries Academy: Responses to *Peter Pan*

HUGH McMILLAN

Just after the Moat Brae Trust was formed in Dumfries to preserve the house and garden that had, in Barrie's own words, inspired the story of Peter Pan, Flora Burns, then Deputy Head of Dumfries Academy, approached me with the idea of raising funds for the Trust by putting together an anthology of poetry from current students and staff of the school. It seemed a great idea, not just to raise a few quid but also to put down a marker about the kind of creative relationship that might exist between a revamped Moat Brae and the school next door: the continuation in a real sense of the relationship between Moat Brae and the imagination of one particular pupil nearly 150 years ago.

It was our hope that Moat Brae would not simply become some sort of museum or stop on the tourist trail but would continue to serve or stimulate creativity, and the use of the written word, especially in children. Few of the poems we received, on the theme of Neverland, were child-like. They spoke of and from a variety of topics, some highly contemporary and personal. Many of them were stunning and testimony to the depths we have and the need we have to express them, an ageless and timeless concern. I choose four to appear here, a sample, only. What talents there are! As the big money rolls in we should not lose sight of the greatest gifts of all.

The Lost Boy

I have no missing person posters
or parents waiting up
for a phone call
I was lost years ago
refusing the space I was in
determined to return to Neverland
to kiss the sky
one more time
We can fly me and the boys
on a severed track of veins
a bittersweet hallelujah needle
my ship will sail on the white powder line
Wendy grew old
when she was off the stuff
no more the crocodile smiles
when Hook got us hooked
You will not remember me
I am the boy
spaced out on a white wash wall
or twisted under a bridge
with my old purple tin
invincible in the land you cannot see
There are very few Tinkerbells here
but many lost boys.

Blossom McCuaig

Snowed In

Recently we've been captured
held hostage by snow
away from biros and dull monotony
dressed up as work.

In leggings shirts and scarves
we shirk in Neverland,
white as a flickering screen
a blank page that cries adventure.

Then reality calls a mutiny
the snow melts,
we're chased back to life
where we're all lost children
terrorised by the ticking crocodile.

Charlotte Singleton

Sunny Days

She wore her heart on her sleeve,
she made things hard to believe
as some children do.

Grow up, they squawked
as quietly she stalked
the simple pleasures of life.

The birds in the trees
the kiss of the honeybees
surrounded her, though she was never stung.

In Neverland
there was nothing bad or bland
nothing poisoned by the years

the need to panic about money
the hand to mouth as the sunny
days still shone in this girl's eyes.

The children who grew up too fast:
they were the first but not the last
to wish the childlike back.

Margaret Laurie

Neverland

Half forgotten words
turn coffee colour
dissolve to sepia nothings.
Breath is flowering in the mirror
fondant yellow, artificial,
bathing his face in the glow.
These eastern skies are vast,
star upon star.

The mirror's metal breath pools
into the room. Paper skin
jeweled with rubies,
crystals of unrequited love.
Star kissed gashes on
virgin skin breathe from tissue
to scream at him.

Tess Schmigylski

Notes on Contributors

Rosemary Ashton is Emeritus Quain Professor of English Language and Literature at University College London. She is the author of critical biographies of G. H. Lewes (1991), George Eliot (1996), Samuel Taylor Coleridge (1996), and Thomas and Jane Carlyle (2002), two studies in Anglo-German relations, *The German Idea* (1980) and *Little Germany: Exile and Asylum in Victorian England* (1986), and two studies of cultural and intellectual life in London, *142 Strand: A Radical Address in Victorian London* (2006) and *Victorian Bloomsbury* (2012).

Valentina Bold is Reader in Literature and Ethnology at the University of Glasgow, Dumfries, and Director of the interdisciplinary Solway Centre for Environment and Culture. Her books include an edition of *Robert Burns's Merry Muses of Caledonia* (2009), *James Hogg: A Bard of Nature's Making* (2007), and *Smeddum: A Lewis Grassic Gibbon Anthology* (2001). She is currently editing *The Brownie of Bodsbeck* for the Stirling/South Carolina edition of the complete works of James Hogg.

Anna Farkas is Assistant Professor of English Literature at the University of Regensburg (Germany). She received her DPhil from Magdalen College, Oxford, and is currently working on a monograph on British women's drama in the *fin de siècle*. She is the co-editor of *Interdisciplinary Perspectives on Aging in Nineteenth-Century Culture* (2013). Her research interests include British theatre history, law and literature, and J. M. Barrie's drama.

Paul Fox is an independent scholar whose research involves late nineteenth and early twentieth century Decadent aesthetics. He has published on a variety of Aesthetic, Decadent, and Edwardian writers, including Beerbohm, Huysmans, Pater, d'Annunzio, Machen, and J. M. Barrie. He is currently writing a monograph on the relationships existing between various conceits of temporality and the aesthetics of Decadence.

Douglas Gifford is Emeritus Professor and Honorary Senior Research Fellow at the University of Glasgow. He has written extensively on Scottish literature, especially on Scottish fiction from Scott to the present. He edited *Scottish Literature: Nineteenth Century* (AUP, 1988), *A History of Scottish Women's Writing* (EUP, 1997, with Dorothy McMillan), and *Scottish Literature in English and Scots* (EUP, 2002, with Dunnigan and McGillivray). He is Honorary Librarian of Walter Scott's Library at Abbotsford.

R. D. S. Jack is a Fellow of the Royal Society of Edinburgh and the English Association. He held the Chair of Medieval and Scottish Literature in Edinburgh University from 1987 until 2004. His books include *The Italian Influence on Scottish Literature* (1972) and *Patterns of Divine Comedy* (1989). He has published two books on Barrie, *The Road to the Never Land* (1991) and *Myths and the Mythmaker* (2010). He has recently edited *The Earliest Plays of J. M. Barrie* (2013).

Ralph Jessop teaches Literature and Philosophy at The University of Glasgow's School of Interdisciplinary Studies. A graduate of Glasgow and Cambridge, he is author of *Carlyle and Scottish Thought* (1997), and a number of papers on Carlyle. His more recent research involves philosophy of education and contestations of modernity as a transnational characteristic of Scottish intellectual history and British philosophy, literature, and art.

Margery Palmer McCulloch is Honorary Senior Research Fellow at the University of Glasgow and Leverhulme Emerita Fellow (2013–2015). She has written widely on Scottish literature, with particular interests in Scottish modernism and its international connections. Her most recent books include the monograph *Scottish Modernism and its Contexts 1918–1959* (EUP, 2009), and as co-editor *The Edinburgh Companion to Hugh MacDiarmid* (EUP, 2011), and *Scottish and International Modernisms* (ASLS, 2011). She co-edited *Scottish Literary Review* from 2005 to 2013.

Jan McDonald was the James Arnott Professor of Drama at the University of Glasgow from 1979 till her retirement in 2005. She is currently an Honorary Professorial Research Fellow and Dean of Faculties at that University. Her principal research interests lie in nineteenth- and early-twentieth-century theatre history and dramatic literature. She has also published on the work of contemporary Scottish women dramatists.

Hugh McMillan lives in Penpont. He has five full collections of poetry, the last three being *Thin Slice of Moon: selected and new poems* (Roncadora Press 2012). He has also published several pamphlets: *Postcards from the Hedge* won the Callum Macdonald Memorial Prize in 2009 and *After the Storm* was a winner in the Smith/Doorstep Poetry Prize. He is currently working on a commission from Wigtown Book Festival to write a book on contemporary visions of Dumfries and Galloway.

Jonathan Murray teaches at Edinburgh College of Art, where he is Head of Contextual Studies within the School of Design. He is the author of *That Thinking Feeling: A Research Guide to Scottish Cinema, 1938–2004* (2005), *Discomfort and Joy: The Cinema of Bill Forsyth* (2011) and *The New Scottish Cinema* (forthcoming 2014). He co-edited *Constructing* The Wicker Man: *Film and Cultural Studies Perspectives* (2005), *The Quest for* The Wicker Man: *Historical, Folklore and Pagan Perspectives* (2006), and *Scottish Cinema Now* (2009).

Andrew Nash is Associate Professor in the Department of English Literature at the University of Reading. He is the author of *Kailyard and Scottish Literature* (2007) and his several edited books include *The Culture of Collected Editions* (2003) and *Farewell Miss Julie Logan: A J. M. Barrie Omnibus* (2000). He is completing a book on the Victorian nautical novelist William Clark Russell and co-editing *New Directions in the History of the Novel* (2014).

Index

Lightning Source UK Ltd.
Milton Keynes UK
UKOW03f1255270214

227272UK00006B/72/P